Pearls

of the
Heart and Soul

A Memoir of

Family, Fancy, Freedom and Faith

Pearl H. Flaherty

PEARLS OF THE HEART AND SOUL
Copyright   2008 by Pearl H. Flaherty
All rights reserved.

Cover Design: Virginia Brach

ISBN – 10: 1-4196-8234-2
ISBN -- 13: 978-1-4196-8234-6

Visit www.Amazon.com to order copies of
Pearls of the Heart and Soul.

Dedication

To Bill for his loving and undying support of this memoir.

To our children and grandchildren who have strewn beautiful
 pearls along the way.

To faithful "dear readers" for their constant encouragement.

Contents

Introduction

In *Pearls of the Heart and Soul*, memories often tumble like seashells from the deep. Some of the little gems take the reader to far-away places, but others simply spark precious memories of another time in my life or theirs. These shining symbols known as "words" are meant only for good as I share them with you. If the words are too flowery, they are meant to reveal beauty hidden in the smallest things. If the words erupt like volcanoes, they are meant to evoke thought. The gentle and humorous words hopefully bring comfort and laughter to unseen, perhaps even lonely hearts. Over the years many have asked how the writing of *Pearls* came about. No doubt, it all started long ago when I discovered that daffodils, like little trumpets, dance to their own music.

In the spring of 1937 when I was eleven, while lying on Grandma Mary Hall's featherbed in her log cabin loft in Virgie, Kentucky, I peeked through a crack in the eaves. A panorama of bright yellow daffodils, with faces uplifted to God, stretched across a green hillside. My heart raced as I scampered down the ladder to tell Grandma who acted surprised at such a sight as I described. She wiped her hands on her flowered apron, adjusted a knot of hair at the nape of her neck, and listened. "I gotta write it all down quick so I will remember," I told her. Amused, she handed me a penny-candy poke and a half-used-up pencil. On that little brown paper sack I scribbled my first poem about sunlit daffodils dancing in the morning breeze high on a Kentucky hill.

Then a most wonderful thing happened that same year. Mrs. Cook, my fifth grade teacher slipped into my Christmas basket for poor kids a book of children's poems. In that book, not only daffodils danced, but fairies, elves and princesses also danced! Over and over I read that book aloud, each time thrilled to the rise and fall of meter and crisp sounds of rhyme! With unflagging enthusiasm I began to jot down little ditties about cows and grass and my mountain Momma.

Four years later, Miss Kalter, a 9th grade English teacher, recognizing my interest in words, asked if I would like to be her assistant; namely, grade students' grammar papers. While friends rushed off to the football field to watch heartthrobs practice, I stayed after school each day. To my delight, I discovered the mighty power of gerunds, participles, adjectives and verbs.

However, it was not until I was married and our five children grown that I began to experiment with the power of the pen. Suddenly there was *time, precious time.* Believing that an "old dog can learn new tricks," I enrolled at the age of 56 in my first college class, Creative Writing. Students' works were read, criticized and praised. Lo, a great revelation! College sophomores liked my dancing daffodils! The teacher, Mrs. Ada Williams, greatly encouraged me to continue writing and gave me an A+ on my final exam! Thus began serious efforts in the form of *Pearls.*

Reader response to columns written for two newspapers over 25 years has been my greatest reward. Grandmas have called to say, "I mailed your *Pearls* to my children up north." Gentlemen often express appreciation for a patriotic *Pearl.* One, excited after reading Forever May It Wave, submitted the article to Reader's Digest. And, how thrilling to have a Superintendent of Schools in Nevada share a Thanksgiving *Pearl* with his teaching staff!

So, dear reader, if I at 82 can spread a little joy or perhaps inspire one person, young or old, to try to make a difference in our world, then clicking away now on a computer keyboard all hours of the day or night is worth it. Thank you for peeking through the eaves with me to view dancing daffodils on a far-away hillside.

A word fitly spoken
is like apples of gold
in pictures of silver
Proverbs 25:11

Family

How dear to this heart are the scenes of my childhood, when fond recollection recalls them to view; the orchard, the meadow, the deep tangled wildwood, and every loved spot which my infancy knew.
    . . . Samuel Woodworth, *The Old Oaken Bucket*

A Sunbow Is Born

Of all nature's gifts
to the human race,
what is sweeter than
a child?
. . . Cicero

The night of January 21, 1926 was cold and blustery. Up a dreary, coalminer's holler in Clear Creek, Kentucky a miracle was about to take place.

On the other side of Big Mountain, Granny Henson had just gotten word that her daughter-in-law, Polly, was in labor. She quickly bundled up in Grandpa's worn, brown plaid Mackinaw, straddled his horse, and rode like wild fire across the mountain. When she reached the other side, she drew in the horse's reigns, slowing his pace as they crossed a railroad track. On and on they tramped through a creek bed. Finally, in the before-midnight darkness, she spotted the little cabin.

Lamp lights dimly shone through all windows of Polly and G.B.'s four-room clapboard home. Granny knew that she would soon witness God's fifth miracle in this place.

Howling winds clapped the front screen door against its rough frame as if applauding this night. Granny pushed through and into the kitchen. There, water boiled atop a wood burning stove. Warmth steamed beyond an open door where screams of childbirth silenced even banging sounds of the winds of winter.

Inside a sparsely furnished bedroom, a weary midwife hunched over a writhing, dark-haired woman lying upon a corn-shuck mattress. She wiped beads of hard labor from the woman's brow while whispering to the wrinkled Cherokee Granny who now too hovered near the bedside.

"Won't be long now, Mary," the midwife told Granny. "Let her squeeze your hand to ease the bad pain about to come."

My Momma, Polly Ann Henson, was the woman about to give Birth and I, dear reader, was the baby about to be born.

4

Momma told me many, many times the story of my birth and how she had wept tears of happiness and relief as I slipped out into Granny's strong arms. Momma always beamed when telling how Granny wrapped me in a flannel cloth and held me up to the coal-oil light for a closer look. Then, her black eyes squinted a smile of love for the brown-skinned baby with blue eyes.

"A pearl of a papoose!" she whooped to daddy, my sister and three brothers fidgeting near the open door. And to my dear Momma, Granny gently said, "Just like a sunbow, Miss Polly. God has blessed you with a sunbow."

And so, dear reader, I was named Pearl Hauine Henson, the Indian name Hauine meaning of many colors – like the sky's rainbow.

Dear Reader,

Each and every newborn is a sunbow, arcing across the family circle, connecting parents with the past, present and future.

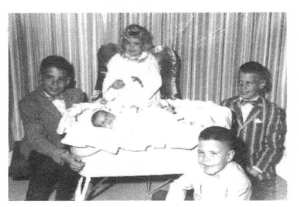

Christmas, 1960 – Pearl and Bill Flaherty Sunbows:
Baby Nicky, Angel Kitty. Left, Tim. Right, Dan. Front, Jef.

I Remember Momma

I remember Momma -
Swingin' in the old porch swing,

Huggin' me close to her side,
Singin' hymns and prayin' for her children
Scattered far and wide.

She, like the sun, arose at dawn,
Walked in the dew to fetch the cow;
She hoed the garden, canned the beans,
Helped Daddy kill the sow.

Momma stewed chicken and dumplin's,
Picked berries for blackberry pies,
Squeezed out sorghum dough just right
For gingerbread boys with raisin eyes.

And I remember my birthday parties
With ice cream made of new fallen snow.
Momma took pennies from her sugar bowl
To buy me a pretty pink hair bow.

Momma liked helpin' sick folks,
Scrubbed their wash on an old tin board.
She took them meals of soup beans
And cornpone - all she could afford.

I remember Momma -
Wipin' away my tears with love
While gently rockin' me in her lap.
She made me warm flannel nighties
And with scraps of wool, a little warm cap.

She stitched patchwork quilts
To keep us warm thru shivering nights,
And when I lay burnin' with fever,
She sat noddin' by the coal-oil light.

Yes, I remember Momma
As an old-fashioned jewel,
Bein' what God intended her to be – Free
To create a home, nourish her children,
And to love Daddy and me.

Momma, Polly Henson, and Pearl, 1945,
up Henson Holler in Ashland, Kentucky.

Where are Yesterday's Little Girls?

Oh, if only innocent, little girls today could just be little girls, trusting their world around them. Oh, if only their childhood could be free of fear - fear of being raped or kidnapped or abused in some other way. Oh, if only in summers they could romp in flowering meadows, walk in clear streams, or safely play in their own backyards as most children could when I was a child. Among my fondest memories between the ages of four and eleven were the many summer hours spent atop our beautiful mountain. In the shade of ancient trees, I learned about nature while playing make-believe in a very special, unusual playhouse.

It was not at all like a real playhouse, one of wood and shingled roof. Feathered friends trilled their joy at seeing a skinny little girl play Momma to bonneted baby dolls. On sunny days, the ceiling of my playhouse was a cloudless blue. Birds sat on every sill with windows that opened to the world. The floor was of ancient gray slate, washed clean whenever the sky shed refreshing, happy tears on the earth. There were no walls to stifle my creativeness, and the furniture was made of the finest wood stumps where mostly imagined friends came for tea. An elegant lace doily borrowed from Momma's old pump organ decorated my low dining table, the stump of an ancient oak felled by Daddy to build a little house down in the holler.

There was no TV for entertainment in my playhouse. The squirrels and chipmunks, my very best friends atop this mountain, delighted me and my baby dolls with their scampering antics. Their scratching and stashing away food for the winter taught me invaluable lessons about survival as well as humans and animals living together in a beautiful world.

Neither were there shelves of books or computers for educating in this special abode. Nature was my teacher. Every hot summer day the shade of large elms naturally cooled my airy abode. Cherry and paw-paw trees provided edible fruits for honored guests in my outdoor playhouse.

Over the years, I learned the names of many species of trees standing like sentinels along the edges of cliffs and streams on the mountain. The sap of majestic rock maples served as seaming for doll dishes made of big maple leaves. These little leafy plates held tiny ginger tea cakes from Momma's oven. Large, beautiful, white catalpa blossoms were perfect for make-believe china bowls. Dark blue huckleberries or ripe red mulberries were served in these when Cousin Mildred paid my make-believe family a visit.

There were no CD players either. But there was music, lots of music. With pines swishing songs around me, I often sang lullabies or ditties to my playhouse "children." Of course, I told them about Momma down in the holler and how she loved us all very much and prayed for us every day. As early as seven I remember standing tall on the mountain, pretending to be our preacher. Loudly I expounded on broken bits and pieces from the Psalms, and then listened to booming echoes bounce back words of praise.

Until age eleven, summer days spent atop my mountain were carefree days. Unlike today, there were no athletic schedules to worry about - climbing a mountain was enough exercise for yesterday's child.

After coming down off my mountain, there were no piano lessons to practice. Momma had taught me to play chords on her old pump organ. Often we would sing hymns in harmony just for fun. Dance recitals were unheard of when I was a child. At three I just started right in tap dancing when my Daddy picked up his banjo and played "Turkey in the Straw, Turkey in the Hay."

Yes, dear reader, life was simple then. I had everything a little girl needed - love, a respect for parents and God, and a natural awareness of the wonderful world about me. And, most importantly, I was safe.

Oh, that little girls today could just be little girls, full of mirth, spending summers frolicking about in a playhouse with a forested cathedral ceiling and windows open to the world.

Even a child is known by
his doings, whether his
work be pure and whether
it be right..
. . . Proverbs: *20:11*

Christmas Love on a Pedestal

Christmas is the time to bring out the family china or perhaps one special glistening serving dish handed down from Grandma. For many, many years one such pedestal cake stand adorned our Christmas table. My children have heard the story many times of the love that shone forth on that treasured cake stand when I was a child.

Christmas dessert in our mountain home was not the pilgrims' traditional pumpkin pie but Momma's Apple Cake, stacked high with seven, thin ginger layers spread with spicy apples. Of course, what made it so special was her use of a beautiful glass cake stand. She had purchased that treasure from the Sears and Roebuck Catalog in 1924 for $1.99. It was the prettiest thing in our Hoosier kitchen cabinet, and I remember how its raised flowers winked at me all year through the cabinet's glass door. A few days before Christmas, Momma would bring out the sparkling stand and set it on our round, oak kitchen table. All five children would squeal with delight knowing that a delicious, tall, sweet smelling cake would soon appear.

Needless to say, dear reader, preparation for her Christmas creation was a labor of love that began as soon as our red-skinned, no-name apples were ripe. To all of us she would say, "Christmas soon be here. Them apples are waitin' to be picked and dried."

With great enthusiasm all within earshot, including cousins Opal and Mildred, would scurry up the hillside and pick until the tree was bare. Some years, four or five bushels of red, juicy apples were lugged to the front porch. At least one bushel was set aside for sulfuring, a method of preserving apples for frying. They were truly delicious in the cold of winter when eaten for breakfast with real cow butter on Momma's hot biscuits. Two bushels were earmarked for Momma's delicious canned applesauce. While bubbling outdoors in a big, black iron pot, she would add lots of cinnamon and sugar. Since Momma always made apple stack cake when "company was a comin" and for our mountain folks reunion, one bushel was immediately prepared for dried apples, the most important ingredient in the cake

What an apple-peeling' party we had every October! My Daddy was a champion peeler! He could peel a whole apple with never a break in the paper-thin peel. As he peeled, Momma cored and the older youngins sliced. The secret of her recipe lay in two months of drying the white-fleshed apples until they turned a deep golden brownish color. Every sunny day she spread the apples out on an old muslin sheet on the smokehouse tin roof, and at sundown she gathered the apples in the sheet and brought them into the kitchen. By December 20, they were ready for Momma's apple stack cake.

Needless to say, I can still smell the pungent, spicy apples cooking on the old wood stove and taste the gingery, tart lick stolen from the warm, oozing apples at the base of the cake. And yes, forever and ever I will remember that beautiful glass cake stand which held stacks of my Momma's love at Christmastime.

If you have a keepsake plate, dear reader, pull it out, shine it up, and use it on your Christmas table. If it has a pedestal, then top it with a special family molded Christmas salad – OR

PRECIOUS POLLY'S APPLE STACK CAKE

BEAT in big crockery bowl: 4 eggs, 1 cup molasses, I cup shortening, 1 cup white sugar, 1 cup dark brown sugar.
ADD: 6 cups flour, ½ tsp salt, 4 tsp ginger, 4 tsp soda, 1 cup buttermilk.
MIX thoroughly with hands, spread with fingertips about ¼" thick in greased round cake tins. BAKE 12 min. at 300 degrees. COOL 10 min. and remove from tins. COOL completely before stacking with cooked apples.

APPLES (modern version of dried apples)

14 apples, peeled and quartered, 1 cup water, 1 ½ cups sugar, 2 tsp. Cinnamon, 1 tsp. Allspice, 1 tsp. Nutmeg. COOK until chunky applesauce. While warm, spread 1 cup of apples on large cake plate, then alternate apples and gingerbread, ending with 1 cup apples on top. Let stand at least overnight. Serves 16-24 people.

Note: A little left over dough makes wonderful Gingerbread Boys. Don't forget the raisin eyes!

Heavenly Snow Cream

At Christmastime when many snowbirds fly back north, I get teary-eyed and long for the sight of dancing snowflakes as well as all the wintry activities associated with Michigan family good times. Reminiscing, my mind becomes a camera, clicking off unforgettable memories.

I vision a string of five children trudging across a tree farmer's white-blanketed field in search of a perfect Christmas tree. After shaking fluff from snow-capped branches, discussions began. Who would help Dad drag it back and who would ride with that pine- scented, prickly symbol of Christmas in the back of our old red station wagon?

I remember the seven of us squished together on an eight-foot toboggan, careening down Holland Country Club hill. Red-scarves clothed squealing children in the crisp January air. Not one, parent or child, complained of the return climb up well-trodden, snow-packed alleys of ecstasy.

Never shall I forget the week Alex Haley's "Roots" aired on TV. In our town of Zeeland schools were closed because of a record snowstorm. Bill crocheted nose warmers to protect frost-nipped noses as our outdoor "Eskimos" frolicked for hours in the snow. They built forts, rolled enormous snowmen, and tunneled daytime shelters through six-foot snowdrifts.

Buttery smells of corn popping filled our family room. Neighborhood children joined ours for a treat and to warm themselves by crackling logs in the fireplace. Never mind the puddles!

But the most unusual and treasured wintertime activity was the making of "snow cream." This tradition began with my Momma. Back in the hills of Kentucky, during a steady fluffy snowfall, she hustled around the kitchen making preparations for this special happening. Then, clad only in a cotton housedress, she rushed out into the icy air and with a pancake turner skimmed fresh, clean snow into her largest crockery bowl.

Back inside, she dipped thick cream from atop a pail of milk and tossed in all other waiting ingredients. With an eggbeater she whipped the mixture until all lumps disappeared. The snow was transformed into a delectable confection. As she heaped frothy mounds into our bowls, the sweetness of vanilla filled our nostrils. She then shooed us off to the fireplace to quickly devour the miraculous treat before it turned into heavenly soup.

When our own children were in their growing years, snow cream was a part of our "Family Fun Time" on snowy Sunday afternoons. No school, no work, no meetings, simply family togetherness.

This memory and recipe I now pass on to you, dear reader, to share with your children and grandchildren living in winter wonderlands. While enjoying the beauty of a snowfall, may they also relish the simplicity of "God's ice cream," Momma's name for her special winter treat.

HEAVENLY SNOW CREAM

BEAT together: 2 eggs, I small Carnation Milk, I tsp. vanilla, I cup brown sugar. ADD: 4 quarts clean fluffy snow. Beat till lumps disappear.

Oh, what precious days, snuggling by the fire with our children, Tim, Dan, Jef, Kitty and Nick while lapping up heavenly snow cream.

This winter relive,
if possible, those
fond memories of
yesterday.

The Other Side of the Mountain

I have never forgotten the words my Daddy often spoke to Momma when I was growing up, "Polly, that youngin's middle name should have been Go." And I can also remember my saying to him, "Daddy, there's a lot more to see and do on the other side of our mountain."

Since retirement in 1980, Bill and I have explored "the other side of the mountain" by participating in *Elderhostel*. *This* non-profit, educational organization was established in 1975 for senior citizens. The courses offered are usually taught by professors at a sponsoring college or university. Programs are available in both the United States and many foreign countries. In addition to acquiring knowledge in a classroom setting, you are treated to afternoon and evening cultural and historical tours of the local area. Participants might live on campus, in a hotel, on a boat, or at an environmental or conference center. All meals are included and there are no books to buy, no homework and no tests. The only requirement is to GO.

These academic adventures opened up new, exciting waterways and by-ways for us. We have cruised on Hampton Roads in the Chesapeake Bay, hiked in the Finger Lakes area of Up State New York, steam boated on the Mississippi, and traversed by foot and rail the great city of Atlanta.

It was in that almost brand new, beautiful city that we joined 45 other retirees from 18 states to learn about Music Masters, Laughter in Theater, and the Civil War. Believing that "once you stop learning, you begin to vegetate," we approached these courses with much enthusiasm.

But why in Atlanta? Who would ever want to GO and stay on Peachtree St. in downtown Atlanta for one week? You would, dear reader, if enrolled in an *exciting* program where you could walk, safely, from the Peachtree Inn to outstanding art museums or to sit in on a live newscast at the CNN Building.

You would, if given a chance to *live* the tragedy of the Civil War in which more men died than in all other wars combined. At Atlanta's Cyclorama, you can feel the heat of battle as you view realistic depiction of the war on a colorful, room-sized painting. After watching Atlanta go up in smoke, General Sherman looked down upon the destruction and said, "Atlanta is no more." If he were here now, he would say, "Atlanta, in all its glory, is here to stay."

You also would enjoy going to Atlanta if interested in visiting Jimmy Carter's Presidential Center where emphasis is on uplifting humanity. You would enjoy taking the night train on the fast, underground MARTA to hear the incredible Atlanta Symphony, one of the top ten symphony orchestras in America.

Oh, Daddy, I wish you could have been there. The first chair violinist didn't play Turkey in the Straw like you did on your banjo. But, Daddy, he and the entire orchestra played concertos by Paganini and Romanoff, composers of music written far beyond our mountain. Daddy, if you can hear me up there, I know you would have been glad for me to GO.

As I sat, enraptured in the 4th balcony of that great concert hall, I leaned over and whispered to Bill, "This is a far cry from Clear Creek, Kentucky." Indeed, it was, dear reader.

Remember, if thou had been
expected to stay in one place,
thou would have been created
with roots.
                    . . . Anonymous.

Blackberries,
Bees and Butterflies

Summertime is a time for picking fruit. I guess, dear reader, you could call me a natural-born picker. During my lifetime I have picked blueberries, cherries, apples, pears and pawpaws. Yes, pawpaws. And I have picked strawberries, raspberries, mulberries, huckleberries, and blackberries.

No doubt, dear reader, my love for picking was inherited from my Grandma Hall who was known to pick everything edible. "A way to survive," she always said. So, every time I enter any orchard, nostalgia calls me back to another very special time in my life, a time of picking big sweet blackberries - h*igh upon a Kentucky hill where sometimes the wind don't blow.*

In my mind's eye I can still see Daddy's old stake-bed truck spitting and groaning in the dusty road up our holler as he fired it up to take us to the berry patch. Momma and Grandma, in their long print dresses, would climb aboard and then hoist me up first because I, at 7 or 8, was the "baby." Then, all the other youngins, garbed in overalls like me, eagerly grabbed out-stretched hands for a lift.

For pickin' each child wore a rope around his middle attached to the bail of a shiny, gallon syrup pail that winked at the sun. What a beautiful sight on that truck - 10 or 12 shiny syrup pails winking at the sun!

I can't remember us kids ever complaining one bit about the truck's hard floorboards as we bumped along rough roads. Laughing and chatting, we happily headed for the peaceful, picky, berry patch - h*igh upon a Kentucky hill where sometimes the wind don't blow.*

The trip up to the berry patch was probably 6 or 8 miles. As the old truck chugged along, we sang country songs and joked about who would fill his pail first. When we reached the top of the mountain, we jumped out, eager to pick those big black berries. All around us bright butterflies flitted from bush to bush and bees buzzed to Momma's humming "Jesus loves me, this I know 'cuz the big black berries tell me so."

My Daddy always said, "After the sky drinks the dew, that's the time to start pickin'. Clean your bush and don't eat too many, else your berries will never rise to the brim of your pail." That's where they had to be, dear reader, to fetch a quarter a gallon. I always listened to my Daddy because he was right. So I didn't eat many, just kept thinking about what he had said. A quarter was the exact price of a little pair of white anklets with two pink stripes! But, my brother Ray would plop one into the shiny syrup pail and two into his mouth. Later, the berries' beginnings poked his belly's insides and we could hear him moanin' all night.

When the sun was straight up over our bush, we crawled under it and ate our biscuit spread with real cow butter and stuffed with a fried egg. Our pint jar of sweet milk, chipped ice still floating on top, soothed parched throats. We would stick out our tongues and die laughing at the purple tell-tale coating.

As the afternoon drug on, the sky's fire sapped our strength. Strands of matted hair stuck to my sweaty brow. Blue-black stains of the wild berries seeped into our palms. Briar scratches on bare, burnt arms looked every bit like quilting stitches done in rust - h*igh upon a Kentucky hill where sometimes the wind don't blow.*

When my two, gallon syrup pails were filled, I joined the other youngins stretched out under the shade of the old truck bed. Soon my weary Momma and Grandma came lugging their four, ten-quart pails. But they pondered not the slump in their shoulders, only blackberry cobbler in the pan. Resting a spell, we all waited for the men folks. Momma talked of cool things, like quart jars of blackberries wintering on high shelves in our dark, damp cellar hugging our home in the holler.

On snow-kissed days the first taste of Momma's delicious blackberry jam on hot biscuits helped youngins forget the bee stings and rusty, briar scratches - *high upon a Kentucky hill where sometimes the wind don't blow.*

Oh, how I wish I could go back atop that mountain, dear reader, and experience this wonderful memory again. Perhaps I could, but there's one big problem. Where on earth would I find a shiny syrup pail that winks back at the sun?

We Did It, Momma!
We Graduated!

In May 2002 I glanced through my granddaughter's high school yearbook and smiled back at the bright and beautiful faces of youth. Then, thumbing through the graduating seniors' comments, I noted one in particular. A young lady thankfully credited her parents for their role in helping her reach this milestone in her life.

Immediately, my own long-ago, topsy-turvy graduation ceremony flashed before my eyes - first, exhilarating happiness, then, earth-shaking disappointment followed by remembrance and tears.

The year was 1944. Sitting on the auditorium stage with the top ten graduates gowned in white, my heart was bursting with pride. I would be the first of my entire family, including many cousins, to graduate from high school. However, while other students smiled and waved to family and friends, my anxious eyes scanned the audience in search of my family members. But there were none. Not even Momma, who had planned to be back from her sister's funeral in the mountains, was there for my graduation.

"Momma," I cried silently, "you always wanted me to be somebody." Then large salty tears rolled down my cheeks. I felt totally abandoned by loved ones. Then, the principal began to announce scholarships and my palms started to sweat. When I rubbed them against the white gown, pleats of my thick crepe dress seemed to cut like a knife. Momma had bought that dress at a second-hand store and dyed it a drab olive green for my graduation. At that moment, dear reader, I hated that dress and I hated being poor. The Valedictorian in her white dress and gown stood to give her address, but the elegant words never penetrated my angry thoughts. "Momma, you promised you would be back in time," I silently repeated over and over.

Through the blur, faces of teachers who had encouraged me along the way appeared. My first grade teacher, buck-toothed, bespectacled Mrs. Chatfield, had ignored my black stockings and homemade, feed-sack dresses. She had placed a First Reader into my hands and said,

"You, Miss Pearl, are going to learn to read." Then I saw Miss Kalter, my strict, old maid ninth grade English teacher who had drilled her students in grammar and spelling and who had taught me to appreciate the power of words.

Just as another tear splashed upon my folded hands, I was jolted back to reality when the principal's booming voice called out, "Pearl Hauine Henson." Without looking up, I hurried across the stage to accept my diploma, a prize for which I had struggled for twelve years.

Upon entering the crowded hall filled with graduates hugging and shrieking their joy, I spotted Momma. Her tired, hazel eyes were searching for me. The black dress she was wearing was rumpled from the long, return train ride home. Strands of chestnut hair fell upon her forehead, marring her beautiful, plain, sorrowing face. Momma had come, but it was too late.

I pushed through the crowd and handed her the long-awaited document. With work-worn hands she opened the shiny, maroon, leather-covered diploma. The white taffeta lining looked fake against the sun-browned hands of a woman who had milked cows, hoed corn on steep hillsides, and scrubbed rich women's floors. A woman who with only a 4th grade education had read to me many times from the Bible, "Wisdom is a shelter as money is a shelter, but the advantage of knowledge is this, wisdom preserves the life of its possessor."

Quietly, Momma ran her rough index finger across the smooth satin purple ribbon in the corner of the diploma on which was printed in gold letters "Honor Student." Happiness shown through the tiredness and for a split second her eyes seemed to sparkle. "We did it, Pearl," she whispered and threw her strong arms around me.

"Yes, we did it, Momma! We did it!" And then I wept on her shoulder. With the strength of her hug, I forgot about the ugly dyed dress and the absence of family at my graduation.

At that very moment, dear reader, I realized that the tears shed on that huge stage were not tears of sadness because Momma had missed my graduation. Those tears were tears of sadness because my dear Momma had missed the glory and honor which by all rights should have been hers.

Instruction increases inborn
worth and right discipline
strengthens the Heart.
. . . Horace, Odes

Smoking Killed My Daddy

In the summer of 2005 I walked into a business office and requested quotes on replacing two plate glass windows in our cottage. I never dreamed I would end up telling the salesman, a total stranger, that tobacco killed my Daddy.

I not only got the quotes I requested, but also much food for thought when I asked, "For how long is the replacement guaranteed?" The very pleasant, burly, middle-aged man smiled and said in a joking way, "Well, 20 years, but you probably won't be around then, will you?"

I smiled back and quipped, "I just might be. I don't smoke, drink or chew nor run around with them that do." He laughed at the old mountain saying. Suddenly, dear reader, our conversation turned from "glass replacement" to "the dangers of smoking" and Daddy's death.

Daddy was only 28 when, after a tonsillectomy, he suffered from an incurable life-long sleeping sickness. Doctors later determined a clipped nerve in his throat was probably the cause of this devastating disease. Because of boredom and inability to hold a steady job, he became a heavy smoker.

Daddy loved the old mountain songs and often sang and picked his banjo while Momma rested on the front porch.

I can still see Daddy untie the yellow twine-like string, reach into the little cloth sack of Golden Grain, take out a pinch of tobacco, place it on a small, thin paper and roll it into a fat cigarette. Smoking among both the rich and the poor was very common during hard times. Sadly, dear reader, no one was alerted to the dangers of nicotine.

Daddy and Baby Pearl

Pick, Daddy...Tap, Child...
Sleep, Daddy...Rest awhile.

My Daddy was a hard workin' coal miner 'til twenty-eight;
When Doc snipped out his tonsils, He had trouble stayin' awake.

Happy times, angry times put Daddy to sleep for sure; Doc scratched his head and said, "I'm sorry G. B., there ain't no cure."

Dynamitin' ended for Daddy; He raised hogs and worked on Model T's.
Moon shined a little, built a humble home for Momma and me.

In a drowsy, dreary world, plagued by a mystery he couldn't fight, Daddy, a lover of mountain music, picked his banjo day and night.

Spirited strings sang "Turkey in the Straw, Turkey in the Hay,"
While his brown-skinned Baby Pearl, tap, tap, tapped away.

Daddy, a cobbler, spent many hours by the cellar door;
Tacks clamped in tobacco-stained teeth, iron shoe last on the floor.

When Baby Pearl's tappin' shoes wore big holes right through, Daddy tacked on a leather, half-sole and they were as good as new.

Like brown soggy oak leaves, fallen and mired in the rain,
Daddy's banjo pickin' fingers bore amber stains of Golden Grain.

When nimble fingers could pick no more, Daddy was laid to rest at sixty-four. Yes, Daddy was laid to rest at sixty-four. A grown-up Baby Pearl cried buckets...and tapped no more.

Pick, Daddy...Tap, Child...
Sleep, Daddy...Rest awhile.

Duct Tape
Ain't All That Bad!

One cool day in February a few years back, I ran into a Florida Home Depot to pick up a roll of duct tape. A buxom, well-coifed lady walked up to me and asked if she could read the writing on my sweatshirt. In her Boston accent, she started to read out loud and then after each statement roared with laughter. Naturally, this attracted much attention. Soon, paint-spattered contractors and do-it-yourself little old men were eyeing my bosom and chuckling as they listened to her read this anonymous expose.

YOU KNOW YOU'RE FROM KENTUCKY:

When your car window is cardboard held in place by duct tape.
When you spit tobacco juice and talk at the same time.
When your family outing is a trip to Wal Mart.
When your answer, "Whatchaupto?" with "Aw, nuthin much."
When your bathroom is out behind the house.
When your home is decorated with yard sale junk.
When you play a saw or warshboard for entertainment.
When your front yard is filled with used tires and concrete statues.
When your drapes are old sheets and Rebel flags.
When you call a gourmet dinner soup beans and corn bread.

I would never have dreamed in a millennium that this gray sweatshirt with dark blue lettering, which I had purchased for 50 cents at a thrift shop, would have caused such a stir. I hadn't laughed this much since my hillbilly brother Leslie and his family visited us several years before. They had roared onto Nettles Island in a small, black pick-up truck with a low, white cap. A large piece of brown cardboard covered a missing window, held in place with - you guessed it, dear reader - duct tape.

And you can bet your Grandma's old washboard that on his grandson's birthday the entire clan, Grandpa Leslie, Grandma May, two grown grandsons and the birthday boy, 14, crammed into that truck and chugged over to Wal Mart in search of gifts. That evening, the last time I ever saw my brother, we joyfully celebrated in our screen room with a country gourmet supper of soup beans, corn bread, and chocolate cake.

Memories rang out that night. We talked of Momma's red and white petunias in a big, whitewashed, truck tire by our swinging gate. Leslie recalled the constant sound of water trickling over the large cliff behind our house and Momma singing while swinging on the porch. As we reminisced, nobody cared a lick, dear reader, whether that old truck in our driveway was trimmed with shiny chrome or - shiny duct tape.

Around the Old Fireplace

Oh, we had such fun in olden days
When firelight lit each face,
Love lifted winter's weariness
Around the old fireplace.

Momma rocked Baby Pearl,
Brother Ray popped Indian corn,
Leslie plinked the juice harp, and
Estil's coon-dog hunts took form.

Sister Bea embroidered dreams
On flour sacks, they looked bold,
Daddy roasted a fresh pig's nose
Amidst red glowing coals.

Oh, we had such fun in olden days,
When firelight lit each face,
Love lifted winter's weariness
Around the old fireplace.

Un-rent Love

A family, like a broad oak tree,
Shades the restless heart;
Its roots bury deep in prairie sod
Where tradition plays a part.

Its trunk is cored with altared faith
And etched with un-rent love;
Rings of gentleness embrace
The symbol of the dove.

Limbs of iron shun idleness
But showers babes with praise.
Sparing neither reed nor rod,
Strong shoots of men are raised.

Leaves of laughter offer dreams
That shimmer through life's prime;
Through veins of selflessness
Runs a trace of the sublime.

A family's seed, like acorns capped,
With wisdom, bursts boldly into youth;
Daring to line a page of history
With a lineage of love and truth.

Whether a Castle
Or Little House on Stilts,
There's No Place like Home.

In 2002 Nettles Islanders in Florida watched in awe as a castle took form on the Atlantic Ocean just south of our mobile-home park.   Finally, details were released.   After three years, when this architectural wonder emerged from a one-story spread-out mystery, I learned that this would be the dream home of a computer software mogul.   His mansion out-classes even the Biltmore in North Carolina.   Total area spans 50,000 sq. feet, not including a ten-car garage.   Reportedly, the estimated cost is eight million dollars.

On the two top floors there are 25 rooms including 10 bathrooms, a game room, bar, music room, media room, library, sewing room, a gym and a lap pool.

The building process was started in 2002 and is to be completed in 2008. This beautiful, man-made creation, with its turreted observation deck overlooking the ocean, makes one pause in disbelief.   Myself? I question whether, indeed, the occupants will have anymore fun than we who live in mobile homes just north of the castle.   We walk the same beach, collect identical oyster shells and star fish and swim in the same white-capped rollers.

Dear reader, home, no matter the size or cost, is where the heart is. Home, no matter how humble, is the place where memories are made. It seems that in a person's latter years the best and most loving memories are of the simple life. As mentioned earlier in this memoir, my first home on a hillside in Kentucky was a coalminer's cabin.   It was small, unpainted, simply furnished. We had 0 bathrooms.   Our gym was the outdoors, our pool, the creek.   And there was music when Momma pumped the old organ, not in a "music room," but in the "living room," where all seven of us "lived."   With much laughter we romped with cousins around this same room playing Blind Man's Bluff. But most of all there was boundless love within those thin walls.

After learning the details of this beautiful monstrosity, I searched and found a poem written in my first creative writing class twenty-five years ago about the little house where I was born. When I read this in class as part of my final exam, college sophomores were amazed at such a simple way of life and asked for autographed copies. And now, dear reader, I share this with you, hoping we will always remember that whether a castle or cabin, there is no place like home.

My Little House on Stilts

My little house on stilts, a front porch and four rooms in all,
embanked Momma, Daddy, me, and four streams of Bill D. Hall.

Birthing was in an old iron bed, slumbering on a flowered
linoleum floor;
A wardrobe hunched in the corner, cretonne curtains covered
its door.

In the living room stood an upright organ, shod in red velvet
pumps;
A library table caressed a Bible and a little glass
chicken with bumps.

The wood stove breathed warmth, cooked cornbread and beans.
Around the old oaken table, happiness prayed, and ate,
and dreamed.

By an unscreened back door, on an unpainted washstand,
sat a bowl and pitcher for washin' youngins' and coalminers'
hands.

A foundation of slender poles was as strong as my Daddy's hug.
A tin shiny roof hovered over us like my dear Momma's love.

After hoein' on the hillside, we sat on the porch, waved
to the engineer;

Life was simple in the little house on stilts - the memories
now oh so dear.

Hog Killin' Time in the Holler

This is a true tale, my friend,
Not of gold or silver dollars,
But of hog killin' time
In a far-off holler.

One morning, long ago, even before the stars dozed in the sky, even before the cock crowed, my Daddy yawned and shook himself awake. His first words to my sleepin' Momma, *"It's Christmas. We're gonna shoot that hog!"*

He plopped his feet onto our cold, linoleum floor, his pudgy body clothed in long underwear. To warm the shiverin' air, he poked up dyin' coals buried under a gray blanket of ashes in a slumberin' country fireplace.

The poker rattled against the grate. The shovel scoopin' ashes scraped the stone hearth, which jarred five little sleepyheads into action. It was indeed Christmas and hog killin' time in Henson Holler.

We scurried into our overalls and splashed warm faces with icy water from a granite wash pan, introducin' us to the crispness of an early winter. Outside, the frozen ground patched with snow looked like a crazy quilt. And my Daddy knew that smokin' and dryin' time was just right.

The jowls of the big iron pot groaned as flames of fire licked its legs. When the water rolled to a scaldin' boil, one shot echoed around our horseshoe hills, tellin' the world that country folks on this special day would soon be eatin' high on the hog!.

The scrapin' and guttin', washin' and cuttin' was a heap of a job, but as the sun peeked over the mountain that Christmas mornin' all were paid a most royal wage, that bein' Momma's hot biscuits, fresh-churned butter, and, of course, Kentucky-fried pork chops smothered with old-fashioned red sop.

This is the end, my friend, of a tale,
Not of gold or silver dollars,
But somethin' far greater -
Hog killin' time In a far-off holler.

Joy and Heartbreak at Christmastime

Not every Christmas memory is a joyous one. On Christmas Eve 1935 a kind, elderly lady played Santa for a nine-year-old little girl bedridden with tuberculosis. The giving neighbor secretly slipped beneath the child's family tree her very own child-size doll. Although the doll was very old and her blue-tucked satin dress faded, the child was ecstatic on Christmas morning and gave the doll the melodious name, Madeline. Joy!

The doll's beautiful porcelain face, encircled with dark, human ringlets, held luminous brown eyes with heavy feathered brows. Her open mouth hinted a sympathetic, sweet smile which day-by-day brightened the sick child's spirits. In their make-believe world, together the new friends sipped nourishing eggnog prescribed for the ailing child by the doctor. Madeline, with her ball-jointed legs and arms, looking like a real child, danced, bowed, and even knelt to pray. After nine months and a million hugs from Madeline, the little girl's health was restored.

Then, just one month before Christmas, 1936, a sad thing happened. It proved to be the beginning of disappointment and mistrust in the little girl's real world. Madeline's arm fell off.

"Don't fret, darling, the man at the doll hospital will make her as good as new," the mother assured her.

So, a few days later, the hopeful child wrapped the precious gift in an old quilt as protection from the cold wind. Then, she waited at the end of their dusty road for a jitney bus to pick them up. When she got in, the stern, black-capped driver demanded two nickels. "But she's only a doll," the distraught child said.

"Two nickels! She takes up a seat!" Then he reached for the fares. She had only two nickels, one for her return trip home, but decided two miles was not too far to walk if Madeline could be made whole again.

"Merry Christmas, you cross old man," the child mumbled as she left the jitney to enter the doll hospital.

When the bespectacled repairman unwrapped the doll, with a solemn "hmm," he lifted her dark brown curls and saw the engraved words "Jumeau Medaille D' of Paris." On a scrap of paper he jotted the words and then pinned it on the fragile blue dress. Peering over his glasses, he dismissed the child with an abrupt, "She'll be ready next Friday." The little girl skipped the two miles home, gladdened by the thought that Madeline would be home for Christmas.

However, when she returned on that Friday, and subsequent Fridays thereafter, the doll could not be found. Finally, on Christmas Eve, the repairman bluntly said, "I'm sorry, little girl. Your doll was stolen."

Heartbroken, the child walked out, fingering the two nickels in her pocket, one meant for Madeline's return fare. But, she couldn't face the harsh jitney driver, so again she trod the two miles, hot tears melting the snowflakes swirling against her cheeks. Mistrust, for the first time in her life, splotched her mind and soul.

Dear reader, I was that little girl. Although I knew nothing of the doll's worth, all my adult life I had subconsciously hoped to someday find my dearest childhood friend, Madeline.

It wasn't until 1984 when I was 58, while visiting a friend in New Hampshire, that I saw her at an auction - at least an identical French Jumeau doll wearing a blue faded dress. My heart leaped for joy, but not for long. I, in disbelief, never once raised my auction paddle because the bidding started at $2,000. Finally, the auctioneer closed the bidding. "Sold," he yelled out, "for $4,500!"

Only at that moment, dear reader, did I fully understand why long ago some greedy person had broken a little girl's heart by stealing her most treasured gift. Surely, that person did not believe in the true meaning of Christmas.

The heart hath its own memory,
like the mind, and in it are enshrined
the precious keepsakes, into which
is wrought the giver's loving thought.
                    ...Longfellow

Remember Grandpa
On Father's Day

Grandpas, though wrinkled, shrunken in stature and have gray coloring their hair, need to be remembered on Father's Day. They have been the object of our love and admiration for many years because of their unselfishness and sacrificial ambition for the sake of their families.

I hadn't thought much of my dear, dear Grandfather who died thirty-six years ago until I learned of a coal-mine tragedy in Kentucky in 2006. Grandpa Joe Hall, whom we grandchildren called "Pap," was not a coalminer though. In fact, during the 70 years of his life he frowned upon the big coal companies destroying the beauty of the mountains, his birthplace and forever home.

When I was twelve years old, I remember visiting his little mountain cabin, sitting at his feet swollen with dropsy and listening to tales of his life as an uneducated father of six. Life was hard. He often traveled by horseback, fourteen days at a time, driving cattle to market to support his family. He was a great father and my much-loved and respected grandfather.

To belatedly honor Grandpa Joe, I share this poetic letter, dear reader, which I wrote ten years after his death:

Dear Pap,

Oh, that you were here.
These dark hills mourn their loss.

You were their mountain stream, uncultured,
Winding through meadows of wild flowers
Where lowing cattle soothed snakes
Sunning themselves upon virgin rocks.

Native soil hugged you to its bosom.
Rain from Heaven kissed your brow.
God blessed your labors with long life
Eternally – then and now.

Old Shep smiled at your gallused frame
Topped by old felt hat shedding sun and rain.
You treasured his faithfulness, while
Shepherding cattle in their waywardness.

Gone with you now are the lowing cattle.
Clear mountain streams are choked with slack.
Kentucky's wild flowers wear a shroud -
Mining scars of which we are not proud.

Ribbons of stone have untied the little cabin.
Gone is the featherbed where I dreamed of
Black ink forming black words, filling white
Pages with forever swaying daffodils.

Oh that you were here, dear Pap.
    Your loving granddaughter,
            Pearl

Dear Child,

My heart grieves in this cold earth
When I feel the mountains shake
And hear murmurings of my beloved
land - dying.

Signed_____ X _____

      Joe Hall

PAP

Daddy's Breath of Spring

Many adult children treasure memories of Easter traditions. In April, 1998 Bill and I received an egg-shaped Easter greeting from our forty-year-old, sentimental daughter, Kitty. Inside, bold black words expressed *her* childhood memories when she was only five:

"I remember Easters from when I was very small...chocolate bunnies and mounds of jelly beans...daffodils and tulips blooming." Then, she added, "I also remember my little navy coat and the new, shiny, black patent shoes. And, Mom, I remember the many pretty Easter bonnets you trimmed, as well as deliciously filled Easter baskets from the Easter Bunny – YOU!"

As I stood holding Kitty's card in my hand, memories of Easter Sunday when I was five trickled down my cheeks. Eventually, like a clear stream in springtime, they freely flowed onto these pages.

Sixty-seven years prior, there was Momma, dark hair knotted at the back, bent over her treadle, Singer sewing machine, her foot operating the scrolled, metal pedal. She was engulfed in a mound of dotted Swiss organdy. "What are you sewing, Momma," I asked? "You'll see," She answered. Because the fabric was of an orchid color, I knew it must be an Easter dress for me.

At first, I stood by her elbow and watched the shiny "foot" feed the sheer, frothy material through the machine to form darts and gathers and seams. She had no dress pattern, but occasionally would hold up a piece of material to my body, trim to fit, and continue her sewing. Then, I sat on the floor, mesmerized by the beautiful design the swift-turning, black, ornamental, iron wheel made as Momma pedaled. She pedaled, then stopped, pedaled, then stopped. In time with the wheel, I recited over and over my Sunday School Bible verse, "He's not here, He's risen, risen, risen, risen."

Bored with waiting for the finished creation, I climbed upon the bed and fell asleep. When I awoke, there, hanging on the door jamb, was an Easter dress fit for a princess – scooped neck, puffed sleeves, and a skirt of three fluffy tiers for twirling.

I heard Momma humming in the kitchen. I ran in and hugged her aproned middle, a delighted child's thanks to a special, tireless Momma. "Mercy," she squealed, holding up a piece of frying chicken with white, floured hands.

On Easter morning I put on the beautiful dress and my new white church shoes with little straps that buttoned. While looking in our chiffonier's full-length mirror, I practiced smiling and looking pretty for my Daddy. He was out gathering eggs, but I wanted him to be the first to see me. Instead of going through the kitchen where my older sister and Momma were preparing breakfast, I went out the front door and around to the back porch. I stood on my tippy-toes and splashed my face with cold water from a gray, granite wash pan. Looking into a small mirror hanging low on the wall, I smoothed my dark, wet bangs until they glistened.

Finally I was ready. I peeked around the corner of the house. Beyond the weathered henhouse I could see yellow daffodils blooming on the hillside and Momma's bed of red tulips by the creek. Suddenly, Daddy in his old denim overalls appeared in the open henhouse doorway. In one hand he carried eggs in a half-gallon shiny syrup pail. Holding high the corners of my frilly dress, I ran into the dusty yard, blocking his way, twirling round and round until I was dizzy. He steadied me with his big rough hand, stooped to hug me, then grinning real big held me at arm's length and said, "Why, Baby Pearl, you are Daddy's breath of spring." Looking back, dear reader, it seems he repeated those words every Easter until I was grown.

Like the card's sentiments from our daughter, most children can remember a special Easter Sunday when they were very small in which their Momma, and Daddy, played a very special part.

To you your father should be
as a god; One that composed
your beauties, yea, and one
to whom you are but as a form
in wax by him imprinted.
                    . . . Shakespeare

Granny and Grandpa Bud

Mary Jones Henson, born in 1871, was an earthy, half-breed Cherokee. Although a gentle soul, she also was as proud and as fierce as a tribal warrior.

She hated Grandpa Bud's still, always ranting and raving that whiskey was destroying mountain families. Granny was known to dump many a gallon of moonshine over the hill. Grandpa's silent spirit attested to his English descent. He would just stand calmly by, his grey eyes hinting a grin beneath a bushy, turned-down moustache. With hands shoved deep into his bib-overall pockets, he never tried to stop Granny's Carry Nation antics.

"You got to live good clean lives," she'd caution while weaving threads of honesty and kindness into the fabric of her children. And to Grandpa she often yelled, "And you, Bud, stay away from devil water and women that don't b'long to you."

Granny could neither read nor write, but her strength for survival in the rugged, dark hills of Appalachia came from a loving family and her unshakeable faith in God.

The house with an old grandparent
harbors a jewel.
                . . . A Chinese Proverb

Jackie Versus Granny

Jackie was married to President Kennedy and lived in a big white house at 2500 Pennsylvania Avenue. I wonder if she ever stitched a patchwork quilt of worn-out woolen garments to cover John Jr. and Caroline at night. My Granny did!

Jackie slept in Abraham Lincoln's bed in the White House and even put a brass plaque there that reads, "Jacquelyn and John F. Kennedy slept here." Well, my Granny was born in the same hills as Abe and tasted the same humbleness that made him so famous, but she never bragged about it.

Jackie was not bad looking in her designer "sack" dress. Neither was my high-cheek-boned Granny in her homemade, "flour-sack" dress.

Jackie later married the very rich Aristotle Onassis, and wined and dined on an exotic Greek Island. My Granny never had a vacation but labored from sun-up to sun-down while "looking well to the ways of her household and eating not the bread of idleness."

These were my thoughts as I sat early one morning watching an auction at Sotheby's on TV. The auctioneer rattled off ridiculous bids on Jackie Onassis's personal belongings. As I listened, I found myself comparing the totally opposite lifestyle of my Granny Henson to that of the famous Jacqueline Kennedy Onassis. One was of ultimate simplicity, the other of ultimate luxury.

When the auctioneer held up Jackie's fake, seventy-dollar pearls, which went for more than two hundred thousand dollars, I began to laugh, dear reader. Then, my laugh simmered to a chuckle and finally a smug smile as I remembered how absolutely grand I had felt the first time I wore a beautiful strand of pearls purchased at a dollar store - for one dollar.

The Great Depression

Times were prosperous. Then,
A dark cloud covered the coal country.
Destitution flooded every holler,
Stripping the hills of their dignity,
Scarring every child, mother, and father.

Work whistles ceased to blow,
Propped-up mountains creaked in the rain,
Brooding coal miners stood idle,
Their faces etched with pain.

Washed between a rock and a hard place,
Strong men bowed with shame,
Clinging to life lines of dried milk,
Dried beans, and dried grain.

Barefoot children cried with hunger and cold.
Bent fathers carved out roads for the WPA,
Picking and shoveling for food and warmth
For one dollar a day.

Tributaries with coal dust in their blood
Trickled north of the Appalachians,
Carrying uprooted proud mountaineers
One step ahead of starvation.
Times were hard.

1929 – The year Daddy and Momma left the coal mining country and moved our family north to Ashland, Kentucky on the Ohio River. Baby Pearl was three years old.

Long Lisle Stockings

Long lisle stockings
Gartered 'bove the knee,
Tan ones for Momma,
Black ones for me.

Poor kids wore black,
Rich kids wore white,
Didn't matter none –
Mine were warm all right.

Momma scrubbed 'em
On the board, hung 'em
'Bove the stove ever night,
Come mornin', they smelled
Lye-soap clean, but
They were black, not white.

Poor kids wore black,
Rich kids wore white,
Didn't matter none –
Mine were warm alright.

My Little Red Coat

I remember the best Christmas present I ever received as a child. I was seven, the year 1933. Times were hard and none of us children expected much more than a few sticks of candy in our stocking.

I can still see my Daddy standing by the kitchen wood stove figuring and fingering crumpled dollar bills in his rough, work-worn hands. "Seven dollars is all I got. Enough for me a new pair of shoes and a few little Christmas trinkets for you youngins," he said, glancing at Momma and me. From a nail by the door, he took down his brown Mackinaw, frayed badly at the cuffs, put it on over his work overalls and headed for the door.

"Get your coat, Baby Pearl. We're gonna have us a very merry Christmas."

It was cold outside. A light snow patched the ground. I ran to the clothes press to find last years' black, hand-me-down coat that barely covered my short-tailed, dark cotton dress. I put it on, along with a little wool cap with ear flaps Momma had stitched up for me. Back in our front room, so delighted he was taking me along, I reached for Daddy's hand and off we went in search of a merry Christmas for our family of seven.

Downtown Ashland, up and down both sides of the single block of shops we trudged, stopping to peer in every window at the holiday decorations. There were red glistening balls, large red velvet bows, and sprigs of holly with red berries. I pointed out to Daddy that the holly was real, just like that growing on the snow-covered hillside outside our kitchen window. The vibrant colors warmed my heart, but the wind whipped my legs with cold and I began to shiver. Daddy noticed, I know.

Suddenly he pulled me into a clothing store. *Oh, Daddy's gettin' him a shiny new pair of shoes.* The thought made me tingle through and through. But, dear reader, there were no shoes in that store. Squeezing my little cold hand with his big warm one, and looking down with a hint of mirth, he asked, "Baby Pearl, how would you like a new coat for Christmas? *A new coat?* A bell seemed to jingle in my heart. Never in my whole life had I had a new coat!

Like magic, the store clerk dressed in a dark suit and red tie appeared. I remember his clean-shaven face spiked with a long pointed nose, and his straight, white teeth as he smiled his best Christmas smile. My Daddy pulled out his wadded-up bills and said straightforward, nodding down at me, "We'd like a $4.00 coat for my Baby Pearl."

The gentleman cleared his throat, then, led us to a rack of children's coats. "We want a right practical, long-tailed coat," my Daddy pointed to the rough, cold, bare space between my dress tail and the black cotton stockings gartered above my knees. The clerk glanced down, nodded and smiled again. He was very kind.

However, each time the clerk pulled out a coat - first a black, then a brown, then a navy blue - I shook my head "no."

"Little girl, don't you like these nice warm coats?" The man's smile suddenly disappeared. I tugged at my Daddy's Mackinaw and he bent to hear my whisper.

Straightening up, he said, "My Baby Pearl likes that red coat, the one on that other rack."

The man cleared his throat again, smiled and then helped me into the Christmas-colored coat. "English herringbone," he sang. I beamed up at Daddy. With no questions asked, he agreed that the red coat was "fine, just fine." While I buttoned the shiny brass buttons, feeling like the brightest star on any Christmas tree, one-by-one Daddy smoothed out dollar bills and handed them to the smiling clerk.

Once outside, he began to whistle and I, in my little red coat, began to skip. Neither of us ever glanced toward the shoe store or Murphy's Five-and-Dime where Christmas trinkets were sold. Years later, dear reader, I learned that the little red coat, the only new coat I would own until I was an adult, had cost not $4.00 but $7.00, all the money my Daddy had to his name.

After dinner on Christmas Day, Daddy, beaming, said, "Show your cousins your present, Baby Pearl." I proudly put it on. Then Daddy, wearing his scuffed-up, half-soled shoes, reached for his banjo. While patting his foot on the linoleum floor, he plinked out "She'll be Comin' Round the Mountain." As family members clapped and cheered, Baby Pearl tap-danced in her little red coat.

Looking back and remembering that merriest of Christmases, I am reminded, dear reader, that a gift of sacrifice and love is a memorable kind of gift to give and surely the happiest to receive.

Circles on the Ticking

Momma cried when we left her in that dark, drab room. But it did have one window. The bathroom smelled Lysol clean, and the moans from the terminal wing were not very loud. Of course, my sister and I felt terrible. Honest. But we were old too. Momma, 88, had a broken pelvis. She needed backbreaking care. What else could we do? She was in the nursing home only four months. Then, she died.

Twelve years after her death, I dreamed of Momma for the first time. In the mist, I floated up toward the old home place nestled in hills laced with dogwood trees planted by God. Beyond the whitewashed picket fence, bleached dish towels and Momma's flowered apron happily waltzed in the Kentucky breeze. The distant colored joy of home was so clear. I soared through the swinging gate, past the Rose of Sharon bush bursting with bright pink blossoms, and then I slowed to drink-in the sweet scent of faded lilacs.

In the dream, yesterday's barefoot children squealed with delight as they chased butterflies. Little girls in cool, short, flimsy dresses and boys in short-short pants raced round and round the big truck tire - the one Momma had painted white and filled each spring with red petunias. I eased on past pots of bright red geraniums seated on the porch railing and felt a grin coming on in my sleep. There, at one end still hung the white-slatted swing where Momma and I, like a million years ago, rested and sang hymns in harmony.

When I pushed the door to the living room open, suddenly elation turned to disappointment. Gone was Momma's red carpet and bold, rose-flowered drapes. There was not one stick of furniture in the room. The family pictures were stripped from the walls. Only a small, silvery Bible-Belt plaque glittered against a creamed wall. The red letters spelled out Momma's faith, *Prayer Changes Things.* Momma lay in the middle of a clean, bare, floor. She was dressed in a blue flannel nightgown, her head propped up on one elbow. Contentment flooded her old wrinkled face.

"Momma," I seemingly cried out, "what are you doing down there? Where's the furniture? Where are your beautiful curtains?"

"Outside, airing," her words floated like clouds toward the open door. "Smell the lilacs, Pearl? Hear the children's sweet voices?"

I drifted over and tugged at her. The frail, shriveled body stiffened a little and in those clouded eyes I saw the same hurt and fear seen when we had left her in that strange nursing home.

"But, Momma, you can't lie there on the floor like that!"

"It's better this way, Pearl. Home is better...better...better..," her voice echoed through the emptiness.

The dream was so real, dear reader. I scooted down very close to Momma and put my little-girl arms around her - just like we slept when Daddy visited his brothers in the mountains. Then, I sobbed myself awake.

The pillow beneath my cheek was damp. Tears had trickled down, for the manyeth time, into my old favorite, feather pillow, the one Momma had given me as a wedding gift. When I turned on the light and removed the pillowcase, I realized, dear reader, that although the memories of home and Momma were only a dream, the circles of guilt on the pillow ticking were real. *Oh, so real.*

Even He who died for us upon the cross
in the last hour, in the unutterable agony of
death, was mindful of His mother, as if to
teach us that this holy love should be our
last worldly thought – the last point on earth from
which the soul should take its flight for heaven.
. . . Longfellow

Remembering
With Flowers, a Flag and a Feather

"I must go back there, just once more before I die," I said to Bill as we made plans in May, 2004 to return to Michigan. It had been thirteen years since I last visited the tiny family plot where my Indian grandmother and English grandfather were buried in Floyd County, Kentucky.

Two weeks later, as we traveled along Kentucky State Road 122, I wondered if anyone ever visited these lonely graves on Memorial Day now that my last mountain cousin had died. Were the weeds pulled, was the grass mowed? Would the engraved names on the two oldest headstones in the plot still be legible and, if so, what living soul would know who they were? These questions were soon to be answered.

At the Hi Hat post office, we turned onto little-traveled 979, a narrow, curvy, black-topped road. When I was young, there was no road here. I remember the creek bed where horses carried coal miners, school teachers, preachers and traveling salesmen to their destinations. Mountain children walked either the creek bed or the railroad track to their one-room school.

Not much had changed up this holler. Many humble homes still clung to the hillsides. The little four-room cabin where I was born, though now covered with white vinyl siding, still stood. It seemed as if the mountains were higher and the holler between them too narrow.

Finally, we located my cousin's home behind which the little cemetery was located. Her husband, daughter and her two children, Andrea 11 and Timmy12, hugged us and hugged us again. With great enthusiasm, the young ones asked questions of how we were related to them and how long ago we had lived in the mountains. Although they knew where the graves were, neither knew that the small, weathered headstones, one on which a little lamb rested, were those of their great-great grandparents.

Even the mother was not aware that her great grandmother was a Cherokee Indian whose ancestors had hid in these mountains to escape death on the Cherokee Trail of Tears.

The children could hardly wait to lead me up the steep hill along a narrow, wildflower path to a rustic, fenced in area. Although the plot had been mowed, long-faded silk flowers, blown here and there by winter winds, lay as dead memories from past visitors. The moment was solemn and the quietness deafening as I stooped to read the name on Grandma's mildewed stone: Mary Jones Henson, Born 1855 – Died 1928. Simple words etched below in a crude hand brought tears to my eyes, "Farewell, dear children, I'm going home."

Timmy placed a tiny bunch of wild daisies on Grandpa's grave and I a small American flag, knowing how he had loved his little mountain home in America.

"What about the eagle feather Timmy gave you?" Andrea asked. "Oh, yes, the eagle feather," I said while stroking the soft, single, black feather, symbolic of the Cherokee's one-feather headdress. I then placed it atop the gentle lamb on Grandma's headstone.

The two children smiled at me. Instantly I knew, dear reader, that there would always be someone to care for Grandma and Grandpa Henson's gravesite high upon a Kentucky hill - and that my loved ones would live on in Timmy and Andrea's hearts for many moons.

To forget one's ancestors is to be a brook without a source, a tree without a root.
. . . A Chinese Proverb

A War-time Wedding

When I was married in 1945 at the age of 19, I knew nothing about traditional weddings - "something old, something new, something borrowed, something blue." But, traditionally, Bill and I were married in a "big church." But, untraditionally, there were only 5 people in attendance, the minister, our two best Navy friends and the bride and groom. Traditionally, I wore a white dress, but it, untraditionally, was short. I did not have a frothy veil either. But my large, shiny, black picture hat blended well with the sailors' white suits and the minister's black robe.

Even though this war-time wedding was not the usual fan-fare for young couples committed to a life-long marriage, the oft-quoted words in a traditional wedding from Corinthians 13:4-8 were read by the minister. These words still ring-out in my heart, mind, and soul as a guide for a lasting marriage.

There are many other traditions brides still consider when planning their wedding ceremony even though they know nothing about how these traditions started or when.

Wearing "something old, something new" to the altar has symbolized for more than a century the bride's leaving her own family and joining another. With the words "I Do" the bride and groom make a commitment to take full responsibility for their own spiritual, mental, and physical future together.

"Something borrowed?" Traditionally in England, something borrowed was given to the bride before the wedding by a happily married woman. Attached to the gift was a hand-written note wishing good fortune for the newlyweds. Good fortune, in a broad sense, as we all know, does not necessarily mean riches but success in our undertakings. A successful marriage is one that is a lasting endeavor.

"Something blue" - The color blue, in ancient times, was a symbol of modesty, fidelity and purity. Therefore, wearing something blue on her very special day was a hopeful symbol of eternal love for the bride. While modesty and purity still rank high for a successful marriage, to me the most important is fidelity. Although Momma never called it that when cautioning me about love and marriage when I was a young girl, I always

44

valued her emphasis on faithfulness to one's life partner, thereby, adhering to one's marriage contract.

No, Bill and I did not have the traditional "rice throwing" after our wedding. Actually that custom, as well as the husband carrying the new bride over the threshold, stems from ancient superstitions. In the olden days people were constantly worried about a wedded couple's new life being darkened by bad luck. So, adding these practices to a wedding ceremony hopefully drove away evil spirits. Both are fun traditions and great for pictures - even if the bride and groom do not know why they are carrying on such a tradition.

The tradition of "wearing the wedding band on the ring finger of the left hand" - The general consensus was that somewhere on that finger, lovers could find a special vein that led directly to the heart. In that respect, Bill and I are more traditional than we thought!

Lastly, the tradition of "throwing the bouquet" - a rather strange tradition, but a fun one. People in bygone days actually believed it was good luck to receive a piece of clothing from a new bride. Can you imagine how tattered a bride must have looked as she waved good-bye to the cheering crowd? Throwing of the bouquet to pretty young hopefuls seems a much better choice.

Since I wore nothing old, nothing borrowed or nothing blue, I only have beautiful memories of traditional wedding vows spoken long ago. A joyful tear rolled down my cheek when we knelt at the altar. The minister's words on eternal love echoed softly from the balcony of that beautiful old church. Today, dear reader, those words form Corinthians still echo within my heart after 62 years of marriage:

"Love is patient and kind: love is not jealous or boastful; it is not arrogant or rude. Love does not insist on its way; it is not irritable or resentful; it does not rejoice at wrong, but rejoices in the right. Love bears all things, believes all things, hopes all things, endures all things. Love never ends."

And the rain fell, and the floods came,
and the winds blew, and beat upon
that house; and it fell not: for it was
founded upon a rock.
. . . Matthew 7:25

Top left clockwise: A war-time wedding, 1945; Our family 1964; Granddaughter Necia weds Jon Ornee, 2003, Grandpa Bill wearing his bargain black suit; Pearl & Bill's 60th Anniversary, 2005; Flaherty home in Zeeland, MI.

Top left clockwise: Silver Lake Cabin, 1966; Grandchildren sailing on Grandpa Bill's Sunbird; Saluting the flag at Kuznz Kamp; Silver Lake cottage, 2000; Grandchildren visiting Grandma and Grandpa; Sunset over Silver Lake and the sand dunes.

How Do I Love Thee?

Whether a lacy card of endearment, a heart-shaped box of chocolates, a bouquet of flowers or a diamond ring, a surprise valentine for your sweetheart on February 14th will surely say, "I love you." The big question is: Would St. Valentine approve of all these gyrations in the name of love? I think so.

After all, St. Valentine was a loving Roman priest who was beheaded on February 14 in the year 270 because of his love for persecuted martyrs. How appropriate that, centuries ago someone - no one really knows who - designated February 14 as a day for lovers and called it St. Valentine's Day.

Second to Christmas, it has become the most loving, and possibly the most commercial, day on our calendar. Even though Ben Johnson, Shakespeare's friend, was appalled at all the frivolous hoopla that characterized Valentine's Day, I'd bet a solid-gold heart that St. Valentine would endorse these earthly goings-on.

What Saint wouldn't thrill to school children frantically pasting, cutting and trimming a homeroom valentine box? If he could sneak a peek, he'd smile at a freckle-faced angel secretly stuffing the box with frilly creations that say, "You're mine, Valentine." Or perhaps he'd blush, along with a tow-headed Cupid depositing his store-bought, "Teacher, this arrow's flying just in time, to claim you for my valentine."

If St. Valentine could tour a florist shop in early February, he'd glory at the heavenly sight - long rows of tables carpeted with a rainbow of bursting blossoms shipped in from all over the world. He'd push through crowded aisles with all other Romeos and Don Juans. There he'd see pink and red carnations fresh from Israel shake their crimped tops at affectionate husbands. He would see scarlet tulips from the Netherlands nod their pretty heads at devoted grandpas, and red sweetheart roses from South America pout for hopeful suitors.

48

Perhaps St. Valentine would even join the chorus of big, tropical plants, whose heart-shaped petals sing, "Take my heart and give me yours, Love will last while life endures."

No doubt, he would be thrilled watching grandmas scouring card racks for the perfect valentine - something like "A loving little valentine, with hugs and Kisses too, for the sweetest valentine of all, Granddaughter, 'tis you."

To the undecided young lover eyeing a diamond engagement ring in a jewelry store, hmmm, what do you think would be St. Valentine's reaction? Being a chaste man, he might hesitate to offer: "Her glance invites, so be not slow; faint heart never won fair lady." However, as the enamored one took that leap and purchased the ring, both gallant souls would experience that "feeling that you're going to have a feeling that you've never felt before."

It's true, dear reader, that card designers, florists, jewelers, and candy stores capitalize on Valentine's Day, but I agree with Webster: "Love is an affection of the mind excited by beauty and worth of any kind." Love certainly deserves a special day on which admirers, including husbands and wives, can express their tender feelings. So what better time to do so than on February 14 in honor of St. Valentine who loved, and loved, and loved?

As for me, I'm not getting too frivolous this year - just a wee-little box of chocolates for my true love. Inside the red satin cover I'm tucking a simple hand-written note:

"Sixty-two years of devotion, Sweet William, is a long, long time. Thank you for being my faithful, special valentine."

Your ever-lovin' little gem, Pearl

The best way for a husband
to clinch an argument is to
take his wife in his arms.
. . . Anonymous

Singing Around the Campfire

There is one thing that is still good in America - group singing of beautiful old songs of the heart. Songs that bind families and friends together and make you feel warm inside. When I was a child, I liked church singing. One Sunday while singing a hymn, a sweet, melodic, strange sound flowed through my vocal chords. Harmony! At that time I thought everyone could harmonize. Not so. To hear and sing any note other than melody, without reading music, is a gift, like learning to play the piano "by ear."

In the fifties when our five children were growing up in Zeeland, Michigan, we harmonized around the kitchen sink. We were no "Jackson Five," but the singing, though amateurish, made dishwashing fun and togetherness heartwarming.

One popular song of that era was "Amen." It was a lively tune. At times, around our summer campfires at Silver Lake, we chanted the words, followed by clapping and singing the "Amens."

However, as time passed, the original words seemed so trite. "No doubt," I told myself, "anyone who loves to sing has an unwritten song in his or her heart." And so I gave it a try, writing new words that bring hope to today's world of sorrow and despair. Singing an old tune with a bright, new message around a campfire is like fanning to life again dying embers. I hope you will share this with your family, dear reader, around a summer campfire.

Chillun, listen up, now we're gonna strive
To sing a joyful chorus, bringin' you chillun alive.
Chillun, when sorrow o'er takes you, no need to faint or cry
Cause we're gonna tell you about a beautiful home on high.
Amen, Amen, Amen, Amen, Amen.

There'll be clappin' and singin', Hallelujahs will roll
When all God's chillun start shoutin' on Heaven's streets of gold.
There'll be no lyin' or stealin' up there where all is bliss,
No wheelin' and dealin', no blacks or whites, no sir, no prejudice.
Amen, Amen, Amen, Amen, Amen.

There'll be no abortions, sisters, no murders or divorce.
Just all God's chillun praisin' Him in one great joyful chorus.
The nuclear bombs can't reach us in that heavenly city so fair,
Cause the mighty hand of God will explode them in the air.
Amen, Amen, Amen, Amen, Amen.

Up there, no smokin' marijuana, no shootin' of cocaine,
No AIDS, no battered children, no cancer, no heart-felt pain.
Powerful guns mowing down youth will be no more.
And there'll be no 9/11 up there on that beautiful shore.

A-A-men, Amen, Amen.

In the future when our family harmonizes around the lake campfire, young sweet voices, once small and unsure note-wise, will fill the clear night air with melodic old "goodies" learned by the light of the silvery moon - and Grandma Pearl will teach them this new song with its uplifting message.

Someone has said, dear reader, "if you don't teach kids a good song, they'll make one up." Perhaps, neither their lyrics nor the melody will be worth harboring in the heart. Amen? Amen!

There is no truer
truth obtainable
by man than comes
of music.
. . . Browning

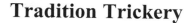

Tradition Trickery

Christmas traditions, which bind families together, are like satin ribbons, not easily broken. These unspoken memory-builders are the arms that reach out and draw the children home for Christmas - a popcorn ball in the stocking, caroling on Christmas Eve or listening to a tree-top angel singing *Silent Night.* If you discontinue one family custom, the voice of tradition blares out in a rebellious whisper that cannot be ignored.

One of our family Christmas traditions, and evidently the most treasured, was a wrapped "special" ornament hidden amidst pine-scented branches. Each year five eager children could hardly wait to open that last tiny, personalized gift, then, hang it on "their" tree.

However, as our family multiplied, there were no longer five ornaments to search for, buy and wrap, but fourteen. A delightful tradition had become a real chore. In 1980, our first Christmas celebrated at Silver Lake, I decided to give our five children their many ornaments and discontinue the practice. Just four days before Christmas, all other gifts wrapped, the red-bowed pine cone wreath hung and candles glowing in every window, I trudged up our circular staircase to the attic. In the cold dark I pulled the light string, bent over Grandma's trunk and began a visual search for the box of treasured ornaments.

"Those kids won't care if I skip the ornament giving," I muttered aloud.

"Oh, yes, they will," a voice seemed to call out in the dusty stillness. Startled, I called out, "Who's there?" I turned toward the open door. No one was there, of course. In the process, I bumped my head on a rafter. "That does it! Tradition! Humbug! We're not even having a tree," I said, rubbing the lump on my head.

Suddenly I heard the front door bang followed by a yell, "Mom, come see the tree." I hurried onto the balcony and discovered our nineteen-year-old son, Nick, shoving a ten-foot Norwegian pine through the doorway. He bounded up the stairs and handed me a stack of Christmas mail. He rushed on by to the attic to gather strings of twinkle lights, tarnished glass balls and, yes, dear reader, the dusty box of "special" ornaments.

I sat on the edge of the bed reading greetings from friends and relatives, half-listening to his chuckles and sentiments being expressed below as he remembered each ornament.

"Hey, Mom, here's that little skier you gave me when I first joined the ski club in 1974," he laughed. "And here's the little Hummel playing a horn - sure was fun playing in the band at ZHS for four years. Mom, no doubt about it, of all our presents over the years, the ornaments were the best." On and on and on.

His memories began to liquefy in my heart and then splashed upon the P.S. of my dear Momma's Christmas card held in my hand, "What ornaments are you giving the children this year?" That scribble settled the wrenching in my soul. With the tail of my apron I dried my tears and quietly tiptoed down the stairs and eased past the enthusiastic tree decorator. I bundled up, pulled on my boots and sloshed out through the snow to the car – en route to the nearest Hallmark Store.

Driving along on the slippery road, my thoughts were not of danger but of finding fourteen ornaments, one of which must be an angel for grandbaby Necia's first Christmas. On the eight-mile return trip, ornament problem solved, I realized that I had bowed to the voice of tradition.

Nine years and six grandchildren later, though, I stood up for a weary Grandma's rights and dropped the ornament giving. No one at our family Christmas party seemed to mind. Or so I thought. Shortly after arriving in Florida for the winter, the telephone rang. Our fourteen-year-old grandson Shawn's first words were, "Grandma, you forgot to give us our best present!" As soon as I hung up, I rushed to the mall, singing Joy to the World all the way, purchased and mailed twenty beautiful, shiny, brass ornaments.

Yes, dear reader, tradition had tricked me again.

The coming together of three
generations at Christmas
time gives a child a sense
of family and belonging.
. . . a pearl

Art Is In
The Eye of the Beholder

One summer while rummaging through our Silver Lake attic, I came upon something I had hidden in an old chest more than 30 years before. In the half-dark, I examined the 11 x 14 unframed winter scene painted in a Community Education art class at Zeeland High School.

Although I had failed art in 5th grade, that first night in class I felt very confident that I could now, at 43, whip up a Rembrandt masterpiece in 3 hours and hang it on my wall for guests to admire on the weekend. After all, doesn't enthusiasm make up for lack of talent? Not so, dear reader.

"First, students," the teacher said, "you must sketch lightly the three bottles you see on the table. Next, try to catch the light." Well, this is going to be a cinch, I thought joyfully. With pencil in hand, I sketched those bottles. They looked a little lop-sided, but the teacher said that was o. k., original.

Then, it was time to watercolor those bottles. I worked feverishly as I watched the clock tick away. But something went awry. The more I painted, trying to catch her "light" that I couldn't see, the rougher the paper-like canvas became. Just as the teacher approached my easel, she put her hand on my shoulder and said, "Pearl, I didn't realize you had never painted before. Perhaps acrylics would be a better medium for you." And with that, she reached for my painting and ripped it in strips. I could have wept.

However, she patiently introduced me to a "beginner" book from which I chose to paint the aforementioned winter scene. Step-by-step I followed the book. By the end of the 3-hour class I had not applied one brush of paint to my creation, only penciled in a faint horizon line, a few vertical sticks for trees, and a winding stream down a mountainside.

Determined to overcome failure, I struggled for five more weeks, each night the teacher praising my efforts. Gradually, patches of snow on bare birch limbs began to look real against the blue sky. My purple shadows on a snow-covered ground, created by sunlight streaming through virgin trees, were indeed awesome. Icy banks holding back the dark water of a winter stream were perfect. Well, so MY artistic eye thought.!

Having completed the course, I rushed home and stood the unframed painting upon the couch so all who entered could praise my work. Our son Jef, a sophomore in high school, came into the room, put his hands on his hips, like any art critic might do, and grinned down at me. "Yeah, Mom, that's a nice picture, but your river bank's not right." *What does a fifteen year-old know about high-class art anyway?* I disgustingly ignored him.

Fifteen minutes later, my husband Bill walked in. "That's a great picture, honey, but you need to work on your bank."

What on earth were they talking about? I couldn't see anything wrong with my bank. I went right to the phone and said to the teacher, "Joan, Jef and Bill say there is something wrong with my picture."

"Oh, you mean the bank, Pearl?"

Well, dear reader, I cried. She offered to help me fix it, but instead, I hid my failure in the attic and never painted again.

But, alas! That day in the attic I remembered the teacher saying it was "one of a kind," and so convinced myself that bank or no bank, I was hanging up that picture. So, I took the curled-up picture downstairs, signed it, Bill framed it and I proudly hung it in my bedroom.

A few days later our thirteen-year-old granddaughter, Meagan Pearl, sauntered into the living room and asked, "Grandma, did you really paint that picture in your bed room?" I nodded. "Why Grandma, you could be another Grandma Moses!" Needless to say, that picture will hang there until I die.

Dear reader, each of us is an artist in our own way, so if you have created something new, authentic – a painting, a poem, a piece of needlework, or any hand-crafted item - don't hide it in the attic. Frame it, hang it or display it in some way for the world to see, but mainly enjoy it. After all, "art is in the eye of the beholder."

Self confidence is the
first requisite for great
undertakings
    . . . Samuel Johnson

Seeds for Life

Dear reader, you'll never believe what Grandma Pearl is up to now. At 81 years of age I have become a fanatic on seed collecting. Whether it be an acorn from a giant oak, seeds from a juicy apple or a single seed from a tall, smiling sunflower, I am obsessed with capturing, planting and then watching any and all seeds develop into a living miracle.

Hanging in my garage at Silver Lake is a large, brown paper bag full of flower seeds collected over the last five years. In September, 2006, just for fun, I sprinkled a "few" of these miscellaneous seeds into my perennial flower garden. Wow! So many yellow and white daisies, purple bee balms and tall white "whatevers" came up among my perennials that I actually pulled up many of the new plants. But, what a beautiful sight to see – all from a little seed that cost me nothing!

In the summer of 2007, after beautifully reaping what I had sewn, my thoughts were, "Why not save apple seeds?" I cut a red, juicy apple in half, and then paused to study for the first time the star-shaped core containing 5 seed pockets. I removed 5 brown seeds and rushed out to plant them, hoping to see a sprout before winter. Yes, I know, dear reader, it would be much simpler to purchase a 4-foot apple tree, hoping to be able to pick an apple from my very own tree during my lifetime. But, I would miss the unfolding miracle of what a seed produces, generation after generation.

A few years ago I donated a 4-foot maple tree that came up from seed in my backyard to the Mears Historical Society. Now that tree is at least 10 feet tall and helping to beautify the grounds.

In May, 2007, I ambled along the Silver Lake State Park fence and marveled at the height of two beautiful maple trees that I had babied along for five years. All summer I would push their spindly limbs and leaves back through the chain link fence so they would grow straight and tall. Already they branch out well above the fence and offer a little shade for campers.

While inspecting those maples, I found a sprouting acorn. Immediately, I planted it in our tiny, sandy backyard. Two months later that sprout had grown to a straight, five-inch oak tree with 8 big green leaves, a miracle in the making. As I have no room in my little space, when that tree reaches 4 feet I will donate it to a public park to shade weary sightseers. Now, that's positive thinking for 81!

Finally, I hope you will be touched by this tale of planting seeds to enhance our life here on this planet. In July of 2007 a little blonde angel vacationing at Silver Lake gave me a single sunflower seed. She was sharing her "snack." I accepted graciously, but explained to Anna, 7, that I could not eat the seed but would plant it and next year we might have a big sunflower taller than she. "Really?" her eyes lit up.

Then I told her the story of planting seeds and watching them grow into something beautiful. She smiled and I began to quietly sing to her, "Oh, who can make a sunflower, I'm sure I can't, can you? Oh, who can make a sunflower, no one but God tis true." She had never heard that little ditty of a song but emphatically assured me that she learned about God and some miracles in her Christian School.

Eagerly, Anna asked when we would plant the seed. Two days later I dug a little hole in the sand, pushed the brown and white speckled seed down with my forefinger, then attached a little marker with the words, "Anna's Sunflower" to a rusty, iron horseshoe. She ran to view her one-seed garden and excitedly read the words. "When, when will the sunflower be as tall as I am?" She asked. I promised to keep it watered and explained that next year when she returns, it might just be as tall as she.

Dear reader, neither you nor I can make an acorn, an apple or a sunflower seed, but we can plant every seed we find to make life more beautiful for little Anna and many other little Annas to follow. Whether a shade tree, a fruit-bearing tree or a bright blossoming flower, all are gifts worth leaving behind.

Flowers have an expression of countenance...
Some seem to smile; some seem sad...
Others are plain, honest and upright, like
the broad- faced sunflower.
. . . Henry Ward Beecher

He that planteth a tree is a servant of God,
He provideth a kindness for many generations.
. . .   Henry Van Dyke

Family Fling, Anybody?

It's family reunion time again! Time for hugging, kissing, joking, laughing, reminiscing. Time to liven up summertime with a back-home family fling! Great Aunt Mary and good old "what's-his-name," are longing for an invite.

Plans for a successful, fun-filled reunion must begin early. Set a date, choose a place, and appoint committees to plan the food and games. Don't forget to include a "special happening" along with traditional goings-on.

THE DATE: Three-day reunions encourage relatives to come long distances and are much more memorable than a one-day affair. Our first Flaherty Fling began on Friday at sundown with a traditional campfire by the lake. Grandpa popped corn in an old wire popper and little ones roasted marshmallows on fresh-cut, green sticks. The warm buttery smell and squeals of delight were the invitation to a jam-packed weekend of food and fun.

THE PLACE: Of course, "Y'all come" for three days means sleeping accommodations must be arranged. Therefore, choosing a site is very important. A lake setting is ideal because of the varied lodging possibilities. There are usually rental cottages, motels, and campsites available. If a lake is not possible, there is always Uncle So-and-So's farm or a rented hall in the city where all can gather.

THE INVITATION: As soon as date and place is decided upon, mail out a questionnaire/flyer. Make the invitation exciting by mentioning plans for special events. Don't forget to include an order blank for "family tree" shirts. The Flahertys, being Irish, ordered a Kelly green with a white tree from a Tee-shirt specialty shop. The more shirts you order, the cheaper. Be sure to follow-up with necessary final details, but remember that the initial invitation creates enthusiasm and assures a big turnout.

THE FOOD. Togetherness is what reunions are all about, so meals should be eaten together. At our reunion, which involved five meals, two or thee families were responsible for one meal for the entire group. They purchased the food, prepared and served it and cleaned up afterwards.

When Irish lads and lassies, wearing their green, appeared for breakfast at 8:30 on Saturday morning, we were, indeed, a united clan.

THE GAMES: If a family sports enthusiast plans the games for both young and old, they are bound to be a success. Libraries provide excellent books on indoor and outdoor games for reunions. The water-filled balloon-toss, sack races, and the paper-plate discus are all popular. Don't forget the children's sawdust scramble for pennies and wrapped candies. If at a lake, the watermelon and egg relays are a wet scream. Whatever, plan lots of activities for the family Olympics, starting immediately after breakfast on Saturday.

When our wild and wet Olympics ended, lunch was served. Then, Grandpa Bill cranked up the old ice-cream maker. Fifteen children scrambled for "my turn" and all happily indulged in his vanilla treat speckled with fresh, hand-picked, sweet cherries.

FREE TIME: A well-planned reunion does allow free time. On Saturday afternoon at Silver Lake, there was time for napping, swimming, canoeing, sailing, sunbathing, and just catching up on the latest family news. Some chose to go cherry picking. The men either rowed across to the high sand dunes or relaxed while trolling for bass or blue gills, pluses for choosing a lake site for a reunion.

A SPECIAL HAPPENING: To make a reunion memorable, plan something very special - a hayride, a sing-along cruise on the lake, or a talent show by the campfire. Saturday night must be exciting and one not to be forgotten.

Maybe the old gang won't be quite as bright-eyed and bushy-tailed for the Sunday morning brunch, but after Grandma's strong brew, they'll be ready for group picture-taking, more free time, and the grand feast at 1:30.

Yes, dear reader, when they all come to greet ye, arms reaching while smiling sweetly, it will be good to touch the green, green grass of home.

> What on earth is half so dear,
> so longed for, as the hearth
> of home?
>   . . . Emily Bronte

Last Will and Testament

To all children I bequeath dunes to climb,

golden sands on which to build castles

and clear, blue waters unmasking

finned creatures from the deep.

I bequeath white clouds that float high

above white birches weeping for joy.

And I bequeath to all children long, bright

days in which to frolic, in a thousand ways,

and many starlit nights in which to marvel at

God's mysterious trail of the Milky Way.

60

Family Fun at beautiful Silver Lake. Top left clockwise: Tubing along high sand dunes shore; Bill finding Love in a Bottle; His new yellow Sunbird; Kuznz Kamp; Roasting marshmallows around the campfire; Building sand castles at the dunes; Inset: Little fisherman, Grandson Shawn; Grand nieces Maggie and Alex.

Love in a Bottle

Oh my, what to give Dad for Father's Day! This year, skip the shirt and socks routine and give him a unique gift in a bottle. You say, bottle? Yes, dear reader, and I'm not referring to cologne, after-shave, barbecue sauce, or booze. First, you must come up with a brilliant idea. Then, be creative in presenting your gift to Dad, thereby making his special day one to be long remembered.

Several years ago Bill received his most memorable Father's Day gift in a bottle - actually a string of bottles. For many years he had sailed a small Sunfish on Silver Lake and longed to have a larger boat in which he could sail dry. But funds were not there for a "step up." So the children and I came up with the idea that if all would pitch in whatever they could afford, we might be able to swing a new boat.

During the winter I wrote letters to the married children, enthusiastically and secretly promoting funds for Dad's new boat. Within days, I received checks in varied amounts. Kitty and Nick, teenagers, each pledged their first summer month's income from jobs at the lake. I had already earmarked my income from a winter, part-time job. In jig time, we reached our goal. But, how were we going to surprise Dad on Father's Day?

I never dreamed of putting his gift in a bottle. But, when we arrived at the cottage the first week in June, I found six, large, empty detergent bottles in a local laundromat trash can. Presto! One for each child's monetary gift. I took all of the checks and bills to the bank and traded them for one dollar bills. Then, I stuffed each bottle and tied them to a long rope. Early on Father's Day, we blindfolded Bill and led him out to the lake. I placed in his hands the end of the rope and asked him to follow it to the end where it was attached to his old Sunfish. All five children and I stood on the dock, prodding him on as he pulled himself along, one bottle at a time. He kept wading until he reached the end. As he gathered up the bottles and rope and removed his blindfold, we all yelled HAPPY FATHER'S DAY!

Needless to say, as he read the notes inside and counted all those $1.00 bills, $2,500 in all, representing much sacrifice, tears welled up in

62

his eyes. Within a week, he was sailing dry in his bright yellow, new Sunbird and did so in that "gift in a bottle" for 26 years.

You don't necessarily need to give your Dad a boat, dear reader, for Father's Day. Here are ten simple suggestions on things you could put in a bottle - or two or three bottles, depending on how many children in your family:

A gift certificate to his favorite restaurant.

A self-written poem or a letter of love.

Tickets to a concert for him and Mom

A child's hand-made card, either hand-written or computer-designed.

A gift certificate to a sports store where he can choose sports equipment or apparel.

Enough cash (in dollar bills, of course) to fill up his gas tank.

Your coupon of promise for his favorite home-made cookies, a pie, or jar of jam.

An airplane ticket to some historical site he has always wanted to visit.

A fishing trip or a championship ball game, arranged by a travel agency.

A child's coupon for a free car wash or lawn mowing.

As you can see, dear reader, the list is endless. Again, put thought into your gift. Bottle it or box it, but be creative in just how or where you will present your love for Dad on his special day. He will treasure the Father's Day memory - forever.

He that honoureth
his father shall have
a long life.
...Ecclesiasticus III, 6

Unearthed Treasures

On Friday, July 1, 2005 at 11:00 a.m. our cottage buzzed with excitement. A nephew born in Japan, and his two handsome sons had just arrived. Jean and Rick Flaherty had never been to Silver Lake and could hardly wait to swim in the deep silvered waters and hike the dunes to search for unearthed treasures. Their black, inquisitive eyes lit up when father Loyd spoke of going on such a treasure hunt many summers before when his missionary parents brought him to Silver Lake for a visit.

Unfortunately, that Friday was the windiest and coldest pre Fourth of July weather in the history of our 39 years at Silver Lake. White caps on the lake rolled in from the dunes and slapped our shores while across the lake, cutting, blowing sand challenged any visitor to hike or even take a dune buggy ride on our famous mountains of golden sand. So, all my plans to make this a special happening for the two boys seemed swept away. But, after a lunch of hamburgers on the grill and all the traditional, good, American picnic fare – baked beans, potato salad, and blueberry pie – all hale-and-hearty hikers were off to the dunes by van where they parked at the State Park access.

Evidently, the eleven and nine year olds had never experienced finding such a marvel on Mt. Fuji, their highest mountain in Japan. Bill chose not to tackle the job of leading the search for the buried treasure on such a cold, windy day. But he knew the boys would be disappointed if they searched and found no "fulgurites." So while the not-so-hale-and-hearty, including Grandma Pearl, waited for the gang's return, Bill, doubting their success because of the weather, pulled out a box of fulgurites collected over the 23 years he had worked as a Silver Lake Park Ranger on the dunes.

After two hours of chilly fun, hiking and swimming, the explorers returned empty handed. But, Bill was ready. When he opened the shoebox, the boys' bright eyes and enthusiasm seemed to warm the whole room. They, as well as uninformed adults, listened intently as Bill explained each little tube of glass and told them the scientific process of lightning striking sand. Suddenly I realized how little I knew of such phenomena.

Fulgurites are formed when a powerful lightning bolt melts the sand into a glass-like state. Although the ones discovered in the Silver Lake Dunes are varied in size and shapes, most are thin, "lightning sticks," typically a tube with a shiny, glazed inside, where the heat is most intense, and a grainy and rough, metal-gray outside. Usually, these can be more easily found in dune valleys where the wind has swept away surface sand.

Were Jean and Rick, two little boys who speak both English and Japanese and hail from a land of chopsticks, rice balls and rice cakes disappointed in their visit to America? Not at all. To them, the sand dunes were as exciting, if not more so, than visiting historical castles from the Shogun Era or the famed 730 year-old bronzed Buddha in their homeland. And, needless to day, they loved not only the fulgurites Bill boxed up for them, but the two little American flags I gave them to share with Japanese friends and their mom, Sacchico.

July 1, 2005 – a perfect pre Fourth of July celebration unearthing joy with loved ones from a distant land, Japan.

What a strange world
ours is! One touch
of the earth and glory
might burst on us.
Oh, what a hid universe!
Anonymous

Mom, We're Home!

Some parents have all the luck. Not only do their grown children love them dearly, but they give them fantastic presents to prove it. Once, a friend told me that their kids bought them a round-trip ticket to Hawaii for their fortieth anniversary. Another's kid surprised them with a $2,500 golf cart - for no special reason.

Well, we don't have kids like that! But that's all right. Come summertime they do all flock to Silver Lake to see us - the kids, the spouses, the grandkids, 20 total - whoops, 23 with dogs.

How do I stand it? Every weekend I put on my back brace, zip my lip - well, try to - sail, swim, play beach volleyball, and cook, and cook, and cook. Now, don't get me wrong, dear reader. They do help and they do bring food - uncooked, of course. And they bring a lot of other goodies, like a beach of sand that sifts through the carpet clear down to the plywood. They bring unlimited fingerprints too, which, when smeared on our six sliding glass doors, distort our beautiful sunsets.

They also bring pop and beer by the case and when they leave, we quietly gather up the empties from the dock, the boats, the balcony, the garage. Now, if I were a cusser, I'd cuss as I unload the cans at the grocer's and discover the beer has soaked the LeSabre carpet, leaving our only means of transportation to church smelling like a tavern on wheels. I vow then and there to give a lecture next weekend on alcohol destroying their brain cells!

But, I love my kids, I really do. So I actually don't say much. Well, once and awhile when our lawn begins to look like it's tiled with cigarette butts instead of grass, I do lovingly just mention, again, that smoking is harmful and without a doubt will kill them.

Then, there are the dogs. They bring big, clawing, digging dogs. Our beautifully varnished entry doors, etched with claw marks, look like a newly raked field, standing upright of course. And the manicured, toiled-over yard looks like all the meteors that ever fell cratered it. Every weekend, same dogs, different craters.

But, dear reader, Bill and I stay calm, honest. After they leave on Sunday night, we collapse. On Monday we shake out the sixteen sandy sheets. Then, along with a mound of wet dish, bath and beach towels we labor, with love of course, washing, hanging out, taking in and folding. Wearily we trudge upstairs to make all seven beds for cozy, weekend heads. On Tuesday we vacuum, Windex the fingerprints, and mop till we drop. Wednesday is rake-up-the-butts and fill-in-the-craters day. Thursday we finish off the leftovers and rest up for the return of the Friday "Let's go to Grandma's" gang.

We know our kids love us though. Long after Labor Day, when we think back to the fun times of a too-fleeting summer, I pull out this treasured letter and re-read what our very loving, 19 year-old, rascal-of-a- son, wrote us at the end of his first year away at college:

Dear Mom and Dad:

I'm writing this letter to tell you just how glad I am that you are my parents. Things often get so hectic day-to-day that I've never told you how special you are. So I thought I'd put it in writing for you to read and remember.

I know that it isn't easy being parents and that we don't always agree. And yet I know that you want only the best for your children. It's obvious from the sacrifices you've made. The things you didn't buy for yourselves so that we kids could have the things we wanted or needed. Or the sacrifices of your time making Halloween costumes - I won first prize as Jack and the Beanstalk, remember?

Just so you'll know it was all worthwhile, please believe that I remember every story and poem you ever read or wrote to me, every lecture on manners, every talk about honesty and doing things the right way, every quaint old "Mother Logic" expression. Perhaps not by heart, but enough. They're the best parts that you've given to me and I'll always be grateful.

I love you, Nick.

So, dear reader, who needs a fancy golf cart or a free trip to Hawaii? Or even a letter for that matter? Like most parents, we love just hearing those words, "Mom, we're home." It is our prayer that their love for us will continue forever to show up on the soles of their sandy feet.

Christmas in October?

Each fall many "snowbirds" struggle with the heart-wringing decision of whether to stay up north to watch little Johnny open his Christmas present or fly south early to avoid the inevitable throes of winter.

Breaking with holiday tradition can cause quite a stir. Kids fret and fume and Grandma cries, but once the tinsel tie is broken, much good comes out of celebrating Christmas early. Although transition without friction is tricky, it can be accomplished with a fun "theme," triggered perhaps by a summer trip you have taken or by the actual day on which the celebration will fall.

In 1986 when we announced to our children, all married with children of their own, that Christmas would be on October 31, naturally they fired shots of protest at their crazy "snowbird" parents. However, we had a secret plan for a memorable Christmas celebration and stuck with our decision, hoping that all eighteen would show.

On the eve of Halloween, Bill and I donned Groucho Marx masks and watched through the window as each family arrived. Grins swept across long faces as they spotted the door wreath bowed with wide, orange and black crepe paper ribbons. Then, smiles burst into laughter when two Grouchos greeted them with a "Ho-Ho-Ho Merry Christmas." More laughter rang out when they noticed tiny, orange paper smiley faces, with twinkle-light noses, glistening on our tree. Soon every heart was gladdened by the Halloween-Christmas setting.

The following year we visited relatives in Japan by way of Hawaii. In October our magnificent tree glowed with pink silk hibiscus leis from Honolulu and unusual oriental ornaments from Tokyo. Gifts of Chinese dolls and tee shirts brought shrills of delight from all. No one seemed to mind that Christmas was being celebrated again in October.

In 1988, after a tour of our National Parks, colorful post cards tied with red satin ribbons dressed October's Christmas tree. What a fun way to relive a wonderful summer experience while sharing with children and grandchildren a post-card trip across America. Not only was this an unusual early celebration, but also an educational one.

The following year, however, my creativity waned, dear reader. August was upon us and we had no special plan for an early Christmas. Discouraged, I said to Bill one evening, "Christmas is for the birds!" "You're right, but what a great theme," he said. Immediately we began sketching bird invitations and searching for gifts that set hearts atwitter. Come October 7 the tree sparkled with saran-wrapped packets of birdseed tied with jaunty red yarn. Secretly nesting beneath were red, cardinal bird feeders and antique duck decoys for each family

After the turkey was devoured, all children lined up outdoors for breaking of a Big Bird piñata. Squeals of laughter rang out through the crisp October air as each, blindfolded, flailed away. When Big Bird broke, all scrambled to retrieve cellophane-wrapped candies and shiny silver coins strewn among colored leaves of autumn.

As a finale to Christmas with a theme, on October 10, 1992 our entire family, now totaling 22, celebrated Christ's birth Western style. Bill and I, recalling summer's foot-stomping good time in Branson, Missouri, decorated the tree with twenty-two, red-bowed neckerchiefs, hand sewn by Grandma.

Smells of hot caramel boiling on the stove filled the entire cottage. After each had crafted a popcorn ball, ten giddy grandchildren, ages four to sixteen, all with sticky fingers, laughingly tugged on strands of taffy. Later in the day all cowhands donned neckerchiefs for a hayride with real white horses. I can still hear the clip-clop accompanying happy voices twanging out, "Joy to the World, the Lord is Come" as we circled Silver Lake.

Celebrating Christmas with our family in October, dear reader, proved to be a good thing. It frees loved ones to enjoy their own friends and family during the holidays and it frees Mom and Dad. Now, we fly south, like all smart birds, before the winds of winter hinder flight to sun and sea. Then, on December 25 we join long-time friends and again celebrate the birthday of the Christ Child.

How many observe Christ's birthday! How many His precepts! O! 'tis easier to keep holidays than commandments.
. . . Ben Franklin

Grandma's Prize Box

There are many reasons why grandchildren like to go to Grandma's house. For some, it is to eat her chocolate chip cookies. For others it is to get a Grandma hug or a tickle kiss – you know the one where her eyelash flutters on their cheeks. Our children and grandchildren look forward to playing games around our old oak table, hoping to win a prize from Grandma Pearl's Prize Box.

You will find in this box, dear reader, no money, no jewels, nothing worth playing your heart out for. Still, all are anxious to win one of the unique prizes Grandma has hidden in her bedroom closet. No one is allowed to peek in the box at anytime, not even to choose their own prize at the end of any game of cards played with plastic poker chips. Whatever the prize, it is without question surprisingly interesting when a child or an adult wins – or loses.

Grandma Pearl chooses what she thinks suitable or pleasing for first and last place. More than 20 years ago this idea emerged as I tossed small, new items found at yard sales into my "fun" box.

One summer while dusting, I found childish signatures taped on the bottom of my old, decorative junk, things they were claiming as their inheritance. So, gradually, antique "finds" were added to the prize box.

Sometimes, the prizes are hilarious and the winning moment has been relived over and over for many years. For example, once our granddaughter Angela and her boyfriend Kyle joined others at our cottage for popcorn and cards. Even before the game started, they began laughing about Grandma's prize Kyle had won three summers before–a pair of like-brand-new, yard-sale jeans.

Now, dear reader, when I found those hole-free, fadeless, size 30 jeans for $1.00, I knew that sooner or later a lucky young man would appreciate my great bargain. And Kyle, that night, amidst much jovial razzing, had put them on and driven away, a winner! As they joked about his special prize, John, granddaughter Necia's husband, said, "Well, I can top that! The first time I played here at the cottage I won a really neat prize – an English nut cracker!"

"Yes, you did," said Necia. "But I can top that! Before we were married, I won an antique sterling silver butter knife." *What great memorable gifts*, thought I as a smile played across my heart.

After they left, I hauled out Grandma's Prize Box to determine whether it needed replenishing before the next Family Fun Night at the cottage. *Each little treasure must thrill their hearts so much they will talk about it for years to come,* I reminded myself.

In that box, dear reader, was a sterling silver tray. So what if serving dishes are more casual now and silver tea sets are out? Everyone should have one of these for show – and memories.

Next, a hand-painted, floral, made-in-China candy dish. At least I thought it was when I bought it for 50 cents. But just now I turned this beautiful import over and read, "For decorative use only. Article may poison food." Now, no Grandma would think of giving this to a dear grandchild who couldn't read! But, it still is a great prize for an adult who loves china knickknacks.

Oh, also in that prize box, are five little red plaid, stuffed Christmas angels, all holding a red heart. These I found at a dollar store after the holidays for thirty-three cents each. I just know that any grandchild lucky enough to win one of these will hold me in his or her heart forever.

Next, on sale for $1.00, a pair of black and white, polka dot flip-flops, very fashionable in the year 2005, and just what every teenager loves. So what if they are a little thin and catch on the carpet when you try to run in them – great prize for sure!

The little solid brass bud vase, made in India, is kind of like the butter knife Necia won. After the winner is married and matures, I'm sure she'll appreciate brass, even it does require polishing. In my book, anything brass is a great unbreakable gift.

And there is more in Grandma's Prize Box waiting to be awarded to the lucky winner, or loser: There are the never-used, modern, gray candlesticks that are etched with little black and white animals – so what if you can't recognize the "artsy" animals? They're a conversation piece!

I also have in this box a 25th Anniversary china bell trimmed in silver. It is this Grandma's prayer that someone will stay married for 25 years!

Well, I could go on and on because there is much more in that secret box - some not as exciting as the aforementioned, but still treasures that will keep memories of Family Fun at our Silver Lake cottage alive for the next 50 years.

I hope you, dear reader, will try filling a box of your own and experience the love and laughter my children and grandchildren have for two decades while winning prizes from Grandma's Prize Box.

A Letter to Grandchildren

Dear Grandchildren:

Did you know that on the second Sunday of September National Grandparents Day is celebrated all across America? Many years ago a West Virginia housewife, Marian McQuade, who had 40 grandchildren, convinced Congress that this special day was needed to honor grandparents. One of Mrs. McQuade's primary objectives was to persuade grandchildren to tap the wisdom and heritage of their grandparents. And, so I am writing this to thank you for listening again to endless tales of your ancestors, plus to all the homespun advice we so generously, but cautiously, offered this summer while you and your friends visited at Silver Lake.

Forty-six days of your coming and going were a blessing to us. However, we were amazed to discover there were so many important things that teenagers need to know besides the names of every rock-and-roller, the best suntan lotion and the latest CD equipment.

Grandpa and I trust you did learn one simple fact - that soap and water does a fantastic job of cleaning your face. It was overwhelming when you and your friends, boys and girls alike, came with large cosmetic cases full of waterless gels, foams, sprays, germ blasters and facial scrubs. Why, I never had a zit in my life and all I ever used was plain old soap and water. Makes me smile now, remembering one comment on the subject, "But Grandma, you're old-fashioned!" True, but hopefully, dear child, you gained a little wisdom from the truth.

And, touching on courtesy: When one of you came into the living room eating that bowl of "something," I couldn't help but mention that it is not kind to eat in the presence of others without sharing. Remember the answer? "But THEY never share!" Believe me, I did understand where you were coming from in today's self-centered society, but I thought all children learned sharing in Kindergarten.

We enjoyed teaching one of your friends how to use a potato peeler, as well as how to sew by hand and on the sewing machine. She seemed thrilled with the little kitten pillow she stitched. It will be a nice remembrance of the 5 weekends spent with us at Silver Lake. It is so sad though that these homemaking skills are no longer taught at home or in Home Economics in school.

When we were playing games, or just talking in general, perhaps you thought it silly that we expected all studious young people to know basic facts. Like, the sun always sets in the West, that the Atlantic Ocean is to the East and that forever there are 36 inches in a yard. These are absolutes and once you learn them, you will never forget. Let me thank you now for finally accepting another absolute - curfew at Grandma's house is 11:00 p.m.

No doubt, one of the most satisfying revelations was that you make wonderful teenage job trainees. Although most of you had never washed a window, you sure learned fast and it made me and Grandpa very happy that you did it willingly and enjoyed the challenge. A little belated hint - be sure to always rub the glass dry to avoid streaks.

We also are very grateful for those who volunteered to tackle washing down our wood paneling in the living room. When grandparents are old, they make better supervisors than laborers. The Murphy's oil-soap-good-smell still lingers. And, we will never forget your three friends who drove 70 miles to help clean the high plate rails and shelves. Neither Grandpa nor I can manage step ladders any longer.

I must say that next to our preacher's grandkids, you are the greatest. I wonder if they too make their beds, wash their own dishes, and do their own laundry. By pitching in to help over the course of the summer, you have learned to do more difficult tasks. But most importantly, you have shown love and compassion for your grandparents.

Dear grandchildren, on Grandparents Day we don't expect our mailbox to be stuffed with cards and letters. Nor do we expect the telephone to ring off the hook; however, it is my prayer that you have read, and will abide by, the latest jewel in the *Pearls of Wisdom* jar in the bathroom, "DON'T SMOKE, DRINK, OR CHEW NOR RUN AROUND WITH THEM THAT DO!"

Nuf said.

Hugs,
Grandma & Grandpa

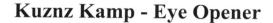

Kuznz Kamp - Eye Opener

Grandparents, if you are concerned about the upbringing of your precious grandchildren, have your own structured cousins' camp next summer. Start planning now. I promise it will be an eye-opener. I learned about such a camp from a grandmother in Alabama. After embellishing her plan somewhat, Woe-is-Me and her assistant, Me's husband, forged ahead with a program that any director of a prestigious children's camp, with a staff of 30, would have killed for. All of our six darlings were under the age of 11, so we scheduled many appropriate, fun-filled activities as well as a few "get- ready-for-life-kid" adventures - cooking, sewing, woodworking, cherry picking, etc., etc., etc.

Upon arrival at the cottage, each cousin was given a red, Big Chief tablet and a navy blue tee shirt - that *fit*. On each pocket Grandpa had stenciled in white the logo KUZNZ KAMP. Every morning at precisely 8:00 when lethargic Me rang a cowbell, six wild Indians spiraled down the staircase ready for powwowing. After breakfast, devotions and kitchen detail, out to the flagpole they marched. Five little maidens, giggling, reminded Eric, their Kuzn brave, that a true patriot does not wear his Tiger baseball cap while reciting the Pledge of Allegiance.

During class time at 9:00, Me and Me's husband watched in amazement as one child, taught a craft. They had been warned ahead of time and all came prepared with materials and know-how. Those angelic children shaped candles, beaded crosses, pressed flowers, sketched birds, and knotted friendship bracelets. No doubt, every Kuzn was a born teacher, just like Grandpa!

Day 1. We toured a local Indian Museum, frantically jotting notes in red Big Chief journals. Lesson learned: "Never forget your heritage."

Day 2. Off to a cherry orchard where they watched the mechanics of shaking cherries onto large canvases. Then, with much enthusiasm, they each picked a peanut-butter bucket full of red sour cherries. Later, with little enthusiasm, they pitted them. Lesson learned: "Work never killed your Grandma."

Day 3. Woe-is-Me and Me's husband taught machine sewing of granny aprons for the maidens and a denim carpenter's apron for little brave. Lesson learned: "Some things cannot be bought."

Day 4. They sloshed sugar and milk in a small Baggie, which was encased in a larger Baggie containing salt and ice, a cool treat that refreshed hot campers and Woe-is-Me. Lesson learned: "Me's Assistant a great Grandpa."

Day 5. Free Time until lunch. Lesson learned: "Don't expect Grandma to plan every minute of your life!"

Daily from 1:00 to 2:30, *you know who* and her assistant collapsed while the six jolly campers rested on their bunks and brought Big Chief journals up-to-date. Afterwards, they sailed, swam, made sand castles, romped on the dunes or competed in beach Olympics with prizes being awarded.

However, on the last day of camp, Me, nearing exhaustion, switched to Plan B, which was a trolley ride through the country, dinner out on Pentwater Bay, and a gazebo-in-the-park band concert. The six, well-mannered darlings, in their matching Kuznz Kamp tee shirts, cavorted among hundreds of concert goers, dancing, singing, or marching to *Stars and Stripes Forever.* Once, Me glanced over at Me's husband who was actually smiling.

Back at the cottage, happy, relaxed moms and dads began to arrive. When all were seated in the living room, six efficient Kuznz, garbed in granny aprons, served the cherry pies they had made earlier in the day. Me heap pleased.

As the blood-red sun plunged over the dunes into Lake Michigan, glowing parents circled our beach campfire for an awards ceremony. Their talented, feathered protégés performed an Indian Corn Dance they had practiced all week. Firelight flickered on sun-drenched palefaces as they sang like robins and read a page from their Big Chief "talking leaves." Needless to say, dear reader, Me proud, very proud.

Then, an antique, candy-filled, "keepsake" for Kuznz Kamp achievements was presented to each camper: A wooden rolling pin for Best Cook. A china cream pitcher for Marathon Champ. A Courier & Ives plate with a grandma's garden gate for Best Craft. A Blue Onion bowl for Best Sailor. A Courier and Ives tin for Best Gymnast and a cut-glass sugar bowl for Best Journalist.

As the finale, Gold Medals dangling from red, white and blue ribbons were awarded for the Most Cooperative, Most Athletic, Most Enthusiastic, Best Journal Writer, Best Computer Whiz, and Best All-Round Camper. All standing in a row, they smiled for pictures. At that moment, dear reader, a very pleased Woe-is-Me decided that most wild angels will survive despite their parents' upbringing.

A Mother's Love Is Special

Why, dear reader, do sons and daughters from Maine to California make a special effort on the second Sunday of May to "go-a-mothering?" Perhaps it is because President Woodrow Wilson in 1914 issued a proclamation that flags be flown as a "public expression of our love and reverence for the mothers of our country." Perhaps it is because a loving, thoughtful Sunday School Teacher, Miss Anna Jarvis of Philadelphia, proposed the same year that children honor mothers by bearing gifts. From then on the observance spread across our nation. Or perhaps - no, without a shadow of a doubt - it is because of a strong love bond that draws children, whether six or sixty, back to the origin of their birth – and to mother.

Poets have never penned enough metaphors or similes to adequately describe a mother's great love. In remembrance of my own dear Momma, Polly Ann Henson, I offer these praises:

A mother's love is like poetry; it portrays the beauty and good in every offspring.

A mother's love is the air and light in a child's life.

A mother's love is like the morning star, shining from birth 'til death.

A mother's love is magic - it changes tears to smiles.

A mother's love is like a soft down comforter providing warmth and security.

A mother's love is the mortar cementing the family structure together.

A mother's love is like a symphony, woodwinds and strings pulling together in harmonious composition.

A mother's love is the center pole in the family circus tent - if it fails, the show cannot go on.

A mother's love is the influence that elevates all who come under its sway.

A mother's love is the holiest passion in a human heart; that which molds pure thoughts and prompts kind actions.

It makes no difference whether a mother is a saintly, silver-haired Madonna or a stumbling young mother rearing children to the best of her ability. She is endowed with special sweet and tender love that is patient, devoted, enduring and sacrificial. She may be a natural mother, a foster mother, a stepmother, an adoptive mother or a single mother; but the one thing mothers have in common is an intrinsic, eternal love for their child.

Each Mother's Day, dear reader, go an extra mile to visit or call your mother. Someone once said, "He who goes-a-mothering will find sweet reunion and violets in his lane."

Tide of Life

The mother crouched upon the sand
A mist concealed her frame
Embedded deep within her womb
Lay birth...or death and shame.

She wrestled with the undertow
As tears fell on her breast
Where once had suckled other babes
When life was at its crest.

To calm the riled winds of fate
And waves that slapped the shore
The words of Longfellow cried out
Above the ocean's roar:

"Oh what would the world be to us
If the children were no more?
We would dread the desert behind us
Worse than the dark before."

Horizon's arms engulfed her thoughts
In one great purple sweep;
The light, a buoy to her mind,
Stirred treasures from the deep:

Memories of cradled smiles,
Of gurgling, cooing mirth,
Like sunlit tides dispelled her fears,
Aborting death...assuring birth.

Mom, You Are
Exactly What You Shoulda Been

We all know, dear reader, what makes a mother – her patience, cheerfulness, thoughtfulness, kindness and her endless love for every little soul she brings into this world. I'm sure that my own five children realize that I did my very best to bring them up to be decent human beings. But, as I look back to those nurturing years, I often think of the little humorous quips I occasionally tossed out about what "I shoulda been."

I had kind of forgotten about that long list of "shoulda beens" until Mother's Day, 2005 when I received a hand-written note from our 45 year-old son, Nick. He thanked me for sticking with him to the end during his teenage years and then ended with these touching words: "Mom, I know you have always said you should have been many things, including a doctor, a teacher, even a preacher. But, you know what, Mom? You are exactly what you should have been – my Mom." This, indeed, was one of the greatest hand-written Mother's Day Greetings that I, or any mother, could ever receive.

As I look through that cloudy window of remembrance at 81, it is clear that I no longer need to say "I shoulda been," because I WAS!

Yes, I WAS a doctor on duty twenty-four hours day and night, attending to hurts whether they be scrapes cured with a band-aid or fevers cured with cold cloths and aspirin. I diagnosed measles and mumps, which were treated non-professionally with bed rest. Tonsillitis was treated with a saltwater gargle. Like other mothers, I was a doctor with an M.O.M. degree – Mother Offering Mercy; i.e. kind and compassionate treatment with innate divine wisdom.

Of course, as teenagers, there were sprained ankles, broken bones in the feet, and pulled ligaments while playing basketball. Our youngest son had emergency hand surgery after jumping out a two-story window following a nightmare. Son Dan suffered a football concussion and Kitty had mono. More serious injuries, of course, required a doctor's examination and treatment.

78

But, dear reader, the long-term attending physician with loving hands and a gentle heart was none other than MOM.

This Mother's Day, I also realize that never again do I need to say, "I shoulda been a teacher." I WAS a teacher. Realizing the importance of books and the joy gleaned from reading, I took all five children to the library once a week and each came home with five books on their level. During the week I read all books to the two pre-kindergarten children and the others read all 25 while lying on the living room floor – no TV. Homework was checked every evening by you know who – the "teacher" MOM. As they left each morning, homework in their book bags, it was Mom who, with a pat on the back, encouraged them with my famous original "Do your best today, in all you do and all you say." And seemingly, they did!

It's up to MOMS to teach the importance of education, good manners, respect for others, and many other "musts" in order to reap responsible children. So, needless to say, I don't ever need to repeat, "I shoulda been a teacher." I WAS!

Now, as for "shoulda been a preacher," the presence of God could be felt in our home. At a very young age, the children learned the simple prayer, "God is Great, God is Good." And even today, they and their children often repeat this at the dinner table when they visit at Silver Lake. Although they learned The Ten Commandments in Church, we tried to enforce these great truths in their daily lives. Should I have been a preacher? I WAS!

So, on Mother's Day I encourage all mothers to enjoy their children while rejoicing in the fact that "You are exactly what God created you to be - A MOM."

A man loves his sweetheart
the most, his wife the best,
but his mother the longest.
. . . Irish Proverb

A White Elephant for Christmas?

According to Noah Webster, "A white elephant is rare and sometimes regarded as sacred." It also is "something from which little profit or use is derived."

A little ceramic white elephant, given to me at a Nettles Island Christmas party a few years ago, still adorns my kitchen counter. True, it has no monetary value, but serves as a constant reminder of a joyous time with friends. Perhaps, this inexpensive treasure, as well as utterances out of the mouth of babes, triggered a switch from our giving store-bought gifts at our family Christmas parties to giving "white elephants."

For several years I had heard many disturbing comments, such as, "Mom, I have two denim shirts already." "Grandma, nobody wears those anymore." "Grandma, I wanted one like..." These quips heralded an end to my tireless effort of searching for just the right gift for 23 people, which I had done for many moons. When I mentioned to my daughter that the shopping, buying, and wrapping had become overwhelming, she suggested doing away with presents entirely. Thus, at our annual Christmas celebration at Silver Lake in October 1997, disguised white elephants marched in as an alternative.

Each family member brought a gaily wrapped, used but useable, present for his or her age group. After a spiraled ham dinner served on once-a-year china, the varied surprises were piled high in the center of the living room floor. All, trumpeting like a jungle herd, gathered around the white elephants. Forgetting momentarily that a chosen treasure could be snatched up by someone else during the second-go-round, both children and adults poked and squeezed and shook the hidden secrets.

I kept urging our teenagers, who always need money, to choose *my* cleverly wrapped gift. I had padded a huge, black plastic garbage bag, filled it with 56 recyclable pop cans worth $5.60, and tied it with an over-sized red bow. But, remembering Grandma's past shenanigans at parties, they all ignored my advice. And so, my clever gift was the last chosen.

80

However, after the bag was opened, everyone begged the lucky owner to trade for their "lemons." But it was toooo late.

Actually, many of the white elephant gifts were worth fighting for. Like the two green and yellow tie-dyed tee shirts - not exactly the intended Green Bay Packer colors, but a perfect camouflage for a hunter. Or, the solid iron antique vise - not useful to a child, but perfect for some woodworker. Then, there were many "partial" rolls of bright Christmas wrapping - perfect for any *tiny-gift* giver. The one that summoned the most laughs though was a racy night shirt on which was printed a sexy female wearing red, lacy undergarments accented with black garters - perfect for shocking an unexpected, visiting mother-in-law!

As for me, I simply loved my gift of gaudy earrings and necklace - a must for a prize-winning Genie on Halloween. And Bill, he absolutely could not have lived without *his* new, white elephant, black with white print, nylon, loose-fitting boxer shorts. They are not only great for lounging for eight hours, but the thousand glow-in-the-dark skeletons light his way from Lazy Boy to bed.

One thing for sure, dear reader, Grandma Pearl's burden was lifted. No more agonizing over what to buy while tramping through the mall, no more scrounging through the attic for suitable boxes, and no more wrapping, bowing, and tagging 23 choice gifts that are often not needed nor wanted. So, what does it matter whether your gift is expensive or perhaps worthless? In the end, it is the love and laughter shared while celebrating Christmas that really makes togetherness special and a time to remember.

A little nonsense now and then
is relished by the wisest men.
. . . Anonymous

Until Death Do They Part

On Sunday, June 13, 2004, a bell tolled twenty-one times at our little, red brick church in Mears, Michigan - a fitting remembrance and farewell to a much-loved President, Ronald Reagan. The thought came to me during this time of ringing silence that the tolling bell could also be deemed a tribute to Nancy. Her love for this great man sustained her through many years of "holding on where there was seemingly nothing left to hold on to." She faithfully cared for him while waiting and watching as the devastating disease, Alzheimer's, crippled his mind, destroying the memory of his greatness and those whom he loved. During all this time, Nancy was by his side.

A few years back, Peggy, a dear friend of mine, was diagnosed at the age of 66 with Alzheimer's. Her devoted husband, Jack, like Nancy, was there for her. He never asked for help. In fact, at first he kindly refused offers to lighten his load. This much dreaded disease comes on gradually. The doctor had somewhat prepared him for the inevitable, but not for the burst of sadness and silence that eventually entered his world while caring for his beloved wife.

Gradually, their dreams of an active life together in retirement were shattered. Fun times were reduced to a swim in the pool or a ride in their golf cart to the ocean to view the sunset. Then, one day the light of love and recognition in my friend's beautiful blue eyes went out. Soon she was unable to walk without help, eventually not at all. Suddenly her devoted husband's life was consumed with around-the-clock care.

Although he did finally accept some assistance with her personal hygiene, basically his waking hours were spent cooking, cleaning, doing laundry and shopping for groceries. When Jack was hungry, he fed her first. When her bed was wet, he changed it. When she fell out at three a.m., he lovingly placed her back beside him. When she cried, for unknown reasons, he held her close.

I spent one morning a week with Peggy. Most of the hours were marked with sadness from lack of response when I talked to her, but once during the holidays when I played Silent Night on a tape recorder, her smile and tears rolling down her cheeks, as if remembering Christmases past with her family, cheered my very being.

Why do husbands or wives spend long, heart-wrenching years caring for a spouse at home? Perhaps sometimes out of necessity, but more often, dear reader, it is out of love and commitment. In this case Jack, married to Peggy for 46 years, was her primary caregiver for eleven years. But why, the younger generation might say, such love? No doubt, because, like Nancy, he cherished and remembered their marriage vows, "until death do us part." and honored them until the end.

Alzheimer's, of course, is not the only debilitating disease requiring undying love. For twenty-seven years I have observed countless devoted caregivers. Never to be forgotten is the well-dressed, elderly couple encountered in a Wendy's restaurant. There was only one available seat. They asked if I would like to join them. She was 81, in good health, and he 82, suffering from Parkinson's disease. When saliva eased from the corners of his mouth, with a napkin she tenderly wiped it away. When he dropped his sandwich, she lovingly rewrapped his hands around it.

"I hope sitting with us has not spoiled your lunch," she said softly as she rose to leave.

"Oh, not at all," I choked back the tears in my heart. And, it had not, dear reader. Instead, she had aroused in me an awareness of true devotion "in sickness and in health" that I was again witnessing up close.

"You know, many of my friends say I should put him in a nursing home, but I can't. We've been married 56 years. We've had the better. And now together we'll face the worse." Smiling, she waved a quick goodbye as she left to help him out the double doors.

It is now 2007. I will always remember, not with pity but with admiration, Peggy's husband, and Nancy Reagan. I also will always remember the tolling bell and how it reminded me of the many tireless caregivers in our church and community, both in Mears and at Nettles Island. At that moment, dear reader, bits of Thomas A. Kempis' touching poem came to mind:

"*Nothing is sweeter than love ...Love often knows no limits but is fervent beyond measure. Love feels no burden, thinks nothing of labors, attempts what is above its strength, pleads no excuse of impossibility...Though wearied, it is not tired; but as a lively flame and burning torch, it forces its way upwards and passes securely through all.*"

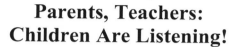

Parents, Teachers:
Children Are Listening!

In May 2004 while visiting relatives, I encountered a most remarkable little boy, Timmy Tackett. He lives in a remote, mountainous area in Hi Hat, Kentucky. It was very evident that he had been safely guided by parents and teachers along the way, but 12 year old Timmy also had been touched in a very unusual, cultural way by one special, 5th Grade teacher who was unaware of her influence on his young life. This is the story, dear reader, I must tell. But first...

One evening after dinner, I asked Timmy's Mom if I could have a family picture. Immediately, the little boy enthusiastically ran to the computer and invited me to view a pictorial family album he had developed himself. I was amazed as he clicked away and expounded on his relationship with his Grandma and Grandpa, his aunts, uncles, and cousins and their importance in his young life. I viewed and reviewed the photos, finally choosing one, which he promptly printed off on an 8 x 10 sheet for me.

A 12 year old! Many 12 year olds I know spend endless hours "shooting it out" on video games! But not Timmy! His mother, I learned later, monitor's what he and his sister Andrea watch on TV, as well as on the Internet. It is apparent that both children, outstanding students, are listening to parents as they guide them along their journey of learning.

That evening the family gathered in the living room. Timmy, wearing earphones and unaware that anyone was watching, dramatically waved an imaginary baton while listening to a CD.

"Timmy," I motioned for him to remove the earphones, "What are you listening to?"

"A Mozart symphony," his eyes lit up. "You gotta listen to this Grandma Pearl! I want you to listen to the difference in Mozart's, Tchaikovsky's and Beethoven's CDs."

Mozart? Tchaikovsky? Beethoven? Needless to say, I was totally astounded at this little mountain boy. His school had never offered music instruction and, therefore, he could not read a note of music, but he had gone out and bought, on sale, four concert CDs and could now differentiate between the sounds of flats and sharps in the greatest classical music ever written. And, Timmy had studied the composers' biographies. As he reiterated their life histories, I felt ashamed that this child knew more than this grandma about Mozart, even though I had visited his home and museum in Salzburg, Germany several years before.

"Timmy," I calmly asked, "How did you ever become interested in classical music?" He then told me about a former 5th grade teacher, Misty Little, who had played classical music during their creative writing classes and how he had become "hooked" on it. "Timmy, is Miss Little aware that you are into this music?" His answer was simply "No."

"She sounds like a remarkable teacher. Would you please write down her address for me?" I asked. He did and when I arrived home, I wrote to Misty Little and here are excerpts from her reply.

Dear Mrs. Flaherty,

"I received your letter and was in awe. You reminded me of the importance of being a teacher. Children are very impressionable and watch your every move. I was unaware that I had a positive influence on Timmy. Most of my students are skeptical at the beginning of the year when I play the classical music; they often giggle and whisper to their friends. Many have never heard classical music and they think listening to it is not "cool." But after a few days, the giggles stop and students really get into their writing. If I don't play the music, they will say, "Miss Little, where's the music?" Naturally, these are words I love to hear."

Sincerely, Miss Little

After adding that she is personally alerting Timmy's 7th Grade music teacher of his extreme interest, she is also checking into music lessons at the Mountains Art Center for him. "I hope that I have been a positive influence," she said, "but in reality, Timmy's remarkable parents, who want the best for their children, are the true inspiration in their children's lives."

Yes, dear reader, remarkable parents, remarkable teacher - and one of many remarkable children – Timmy, listening.

Grandma's Junk,
Grandchildren's Treasure

Stop! Don't throw away that old cracked pitcher or that old barn-board painting of the soldier with the too-short legs. You just may be destroying a grandchild's greatest memory.

What a shock I had while dusting in the summer of 1999. I turned over an old blue, dented milk can and found a piece of masking tape with a signature taped to the bottom. Our No. 8 grandchild, Carly Anna, without saying a word, had claimed this as her inheritance. Then I began to check behind cheap, decorative pictures on the wall, as well as under pieces of old-old furniture and "chipped and not-chipped" cream pitchers high on a dining room plate rail. Both Bill and I chuckled to think that grandchildren were secretly claiming a memory - such as the old milk can and the refinished wooden youth chair in which all had sat as tots.

As I recall, several summers before all ten grandchildren had asked at one time or another about the decorative "junk," most of which had been bought at yard sales. I had given them permission to put their names on one memorable item. Most had chosen a blue and white plate from another plate rail, or one of the antique cream pitchers. Evidently colorful collections had caught their eye while eating around our big, seven-leaf oak table. Each had taped his or her name to the bottom of their favorite and then forgotten staking that claim - or so I thought!

As I continued to dust, I found a name taped to most every moveable item in the cottage. The 36" barn-board painting of a captain sailing into a Silver Lake sunset also had been tagged. Although this was very amateurishly painted several years before by our son Dan as a Christmas gift for his dad, it was now being claimed by Erin, her memory of sailing many summers with Grandpa.

Then, there was my Momma's wall-hung, wooden coffee grinder, my own memory mounted beside our Hoosier cabinet. Why would a teenage grandchild want that as a keepsake? No doubt, she remembered hearing the story of how I, as a child, watched dancing beans through the little glass window. Now, she wanted to capture that as her own memory and had boldly taped her name on the back of the grinder.

From room to room I wandered, joyously reliving wonderful moments we had shared with the grandchildren over the past 27 years. On the balcony, another barn-board painting of a British soldier with too-short legs, painted by non-artist Grandma Pearl, had been claimed, as well as the gold-framed "fake" print of Mary and the Christ Child that I had purchased at an auction for $2.00.

What's a grandma to do? As I discovered these names, I told each culprit that Grandpa and I couldn't allow this as it was not fair to our children or the other grandchildren whose visits were not as frequent. This was a good excuse, but frankly, their parents, our own grown children, have shown no interest in our old junk that was acquired after they had left home.

However, there is one exception. Hanging on the dining room wall is a 1905 cross-stitched prayer titled 'Bless This House.' The tiny words are so heart-rending and the blue birds, pink flowers and beaten pathway to a country cottage so beautiful. When a daughter-in-law expressed a desire to put her name on that prayer, I discouraged her saying no adults were allowed to put names on anything. But she laughed, marched over, took it off the wall, and then I heard her exclaim, "Darn, Kitty has her name on it already! Kitty, our only daughter, who never wanted any of Mom's old junk!

In conclusion, Grandma Pearl is certainly going to have to draw up a new will listing at least one piece of worthless "junk" for each grandchild. After all, dear reader, there is no greater legacy a grandma can leave than priceless, treasured memories.

Where we love is home,
home that our feet may
leave, but not our hearts.
. . . Oliver Wendell Holmes

A Monumental Birthday

My 78th birthday celebration started out in a very common way. Flowers and gifts from my children, as well as a "Happy Birthday sung over the phone by my Great Granddaughter, little four-year-old Kelsey. The previous evening a group of friends at Nettles Island had joined us for dinner out with the usual tiny complementary cake aglow with one candle. Their singing and friendly toast to my health were very special to me. However, the best was yet to come on the actual day of my birth, January 21.

When we returned from the birthday dinner out, January 20, I checked the e-mail. There were several special greetings from friends, children and grandchildren, but the "hugging bear" one from my granddaughter Necia in Holland, Michigan turned out to be the one that triggered a first-in-my-lifetime thought. "Grandma, did you know that the 21st is also National Hugging Day?" National Hugging Day? No, I did not know that until that very moment. Well, I thought immediately, why not scamper around the island tomorrow and give, as well as get, 78 hugs?

As I lay down to sleep that night, I was so excited and began to plan the most interesting day of my entire life. I had to take an extra sleeping pill and an extra swig of cough medicine to get the rest I needed for my hugging birthday celebration.

Bill, of course, was my first victim. I hugged him, ate the breakfast he had prepared for my birthday and then made a little chart on a 3 x 5 card with 78 spaces. I checked his hug off, grabbed my tennis racket, jumped in the golf cart and chugged along, the adrenalin flowing. As I turned the corner, I just had to stop and hug two neighbor men as they stood in the street talking. Naturally, they were shocked that I was giving them a hug, but laughed when I said, "It's National Hug Day - and my 78th birthday." This was to be the joyous greeting to all whom I met that morning, reminding each to pass the hug on.

At the tennis courts, I first hugged my group of "over-the-hill ladies" and then collected four more hugs from "over-the-hill" men on the other court. At the Condo Office, I hugged the manager, the bookkeeper, the secretary and a security guard. My chart was looking good!

Back at the Commercial area, I stopped to hug two fishermen by the bridge. They laughed, and promised to hug their wives when they got home. At the grocery store I hugged four hefty, road construction men wearing orange protection vests. My first "dusty" hugs! I hugged them all, black and white alike - the pipeline digger, the Cat loader operator, the street sweeper, and even the tall, handsome "whoever" that couldn't speak a word of English. I showed him what the word HUG meant. He smiled, his big gold tooth showing. Then, sort of embarrassed, he hugged me back. "God bless you, young man," I said and hugged him again.

I also hugged the laundromat owner, the beautician and an 81 year old, pudgy little friend getting a pop out of a machine, as well as a big Canadian guy I knew from church choir. Card filling up fast!

Spurred on by hugging results, I hopped in the golf cart and zoomed back to our Island Snack Bar, more good luck and joy! First, I hugged the waitresses and Jan, the owner. "Well, what about the cook?" she said. O. K. And the cook said, "Our dish washer needs a hug." So, he shook the water from his hands and I had my first "wet" hug. The laughter that rang out in the restaurant was infectious. The word had spread that Pearl was celebrating her 78th birthday with hugs, so people trickled in from all over. As I left the kitchen, people from different states, different walks of life, and different ages hugged me and I hugged them. One gentleman, a total stranger named Guido, from Switzerland, stood, hugged me with gusto, and then smiling went back to finishing his lunch.

By this time, dear reader, I was beginning to wear down and Jan said, "Sit, Pearl." She called Bill and he joined me for a birthday lunch on the house. I showed him the card - 99 hugs. Before I made it home and collapsed in bed, the total was 110. So what started out as a common birthday celebration in my life turned into an uncommon phenomenon - friends, old and new, here on our little island by the sea, giving and receiving the precious gift of love on my grandest of all birthdays, number 78.

George Washington Carver once said, "When you do the common things of life, in an uncommon way, you will command the attention of the world."

Whether with peanuts or hugs, 'tis true, dear reader.

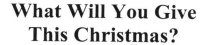

What Will You Give
This Christmas?

I once read: "The only true gift is a portion of thyself." It's true that not everyone can pen a poem or paint a masterpiece. Not everyone can carve a unique sculpture or compose a melodious song. No, not everyone can write, as his or her gift at Christmastime, a few joyous ribbons of truth heralding the birth of the Christ Child. But a gift, no matter how simple, that comes from the hands and heart of the giver will reflect love and be remembered and treasured for many years.

One Christmas morning in 1932, when I was six years old and bedridden with tuberculosis, I received the two most memorable gifts of my young life. Memorable because it was depression years and the only gift my parents could afford was a stocking filled with hard candies and an orange. That Christmas so long ago I awoke to find a beautiful, child-sized doll sitting at a little shiny, red table with two chairs. The doll's arms were outstretched and her satiny, porcelain face wore a smile of love for a sick child. These unexpected gifts had been secretly placed beside our tree on Christmas Eve by two elderly neighbors. Although the doll was very old, Mrs. Martin had hand-stitched a new blue-tucked dress and lace-trimmed bonnet for her and Mr. Martin had crafted and brightly painted the little table and chairs. "The seamstress gave her stitchery and the carpenter gave his skill."

Two years later at our 3rd grade Christmas party, I received a pair of warm red mittens in my "needy" children's basket. Although I remember the other gifts in that basket - a green plaid hair ribbon on a clasp and a book of nursery rhymes - I especially remember the warmth of those mittens on mile walks to school in blizzards. But you know, dear reader, most of all I remember my beloved teacher, Mrs. Cook, who had knit them just for me.

It matters not whether a gift is large or small, expensive or inexpensive. One Christmas treasure I received at age 60 was a red and white potholder crocheted by Ida Barr when she was 89.

For many years I have hung on my Christmas tree a little stuffed bell covered with holly-berried cloth, hand-sewn by Ida's daughter, Rosemary Lower. Like the gifts from my long-ago neighbor, Mrs. Martin and my teacher, Mrs. Cook, these gifts will long be remembered because they were made special for me.

One November as we were preparing to leave Michigan for Florida, Esther Viterna, a long-time friend in Mears, placed in Bill's hands a Christmas gift. "Just for you, Bill," she smiled, knowing that he loves homemade fudge and that I never make it because I am allergic to chocolate. "The candy maker gave her candy."

And, oh, how could I ever forget the Christmas gift I received from my precious Momma in December 1978 when she was eighty-one? When I hurriedly untied the crude twine knots and tore away the brown, paper-sack wrapping, I immediately recognized Momma's loving gift made with arthritic hands. A flood of Christmas tears streamed down my cheeks as I read her simple, penciled note scribbled on a scrap of paper and tucked inside:

"Dear Children:

I have made gingerbread pones until I can hardly set up. I know you all have money to get what you want and I have a little money to buy, but you can't eat money. So I hope you will enjoy this Christmas bread, every piece made with a heart full of love." And, "The baker gave her bread."

Looking back, dear reader, I do believe that "The only true gift is a portion of thyself."

One cannot find any rule
of conduct to excel
simplicity and sincerity.
. . . Anonymous

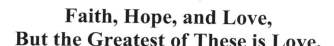

Faith, Hope, and Love,
But the Greatest of These is Love.

No doubt, the most important telephone call of my life was early in March, 1945. Bill proposed to me by phone from his Naval Air Base in Florida. His simple words were, "Come on down to Jacksonville and let's get married." I was only 19 and my sailor Bill 20.

I had known him for barely 6 months when he was transferred from Oklahoma to Jacksonville. I had cried when he left, thinking I might never see him again. But we had exchanged many letters declaring our love for each other. Naturally, and enthusiastically, I promised I would be on the next train out. "But we can't get married without your parents consent," he cautioned. And so, the journey to the altar instantly became complicated.

When I phoned my parents in Kentucky and asked them to mail Bill the consent, Daddy refused, saying to Momma, "Every sailor looks alike, and Pearl can't tell the good from the bad." But, Momma finally convinced him that unless he signed, we would have to go all the way to Georgia to be married. Funny. At that time, neither they, nor I, knew that Jacksonville was only across the Georgia line.

Now, it is 62 years, dear reader, since Bill and I on April 4, 1945 stood in that BIG Methodist Church in Jacksonville and said, "I do." But, I dare say it was no BIG wedding – only Bill and I, his sailor buddy and wife, and the minister. There were no beribboned candelabras, no organist playing The Wedding March, and no guests to hug us after the ceremony or lavish us with gifts. But nothing mattered as we stood there, he in his white sailor suit and I in a white linen short dress accented with a red rosebud corsage. Nothing mattered except our promise to love and cherish each other "till death do us part."

Bride and groom expectations for gala weddings are so different now. Five to twenty thousand dollar weddings seem to be more and more common. But a war-time wedding sixty years ago was different. I had exactly $25 and Bill, four U. S. Savings Bonds worth a total of $100. I recall so vividly our one-week honeymoon in a $6.00 a week, rented room in an old wooden, two-story house overlooking Jacksonville Beach. Our attendants had an adjoining room and we shared a bath. Since we could only afford to eat dinner out, we purchased 2 spoons for five cents each and ate corn flakes for breakfast. A ten-cent can of soup, which we heated over a kerosene heater, was our lunch. But no other honeymoon in the world was more beautiful - swimming in the ocean every day and surviving on love and laughter.

As I write this, so many treasured memories echo across my marriage valley. Over the years, on various occasions, Bill has presented me with flowers, none being more appreciated than after giving birth to a child. For many years before church on Mother's Day, he would surprise all of us by proudly pinning red carnations on the five children and white ones on the two of us. Naturally, his everlasting devotion to our family endeared him to me more than ever.

But, dear reader, we all know there is more to a lasting marriage than flowers. In late March 2005, aboard a beautiful Italian ship in the Caribbean, with a band and soloist serenading us with love songs, we renewed our wedding vows. Although the flower in my hair was one made of bright pink, crepe paper, made in a craft class on the ship, I felt beautiful and warm, loved and blessed. Three of our children, two grand children, a niece and her family, as well as many friends, shared in this ceremony. As the minister read from 1st Corinthians the chapter on Love, all couples joined hands and, many with tear-stained eyes, reaffirmed these words on love and marriage:

"Faith, hope and love – these three ingredients make for happiness in a marriage. And the greatest of these is love.

Love is patient and kind, never jealous or envious, never boastful or proud, never haughty or selfish or rude. Love does not demand its own way. It is not irritable or touchy. It does not hold grudges. Love is never glad about injustice, but rejoices when truth wins out.

Loving someone, you will be loyal to him or her no matter what the cost. You will always believe in him, always expect the best of him, and always stand your ground in defending him.

Faith, hope and love – but the greatest of these is love."

Fancy

Many a true word is spoken in jest.
. . . An Old English Proverb

Skinnin' a Cat

A serious social problem has puzzled me for years - why today's marriages don't last. Since biologists, psychologists, and sociologists have failed to come up with a solution, I took this problem to our Nettles Island hot tub.

"Why do you think so many marriages today end in divorce?" I asked four soakers, all married over 40 years.

"No question about it," said one bald gentleman jetting his aching neck. "They start out in the wrong place. When I was young, you met a respectable young lady while sipping a soda at the roller rink or when at a ball game with her brother. And, she had clothes on!"

"Yeah," added another. "Nowadays young whipper-snappers meet in bars and guzzle Harvey Wallbangers or they frequent beaches where half-naked girls are sunning themselves. Why, that's no way to meet a future dependable mate."

Hey, good points, I thought. My sentiments exactly! "How about you?" I asked the white-haired lady whose swimsuit skirt was ballooning to the top of the bubbly water.

"I met my husband at Ford Motor Company while working on the assembly line."

Great place to meet. Both industrious, no doubt. "And you, sir, how did you meet your wife?"

"In church," said the round-faced little man as he slid a little deeper into the water. "She had a figure like a post, but she was a good girl."

Good girl, in church. That certainly beat hanging around discos, high on everything but hymns and true love.

Suddenly, the man jetting his neck looked at me and said, "How did you meet your husband?"

"Me?" Oh, well, might as well blurt it out. "The first time I laid eyes on my Bill I was skinnin' a cat."

"Skinnin' a cat?" one red-faced hot tubber shouted as the others quickly floated to the edge of their watery seats.

"Yes sir." Then I quickly explained. "But there is, as you know, more than one way to skin a cat. One way is actually skinning one, and the other way is done on metal monkey bars. You know, like the high bars kids play on in parks? You jump up, grasp a bar, pull your feet up between your arms, then, you flip through to a standing position. That's what I was doing. But it was respectable and all."

Nobody said a word. Feeling a little uncomfortable, in hotter water than I wanted to be, I tugged at my bathing suit strap and slid under to my chin. "But I was being helpful, teaching little kids at poolside to do tricks on the bars," I added. "My suit was very decent, not cut up to the arm pits and down to the navel."

Why am I telling them all this? I asked myself. I'm the interviewer.

"Go on, when did HE come into the picture?"

"Who?"

"Your husband?"

Quick recall, dear reader. 56 years ago. At an amusement park pool in Oklahoma City. When he had hair on his head.

"Oh! Well, half-way through the skinnin', while hanging by my knees, this handsome, blonde, muscular young sailor, wearing bathing trunks and a Navy dog tag, appeared within my upside-down vision. He thought I was a kid and had come over to play and teach me a trick or two. Being a country girl of 18, naturally I was embarrassed, so I quickly flipped to my feet."

The hot tubbers leaned closer. "Then what?" One questioned.

"Well, let's see. Oh, he said, 'Bet you can't do that again.' He blushed when he suddenly realized that I was not a kid, but a cat-skinnin' young woman." They laughed and I continued. "Would you believe that no matter how hard I tried, I couldn't skin one more cat? My knees had become like jelly and a twinge had pierced my heart."

Again, they laughed and I quipped, like our preacher, "Now that's a true story."

Problem solved, dear reader. If today's young people want a lasting marriage like Mom and Dad's, they need to look in the right places. And, be sure to look side-ways and up-side-down at their choice of a lifelong partner. Finally, once the knot is tied, they should hang in there. It's kind of like skinnin' a cat.

Every wise man
loves the wife
he has chosen.
. . . Homer

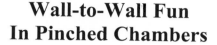

Wall-to-Wall Fun
In Pinched Chambers

*"Seaside lodgings are not
very comfortable, but who
would not be a little pinched
in his chamber if his windows
but looked upon the sea."*
    . . . Anonymous

Like most Snowbirds, as soon as the geese honk across October skies,
we leave for a little spot on the Atlantic Coast called Nettles Island, a
recreational park in the Intra-Coastal Waterway, about 50 miles north of
West Palm Beach.

The first 10 years of retirement Bill and I were thrilled with our
postage-stamp lot and 31-foot, doll-size, travel trailer with doll-size twin
beds and a screened porch. We had many laughs while falling into our
bedroom storage closet that could be reached only by leaning across a
single bed. We ignored near concussions acquired on a low-ceilinged
tip-out. When grandchildren visited, we had wall-to-wall family fun and
counted our blessings each day.

Then, the county approved park-model trailers with add-on rooms.
This sent Bill to the drawing board. After all, who wouldn't long for a
peaked roof, without leaky seams, and a bathtub big enough so we could
soak tennis knees and hemorrhoids? And who wouldn't want a wider
living room so that when sitting opposite guests you could avoid playing
kneesies? And, oh, for two bedrooms! Why, when the kids come, you
could shove them, their duffel bags full of sweat sox, sweat suits, sweats
whatever, along with smelly tennis shoes, into the spare room, close the
door and relax.

It sounded perfect, the big little house. But, we discovered, dear
reader, that upgrading to a so-called custom castle on wheels triggered
nerve-wracking hassles. At the factory, for nine hours we wrangled with
the manufacturer over choice of colors, paneling, carpet, and appliances.
As we signed on the dotted line, the salesman cooed, "Just call us collect

if you want to make changes." I did many times, dear reader, and he always blared back, "Well, there'll be a charge...a charge...a charge." That was when sleepless nights began, wondering if we had made the right decision to upgrade.

Finally, the day of delivery - and discovery - arrived. When the dealer called, I calmly asked, "Is everything as we ordered?" "Oh, yes, ma'am, a beautiful coach," his exact words. I felt a smile creep across my weary face and thought to myself, *My worries are over.* As our forty-foot palace rolled onto our circle, I danced all the way to greet the deliverer.

"I can't set it on the lot," he mimicked his boss, "till I get the check in full in my hand."

"Can't I just look in first?"

"No ma'am," he reached for the check.

One hour later I slid open the glass door, peeked into the rosiest of rosy rooms and honestly thought heaven couldn't be more beautiful - almond and white furniture resting on deep pink carpet, like whipped cream on a strawberry tart.

But upon inspection, my spirits fell. No linoleum in the kitchen? Why, everyone knows I'm a slob who occasionally drops a raw egg on the floor! Upon entering the bedroom, I banged my shin against the corner of a built-in bed base that was 10 inches too long. Dumb me for handing over that check!

In less than two months, dear reader, the egg and visiting grandchildren droppings had gooed the plush kitchen carpet into a pink pavement. The black, green, and yellow bruises on my shins could have passed for camouflaged socks. But, I must confess I slept almost as well as before that nightmare-of-change started; that is, until the night I awoke with a terrible scream. I dreamed that Hurricane Hattie had blown away our elegant pink palace while all around us other families were still having wall-to-wall fun in pinched chambers with windows to the sea.

Is not a small house best?
Put a woman into a small
house, and after five years
she comes out large and
healthy.
　　　. . . Emerson

Grandchildren and Belly Belts

I've seen a lot of unusual things at flea markets, but never a rhinestone "belly belt." In fact, until shopping with two teenage girls, I never knew there was such a thing.

One spring vacation our beautiful granddaughter Angela, and friend Ginger, both 16, flew down from Zeeland, Michigan to visit us in Florida. For ten days they sunbathed and frolicked in the turbulent sea on boogie boards.

On Saturday morning, I shook them awake, and shortly we departed for the Flea Market eight miles south. After parking the car in an open field, we hopped on a trolley that took us to the first row of many rows of bargains. We planned to meet at the hot-dog stand in one and a half hours. However, five minutes later, they ran back to show me their first "great find." Out of a plastic bag, they each excitedly pulled out a long, glittery, string of something.

"Grandma, what a buy! Only five dollars! Up home they cost $25.00," Angela exclaimed.

"What on earth is it, a rhinestone necklace?" I questioned. Looks like the one my Aunt Myrtle wore back in the fifties."

"Grandmaaa, these are not necklaces, they are the latest things for girls. They're called belly belts! Everyone's wearing them, Grandma."

Now, dear reader, when I was young, a "belly belt" was that strip of muslin you wrapped around a newborn's tummy to hold his navel in. But I knew commenting on that would be Greek to these fresh-faced, Twenty-first Century beauties.

Honestly, I tried, for their sake, to be enthused, but didn't quite get the "belly" connection until Angela, much to my shock, pulled up her skimpy little tank top, exposing her bikini-tanned midriff - right there on Row I. Yep, right in front of moms, dads, grandmas, grandpas, and even a few young male onlookers. Well, you can guess what I said next. "Girls, you don't wear those on your bare skin, do you?" They responded in unison, again, "Grandma, everyone does!"

"Well, girls," I swallowed as I measured my words, "the belts are beautiful and a great buy, but promise me you will not wear those back on the island in the presence of my friends. They would dub you 'loose'." From the pained look they gave me, I knew, again, the expression "loose" was Greek to them. Without answering, they pocketed their rhinestone treasures and ran off headed for Row 2 or 3 or whichever.

Killing time, I roamed around looking at practical grandma things, like towels and socks. Then, while sipping a Coke at the hot dog stand, needless to say, I began to wonder how I would handle this navel-novelty dilemma back at our Senior park.

However, on Sunday morning these beautiful, mature, modest young women emerged from their bedroom, ready for church. Each was clad in a smart, short, strapless dress – one black, the other white. They looked very chic. And, encircling both "covered" middles, dear reader, was a thin strand of sparkling rhinestones - their brand new belly belts.

All I can say is, "Never underestimate the integrity of grand kids!"

We were as twinn'd lambs
that did frisk i' the sun,
and bleat the one at the other;
what we chang'd was innocence
for innocence; we knew not
the doctrine of ill-doing, nor
dream'd that any did.
. . . Shakespeare

Stuff

I finally have a solution to a real Grandma problem. Since myalgia rheumatica attacked my well being, I've been struggling with how to simplify my life. Well, not the play part, just the work part. Took a lot of thought and a lot of guts, but this is my final answer, GET RID OF STUFF! You know, that gosh awful STUFF that one can live without.

First, dear reader, all that STUFF has to be dusted! Charming, framed scenes of yore, no longer in vogue, as well as hand-woven, wall hangings, now faded, that must periodically be vacuumed. At age 70 I simply adored all the decorative items cluttering up our Silver Lake cottage. But that was twelve years ago. After Bill fell off the ladder while dusting eight iron horses pulling a German beer wagon, I began to declare war on STUFF.

And, oh yes, those crafty gifts, - like the two miniature baskets with tiny balls of yarn and 2 nails for knitting needles that really have no value. When you get right down to it, they are tacky, tacky in any decor. All this STUFF I have collected and admired for thirty-seven years!

Every house, for a homey effect, needs several white wicker baskets filled with something, like old magazines, plastic flowers, or whatever. Right? Wrong! Those beautiful dust-collector baskets had to be doused once a year in a huge white, dry-wall plaster bucket full of chlorine bleach. That got rid of the dust mites and any other varmints hiding in the woven wicker, but it also broke my back. No more!

Now, dear reader, how can a Grandma possibly part with those garlands of silk ivy with little burgundy flowers strung across her plate rail? That ivy provides class while it frames eight, old, blue and white plates. How can I part with the soft, silk greenery above the lace valance at every dining room window? I admit I haven't dusted those suckers since I put them up 4 years ago. They are looking faker by the minute. Now that I'm on this "make life easier for Grandma" spree, I'd better just box up the garlands and donate them to a thrift shop where someone younger will enjoy dusting, dousing, and dumping.

After doing a lot of all three of the aforementioned, my next move was to clear the refrigerator door of STUFF. I promptly removed those ancient, "darling" grandchildren pictures and cutesy magnets holding famous quotes. Now, I can swipe a dishcloth across that door, and zippo, it's shiny clean!

That about takes care of the inside dusting, dousing and dumping at our home in Michigan. Now, let's go on to cutting down and pulling up STUFF around our mobile home in Florida. No one sees those old bushes in the back. Pruning those several times a season is back breaking. And the scheflera, once a three foot house plant, is now a leaf-dropping, fifteen foot giant that sheds constantly and covers my four-foot back alley of creeping grass. This is another one of those scary, climb-a-ladder-at-80 chores. No way!

A friend of mine was astounded to learn that I actually pulled out four banana trees last week! "No more banana split parties?" she questioned, remembering the year we had a party with thirty-three bananas from my plantation. But, the time had come. I had to do it. Those banana trees had to be fertilized with potash often. Dead fronds needed faithful trimming. And usually, the neighbors ate the fruit while I was gone in the summer. No problem there, just too much work when I could be collecting starfish along our Treasure Coast beach!

Wish I'd thought of getting rid of stuff 25 years ago. Then, I would have had more time to play tennis - perhaps even win a Class A trophy. Woops, scratch that idea. Trophies have to be dusted!

Let your conversation be
without covetousness;
and be content with such
things as you have; for He
has said, I will never leave
you nor forsake you.
. . . Hebrews 13:5

If You Want to be Famous, Hang Out Your Fruit of the Looms

I was never going to admit this, but it's time my readers knew. Bill and I are quite well-known on Nettles Island where we spend our winters. It's true. Not because of any great talent we might possess, but because Bill has the whitest Fruit-of-the-Loom underwear on this entire Florida island. Strange thing to be famous for, but having been brought up to appreciate and use God's great gift of sunshine, we always hang out our wash - both here and on sunny days in Michigan.

Now, in the "good old days" a woman's Monday was measured *not* by the clock, but by the sun and whether it was a beautiful day to do the family wash. Before my Momma acquired one of those new fan-dangled miraculous washing machines, doing the wash was a back-breaking chore. But she went about it cheerfully. Wearing a sunbonnet to protect her beautiful face, she hummed hymns as she plunged a broomstick into the whites boiling in a big oval copper kettle outdoors.

Ages ago, I ran across this old, sunny-washday "receet," of unknown origin, which sparked my memory of a by-gone era. At one time, this method of doing the family wash, especially in rural areas, was handed down from mother to daughter:

1. bild fire in back yard to het kettle of rain water.
2. set tubs so smoke won't blow in eyes if wind is peart.
3. shave 1 hole cake of lie sope in bilin water.
4. sort things, make 3 piles: 1 pile white, 1 pile cullord, 1 pile work briches and rags.
5. stur flour in cold water to smooth, then thin down with bilin water. rub dirty spots on board, scrub hard, then bile. Rub cullord but don't bile. just rench and starch.
7. take white things out of kettle with broom stick handel, then rench, blew and starch.
8. bleech tee towels on the grass.
9. hang old rags on fence.

10. pore rench water in flower bed.
11. scrub porch with hot sopy water.
12. turn tubs upside down to drane.
13. go put on clean dress, smooth hair with side combs, brew cup of tee, set and rest and rock a spell and count your blessins.

I especially like No. 13. So anytime you are out and about, dear reader, check out the Flaherty wash utilizing nature's breezes as well as Old Sol's drying power.

Most importantly, if you are lacking for notoriety, try the old-fashioned method of drying your laundry. Not only will your undies be as white as Bill's, but you will save enough money for an extended cruise on the high seas.

Home,
Where the Heart Is

Home is where the heart is,
And friendship is a guest;
A book, a fire, a handclasp,
A place where one can rest.

Home is where the heart is,
Where children's voices ring;
A blossom at the window,
A tiny bird to sing.

Home is where the heart is,
Be it mansion on the hill,
Or cabin in the valley,
Or cottage by the rill.

Home is where the heart is,
Where laughter is a welcome guest,
And love and faith and gentleness
Can soothe a heart to rest.
                    . . . Anonymous

Old Dogs
Can Learn a New Trick

Never believe that an old dog can't be taught a new trick! No matter what your age, you can amplify your mind with a six-week course in personal computers.

When I was 66 and Bill 67, we decided to enroll in a Community Education course and learn the basics of a "new" language our children and grandchildren were speaking. Two mornings a week we replaced watching flophouse floozies on the Phil Donahue Show with fooling around with "floppy disks" in a kennel of old dogs seated at personal computers.

In only one session we learned basic PC terminology. "Bytes" were not what dogs do, but the number of letters, numbers and spaces that can be stored away on a disc, a small flexible record. We also learned simple techniques on the keyboard that all puppies are now learning in first grade.

After two sessions on that magnificent, magic machine, the instructor had a class of twelve old dogs perking up their ears to such commands as "Insert the hard drive," "Wait for virus checks," "Retrieve," "Save," "Enter," "Delete," etc.

Four sessions later, we male and female mongrels were creating our own personal files and yelped for joy when holiday card lists emerged from the printer at a tremendous rate of speed.

By the end of our program, we were processing letters, "Word Perfect." Fantastic! Old dogs not only learning new tricks, but getting treats of perfection for a loyal performance!

Bill, along with other inexperienced mutts, was in his glory working with "spread sheets," that is, charts and graphs. He learned that by simply changing the price or the interest rate of various items on a chart, the machine instantly recomputed all totals on the entire chart. Amazing!

And to whom are we human canines indebted for this information-processing machine? A Mr. Charles Babbage. During coffee break, we discussed the history of computing and learned that Babbage designed a mechanical calculator more than 150 years ago and is considered to be the forerunner of such a mathematical tool. However, not willing to let sleeping dogs lie, it was his faithful assistant, Countess Ada Lovelace, who is credited with translating and publishing his notes and illustrations. In addition, she wrote programs for his machine, introducing information processing. All this was a beginning perhaps of today's computer technology worldwide.

So, dear reader, if your knee joints are wearing out and your hind legs are torn and tattered from years of muscle stretching, don't just lie down and roll over, switch to mind stretching.

Most Community Education programs are willing to throw a few bones your way in a Computer Class and the courses are almost "free to a good home." Never miss out on an opportunity, dear reader, to learn a new trick. I promise that your family and friends will sit up and take notice.

Jesters do oft prove
to be prophets.
. . . Shakespeare

To finish the moment
to find the journey's end
in every step of the
road, to live the greatest
number of good hours,
is wisdom.
. . . Emerson

Goofballs on this Earth Ball

Perhaps it's time to rethink what is important in life. Is it baseball, football, basketball?

A few years ago at the end of baseball season, when the Toronto Blue Jays tucked a third win under their wings, I chirped for joy because one "playoff" had ended and I could fly on to the Cardinal's nest to waste more time.

"Thank goodness, that's over," I warbled as I flipped off the TV.

"What do you mean?" Bill looked shocked at such a statement from an old seasoned softball pro.

"That's three out of five for the Blue Jays - they've won it!"

"It's the best four out of seven games now," he informed me.

That four-out-of-seven new baseball ruling was like a shot wounding caged birds. America was then, and still is, either playing ball or watching ball night and day, seven days a week. Round and round it goes; where it ends, nobody knows.

Please don't get me wrong, dear reader. Ball playing of any kind is good sport, but when it becomes an obsession that dominates our leisure, our thinking, our very life, then, self-control must be exercised. Otherwise, we birds may never sing the song we were created to sing.

Now, dear reader, I played softball when I was a young chick in Ashland, Kentucky - a few years back, like 60. But when summer ended, we went back to school to get educated. When I became 18, I packed away my cute little green satin shorts and flew across the mountain to get on with the serious business of living.

Later, I must admit, during childbearing years, I became a dedicated parent spectator. I watched thousands of games in which our children were involved - tennis, soccer, volleyball, basketball, football. I learned a lot of "ball" terminology as well as strategy of many different games. This helped me to enjoy a few, and persevere many long, drawn-out, boring evenings as sports commentators spluttered over Redskins scalping Lions or Tigers devouring Giants.

Play ball! Play! Pitch it, bat it, throw it, catch it! Run with it! Shoot it! Score! Play ball! Ball on Mondays, ball on Tuesdays, ball on Wednesdays. Ball every night of the week. Whether your child is in elementary school, middle school or high school, some form of ball fills his free time as well as that of many, many adults. Watch ball – in the stadium, on TV at home or in the bar. Sit. Eat. Drink. Round and round it goes; where it ends, nobody knows.

And another thing, dear reader, for the life of me I can never understand how any ball player is worth a million dollars or more. Money, strikes, more money! Beer, drugs, more beer! Times are sure a changin'. In the old days when our softball team finished a game, the coach patted us on our satin backs and treated us to a soda pop. Then I went home and milked the cow. Now, players are off to the bar for a few with the gals - or guys. Rah! Rah! Rah!

Strike outs, fly outs, sell outs! Grounders, sliders, homers. Cracked bats, cracked shins, cracked skulls! Cracked, cracked, cracked! Rah! Rah! Tailbacks, running backs, quarterbacks. Kick it, punt it, pass it. Hit 'em hard! Tackle. One down, two downs, three downs, touchdown! They're all down! Rah! Rah! Rah! Round and round it goes; where it ends, nobody knows.

In Spring ball, in Summer ball, in Fall ball, in Winter ball. It seems that four-letter word B-A-L-L has turned us all into goofballs on this earth ball.

I must admit that I don't recall who, the Jays or the Cardinals, won that playoff. But one thing I know for sure, dear reader, I will remember until my dying day the outstanding fly-ball catch yours truly made on 3rd base at summer's end in 1943. "OUT!" The ump yelled, signaling the end of our Tri-State Championship Game. Who won? Why, Kentucky, of course. RAH! RAH! RAH!

"What then?" you ask. Well, this middle-of-the-Twentieth- Century softball player went straight home, hung up her little green satin uniform for the last time – I thought.

Now, dear reader, it is 2007, and I have a confession to make. Fifty-four years after that great catch, I took up tennis. For 17 years I batted that little green ball back and forth, back and forth over a net – another goofball on this earth ball at 62.

Twenty-seven years of Fun in the Sun at Nettles Island in Florida:
Top Left clockwise: Chorus Line (men); Red Hot Mamas; Tennis,
Anyone? Queen of yard sales; N. Is. Red Rockers rockin'; Birthday
surprise from a Jill in the box, Hawaiian style; Leis, ukuleles and
Wahinis; Roaring Twenties. Center: Pastor L.C. as the Turkey, and
adorable Winston.

Winston Celebrates First Birthday

Now, I've done it all. Approaching my 76th birthday, I attended my first dog birthday party. Good friends, Ray and Mary Ann Schoonover, threw a humdinger when their dog Winston turned one. It was just a small gathering of Nettles Island neighbors honoring a new dog on the block.

On this gala occasion, Winston, an over-zealous Jack Russell puppy, received the biggest birthday dog card ever, 16 x 20 inches, which was signed by 60 guests. The food was delicious and both Momma and Papa Schoonover were in dog heaven because Winston was such a perfect high-class mutt. He didn't pee on one high-class guest during the whole indoor extravaganza.

Dear reader, I don't usually mention human or dog bodily functions in my writings, but not only has Winston, on occasion, been known to pee on a neighbor's palm tree, but he has also been known to pee on a prestigious next-door neighbor's foot. Picture this: Neighbor comes out all dressed up. Winston, excited to see his favorite admirer, leaps up on her. Affectionately she pets him, and then, loveable Winston proceeds to pee on her best shoes. Now I really don't know, but I am inclined to think they were red and he, no doubt, thought her a fancy fire hydrant.

Anyway, when Winston turned two, all neighbors had evidently forgiven all. On Dec. 27, a throng of dog-tolerant, food-and-fun lovers showed up on the lush lawn behind his master's mansion to help Mama and Papa celebrate their adorable Jack Russell's birthday. What a riot!

Jovial well wishers laden with dog cards and gaily wrapped dog gifts greeted a hyper-happy Winston, gussied up with a rhinestone collar. He even received his own silver, personalized, photo album. Proud hosts and guests toasted Winston and the upcoming New Year 2000 before a sumptuous outdoor buffet was served.

Many competitive partygoers lined up to play "Pin the Bone in Winston's Mouth." However, no prize was given because admittedly the winner who hit the mouth dead center had cheated by peeking under the blindfold - as did many other participants.

The finale of this unusual, one-of- a-kind party was a huge one-of-a-kind birthday cake covered with bones of icing. Unfortunately, dear reader, the neighbor with the fancy shoes wasn't there to enjoy this gala affair. I heard she sold out!

Yard Tales

Dear Reader, herein you are about to read some tall tales by the Queen of Yard Sales.

During the last two decades of the 20th Century. I bought everything from a valuable old Red Wing vase for $1 to a practical Sunbeam electric can opener that actually worked for 25 cents. Our garage at Silver Lake has been jammed for years with my varied weaknesses - old rusty toys, ornate picture frames of all shapes and sizes, and spindled, pressed-back chairs. Some of these, along with many other "can't- pass- up" treasures, I finally donated in 2001 to the Mears Church yard sale.

However, with my best "finds" I have furnished our cottage, outfitted an actor fur trader, and occasionally garbed myself with designer clothes. And, behind a few of these super bargains of the century lie yard tales worth telling:

First, let me tell you that some yard sales make you cry. Like the one I stopped at in 1980 in Shelby, Michigan. Four daughters were selling their deceased, 90 year-old mother's furnishings, including a solid oak table with seven leaves. It bothered me so to think none of them wanted their mother's beautiful table. "Why, didn't any of you keep the table?" I asked, remembering the old wooden table around which Momma, Daddy, and we five children prayed, and ate and sang.

"Oh, honey, we all have nice new dining tables. But we did each take a chair for a keepsake."

With a lump in my throat, I bought the table, but all the way home tears welled up in my heart. Now, I sit at this table every day when we are at Silver Lake. I often wonder who will own this indestructible treasure some day. Will they too build memories around this old oaken table as our family has while playing games, eating, singing, and yes, praying?

Secondly, some "finds" you just can't pass up, such as a real beaver coat. Now, dear reader, I can almost hear you say, "Why would Pearl want to buy an old, out-dated fur coat?" I had just finished writing a play about the Cherokees' Trail of Tears and was searching for costumes. At a yard sale near our cottage I spotted a fur coat hanging on a clothesline.

It was just the costume needed for the fur trader singing to an Indian maiden in my upcoming production.

"How much is the old coat?" I asked nonchalantly, not mentioning the word "fur," and looking as disinterested as I could.

"Honey," the lady in charge said from her lawn chair, "That old thing was my Grandpa's and has been hanging in our barn for years. If you will take it off our hands, you can have it for 25 cents."

TWENTY-FIVE CENTS! I didn't yell it. I just handed her the quarter, took the coat to the car, and didn't feel a bit guilty until at home I read the inside label - "PURE BEAVER from J. L. Hudson's Furrier of Detroit." Needless to say, my fur trader looked grand on stage and soon afterwards my preppy grandson, Joey, carted it off to Michigan State to wear to football games. My guess is that this bargain is worth nigh onto $800 - if you could find a buyer.

My third yard tale still lights up my life. One Saturday, I ambled into a yard sale and noticed a solid mahogany floor lamp. A young lady running the sale noticed my eyeing the lamp and called from her front porch. "Grandma's old lamp doesn't work. Been sittin' in our shed for years. It's free." FREE? Now, believe you me, anything that's free, I'm fer it.

Lastly, dear reader, some bargains at yard sales are not what they are racked up to be. Take for instance, the stunning, white, 100% all cotton, $40 Dockers. Like new. I never had a pair of fancy Dockers. What a thrill to find these for $1 at our church yard sale one spring. Just my size too. Didn't even try them on. Big mistake!

When I finally pulled them over my size 44 hips at home, I discovered these "baggies" were for a tall person with a bigger derriere and heftier thighs. Made me look like a ballooning yard saler . So, I put them in my "give-to-the-church box" right away and chalked this "find" up to a bad experience. However, some people never learn.

One year later, I hurried over to the little Mears Church annual yard sale. I got up early, took a Tylenol to ease my early morning myalgia, and drove fast so I could get the best bargains. After pawing through all the racked clothing, believe it or not I found another great pair of Dockers, my size. ONLY 50 CENTS! "I'll take 'em," I joyfully said to Alberta, the dear, 90-year-old clerk.

Got home, tried 'em on, and guess what, dear reader? This Queen of Yard Sales had bought back her own 100% cotton, baggy, white Dockers which she had shortened before donating back to the church a year earlier.

The end of this yard tale is: Alberta auctioned off my Dockers to the highest hippier bidder the following year. At noon, before taking a break, I heard her call out, "SOLD FOR $3.50!"

Crabbin' on Currituck Sound

In late June 2001 while ridding crowded closets and stuffed drawers of unwanted clothing and once-treasured, long forgotten items, I ran across a large wad of twine wrapped around a piece of thin aluminum. I was puzzled as to what this was and tossed it into the "yard sale" pile. Later, Bill identified this strange object and then we began to reminisce about a long-ago fishin'-for-crab experience with strangers.

In 1995 we were en route to Virginia by way of Cape Hatteras National Seashore. At Coinjock, on the mainland, we discovered an RV park on a little point overlooking Currituck Sound. While registering us, the park owner quipped, "Best crabbin' in all North Carolina!"

Crabbin'? I've never been crabbin'. I must try it! Just the thought sent a surge of enthusiasm through me, alleviating the usual van-lag from traveling all day. After settling on our beautiful grassy lot, I hurried back to the park store. "What do I need to catch me a crab?" I said to the crabbin' expert.

"All you need is one of these," and from a peg board he pulled a simple aluminum apparatus that looked like a giant safety pin. Then he tied a long piece of twine on the loop end and said, "That will be seventy nine cents."

"That sure is cheap enough, but there's no hook. How's that going to catch a crab?" I asked.

"Well, Ma'am," he said, looking over his black-rimmed specs," you need one of my special chicken necks."

"A chicken neck? How in the world can a little crab swallow a chicken neck?" I asked. I don't know why, but he laughed 'til I thought his sides would bust.

Suddenly he let up and walked over to his freezer and pulled out a frozen neck. "Only $1.50." *One dollar and fifty cents? Why I could buy a half chicken for that!* "Now, here's what you do, young lady." *Young lady? This crabber is a real charmer*, I thought. *Me with one foot in the grave and the other on a slick crabbin' shore.* As he attached what used to be my favorite part of the chicken to the hook, he said, "See all this fat hanging from this neck?" I saw it. "Well, when a crab comes a nibblin' on that you just lift on your line and net him in." *Net? I don't have a net. Nobody told me you had to have a net! How much is this crabbin' gonna cost me? I didn't say this, just screamed it silently.* "The net is only $3.00, a total of $5.29," he said matter-of-fact-like, not adding his jubilant "young lady."

"Well, I don't know. We're only here for one night," I hesitated. While I was figuring out whether crabbin' would be all that much fun, a middle-aged couple from Virginia Beach intervened.

"Don't buy a net," said Wanda who was waiting to make a purchase from the fat-chicken-neck seller. "You can borrow ours. I caught 23 yesterday."

Twenty-three? I got so excited I almost forgot to pay what's-his-name for the hook, line and chicken neck. Wanda led the way to the crabbin' site overlooking the bay. After one easy lesson in crabbin', she left. Immediately there was a slight tug on the line. Through the clear sea water I spotted a beautiful blue crustacean clawing at my fat neck.

I screamed! "I've got one! I've got one! What do I do?" I'm sure the howl was heard on North Carolina's Outer Banks. Wanda, laughing, scurried from her little camping trailer to the rescue. She gently brought the crab to the surface and when the squirming creature released the neck, she netted him and then plopped him into a waiting pail of clear salt water.

I, of course, had visions of sizzling crab cakes for dinner, so my enthusiasm soared as I hurriedly dropped the line back in. Fifteen minutes, thirty minutes, an hour passed without a nibble. As shadows of darkness dulled the glistening calm waters, I toted my one shimmering beauty back to our camper van. "I'm a big-time crabber," I joked. Bill laughed and snapped a picture for posterity.

Dear reader, if you have never been crabbin', try it sometime. The experience will be a memorable one. So memorable that you will never ever sell your crabbin' chicken-neck holder at a yard sale. Neither will this crabber.

Merry have we met,
And merry have we been;
Merry let us part,
And merry meet again;
With our merry sing-song,
Happy, gay, and free,
With a merry ding-dong,
Happy let us be!
. . . Old English Rhyme

Flesh and Blood Fleas

A flea is a flea is a flea. Not so. Some fleas are jostling, pawing, friendly human beings that wouldn't hurt a dog.

There are many reasons why scavengers flock to flea markets. Economically, it's a cheap way to enjoy some of the finer things in life. Financially, a bargain can surely be sold, sooner or later, for a profit. Socially, it's exciting to mingle with people from all walks of life. Finally, some of the "great" finds enlighten the mind and change the heart.

Once bitten by the flea-bug, there is no turning back to one's neat, organized way of life with no junk to sort through and no bargains to brag about to neighbors.

According to Noah Webster, a flea is "any of several small wingless, jumping, parasitic, bloodsucking insects." A dedicated flea marketer might bristle when reading the ugly word, bloodsucking, because "a bloodsucker is a person who extorts or takes from others as much as he can get."

Actually, the ancient Greek definition of a parasite is more palatable: "One who flatters and amuses his host in return for free meals." Certainly, there is nothing wrong with a little cajoling to congeal a deal. That's part of the flea market game. And if a good bargain is struck, the saving is money in the pocket; therefore, bread and butter on the table.

When my husband dares ask why I bought "that hunk of junk," I rattle off how it's just like new, how much it cost new, and how I saved him a bundle. What does it matter that he already has two shovels and a bad back? Where can one buy a good rusty shovel for fifty cents?

Buying an item, then selling it on the spot is the ultimate in flea marketing. Once I bought for $3.00 an Arabian brass pitcher for my collection. As I ambled on down the aisle, suddenly I felt a tap on my shoulder. "Ma'am," a clean-cut baby boomer in suit and tie begged, "would you sell that brass pitcher?" I truly hated to part with my great import. However, he continued pleading, so finally I asked how much he would give. "Five dollars?" it was a question.

"Oh, Sir, I am so sorry, but this is solid brass and a valuable piece."

"Yes, I know. It matches the coffee server I just bought. Would you please let me have it for ten?" What could I say? I chucked the three plus seven into my carryall bag and a few tables later bought another treasure I didn't need.

Don't you just love haggling with those laid-back vendors at the flea market? When seen behind their rented tables, fellow fleas usually are sharp and eagle-eyed, but they are also regular jocular Joe's out for a little fun in the sun.

Only once have I encountered a suave, but grouchy, old vendor. He wore a white shirt and red tie and operated out of the trunk of his Cadillac. Spotting a shiny bottle opener that I really needed, I ventured a fair offer. "Would you take a quarter?" I chirped.

"Lady," he boomed so all could hear, "I'm a millionaire from New York. Just down here to see how all the slobs live. Thirty-five cents. Take it or leave it!" I left it and later dubbed him a "fleabane," one who drives good fleas away.

On the other hand, there is this grubby little fourteen- year-old who sells tomatoes, corn, and cukes at his father's stand. "What can I do for you, Ma'am?" he sings.

The first time I looked into his Paul Newman eyes, I fell in love with that boy and blurted out, "Young man, you have beautiful blue eyes." His broad, embarrassed grin bared teeth darkened with lack of care, but his clean hands, though rough from hoeing, picking, and packing, gently bagged my vegetables. My day at the flea market was brighter because of this young vendor's pleasant disposition.

Then, there are those beautiful, old books. Although the old yellow pages make me sneeze, the words pleasantly sting my eyes, and, yes, my heart. Words like those of Charles Summer, a great orator and senator from Massachusetts. Words that ring as true in the year 2007 as they did in 1886:

"He is the benefactor and worthy of honor, who carries comfort to wretchedness, dries the tear of sorrow, relieves the unfortunate, feeds the hungry, clothes the naked, does justice, enlightens the ignorant…and by generous example, inspires a love for God and man."

Where else in one day, dear reader, could your mind and heart be touched by so many other human beings while learning lessons from both the rich and the poor? Where else could you find innumerable bargain treasures? And, where else, other than at a flea market, could you trudge up and down dusty aisles and find an almost new box of flea powder for a nickel?

Fabulous House Design

I've got it! The greatest idea ever to emerge in the 21st Century! When architects in the U.S. of A. read this, they will burn the midnight oil while hovering over drawing boards in an effort to top my new house plan! Builders will scramble to get copies, which I will have copyrighted, of course.

In my mind I have designed the perfect house for weary, American homeowners who are tired of dusting, tired of scrubbing, tired of vacuuming, tired of washing windows - just plain tired. This plan is the ultimate in a work-saving abode. When I mentioned this brainstorm to 81 year old Bill, he thought I was a little wacky to waste time on thinking such outlandish thoughts.

But one day while outside pinching my dead petunias, I found a good listener in my gracious, jean-clad, middle-aged neighbor who patiently lent an ear. Step by step I unveiled my plan for selling out lock, stock and our sleeps-fifteen cottage and building a cozy little home where we can relax with our aspirin and ice packs.

"First," I said to neighbor Glenda, "there will be only one large, square room. That's right, one room," I outlined it in the air as I enthusiastically forged ahead. "In one corner will be a small kitchen counter just big enough for buttering a raisin bagel and spooning instant coffee into two cups. No stove. No siree. No stove - just a microwave and a toaster oven that does everything - toasts, bakes 6 bran muffins or grills two chicken legs."

"What about a refrigerator?" My concerned neighbor questioned.

"Well, that will go under the counter as we will need to bend occasionally for exercise. Just a small one, though. That means I will have to shop more often, thereby encouraging Bill to take me out to eat - with coupons, of course."

"But you'll need a bathroom, won't you?" She looked a little puzzled.

"Well, yes," I said. "But no tub. Absolutely no tub. Too much work to scour. When I get down in now, I can't get out."

Glenda frowned and uttered a word of sympathy.

"And, I'm not having a glass door on the shower that you have to squeegee either," I emphatically stated. "Did you know, Glenda, that you can buy a brightly-flowered shower curtain from a dollar store for one dollar? Yes ma'am, one dollar! When the flowers get smudged with mildew, I'll just toss it out and replace with another. Two dollars a year, I predict, is all it will cost me."

"Sounds good to me, I guess," said my confused neighbor.

I rambled on, anxious to get on to the next corner of my fabulous room. "Now, in the other corner, opposite the kitchenette, sets a small, round table and two straight chairs. One for Bill and one for me. The only reason I'm having a table at all is so we will be forced to sit up straight while eating. That way we won't dribble down our fronts. That seems to be a problem lately. Of course, I plan to purchase two Italian, spaghetti-style, large bibs that will be left folded on the table at all times."

"But what about when people stop in for coffee?" She acted as if she might cry.

"Well, I guess they'll just have to sit in the other corner. Yep, that's it. Because in that corner will be two small Lazy Boys with a small table and lamp between. Won't that be grand? Just think, Glenda, I'll have only one lamp shade to vacuum and one table top to dust. No knick-knacks either and definitely no pictures hanging on the walls of me at 18 when I weighed 116 and Bill had hair on his head. I love it! I love it! I'm so excited, I can hardly wait!"

"Where will you two sleep?" She truly was concerned.

"Oh, almost forgot that, but no problem. It's in the plan. In the 4th corner of that magnificent creation of mine there will be one of those Murphy Beds. At night we just push a button and presto! The bed eases down and I climb in. Bill, of course, after sleeping 6 hours in his Lazy Boy, won't know whether it is up or down when he climbs in for his other 6 hours," I howled.

Glenda didn't laugh.

"The best part about that Murphy Bed, you know, is that you don't have to make it in the morning, just push that button," I pushed the air. "And up she goes. Now, whataya think of this super-colossal idea? Great or what?" I bent down to pinch off another wilted petunia. When I straightened up, my now dead-serious neighbor's brow was deeply furrowed.

"Why, Pearl," she exclaimed, "that sounds just like where my mother is." She paused, and then declared, "In a nursing home!"

I thought about her final comment long into the night. Shucks, dear reader, why didn't I think to tell her that nursing homes don't have Murphy Beds and that I am definitely forging ahead with my fabulous house design?

Grandpa's Bargain Suit

It all began when I bought a man's black suit at Hart, Michigan's summer sidewalk sale. I certainly had no intention of telling a soul what I had paid for it, but the news first broke, unexpectedly, on August 9, 2004 at our granddaughter Necia's beautiful, outdoor wedding. The beaming bride in white walked down a path strewn with rose-petals and joined John Ornee under a flower-trimmed arbor where they repeated priceless vows of commitment to each other.

We grandparents were escorted to the front of the tree-bordered cathedral. I must admit Bill looked very dapper in his dressy black suit with floral tie. Of course, like most weddings, there were smiles and tears of joy during the ceremony, followed by much laughter, which is where the suit comes in.

After the groom kissed the bride, guests filed down the path to a large white tent. Following a sit-down dinner, glasses tinkled and the bride and groom kissed many times. Then, the Master of Ceremonies, a college friend of the groom, introduced the glowing couple and commented on their idiosyncrasies.

"Most of you know that John and his buddies are big bargain hunters. They clothed their way through Hope College on cheap deals from thrift shops. It just so happens that I didn't have a suit for this wedding," the debonair M. C. told the guests, "so I went to Goodwill and found this entire hot number for $1.00." Everyone cheered at his bold confession as he strutted across the small, out-door dance floor in his brown tweed suit.

Well, dear reader, Grandma Pearl's old wheels began turning, and I thought immediately, "I can top that story." Bill's suit, although it cost a little more, was not a dull, wintry speckled wool, but a black, classy, summer-weight suit, perfect for this black and white garden wedding.

When the M.C. invited others to sing praises of the bride and groom and tell any related, personal tales, naturally I, as grandmother of the bride, hopped right up, and praised Necia for marrying such a thrifty man. Then, before the 230 attendees, I said to the M.C., "Young man, I love your thriftiness and admission that your suit cost only $1.00. And, John, our groom, will be proud to know that he has married into a thrifty family. Take a look at Grandpa over there," I proudly singled Bill out. "His new suit was a real bargain also. Only .99 cents for the pants and $4.99 for the jacket! Pure, worsted wool too and wrinkle free. I purchased that suit at Hart's sidewalk sales."

Needless to say, when Bill then appeared on the stage, unrehearsed, and out-strutted the M.C., the guests roared and throughout the evening his black bargain suit was the main topic of conversation.

One thing I must confess though, dear reader, Bill's "new" suit was not "brand new," as I may have implied at the wedding. It had been a rental suit for dressy occasions. But, one thing for sure, that suit didn't have a single hole in it, all the buttons matched, and the zipper worked! And, furthermore, there's not a shadow of doubt in my mind that it will see us through all future cruises, weddings - and funerals.

The suit does not make
the man...it's what's inside
that suits the world.
. . .

Be Careful What You Ask For, You Might Get It!

In the summer of 2002 at a family reunion at Silver Lake, my children asked what I would like for Christmas. I jokingly blurted out something I never dreamed I would ever get. Thankfully, that silly request was not granted at Christmastime. But lo and behold, on Valentine's Day, Feb. 14, 2003, a UPS truck stopped at our door in Florida and dropped off a huge box. Inside was the gift I should never have asked for.

I was shocked! Bill, who has the memory of an elephant, had lovingly surprised me with a bright yellow, electric scooter. ME! At age 76! I must admit I was excited. But, while he was sawing off the main steel center post so my feet would safely touch the ground, I began to read the X-360 manual and my delight turned to fear.

"Your X-treme scooter will deliver the best results on a smooth, flat, surface. Avoid uneven surfaces with potholes, cracks, or obstacles." Whoa! I wasn't worried about the obstacles, but potholes? Our entire eleven miles of unnamed streets at Nettles Island had been under construction for several months and the potholes presented hazards to even Seniors out for a stroll.

Reading on, I began to realize that what I had asked for I had gotten, but might not survive to regret it: "Serious injuries can result from the unsafe operation of this vehicle. To minimize assumed risk, the user must wear a safety helmet, goggles, gloves, elbow pads and shoes with sufficient ankle support."

I felt like crying. Wouldn't I look stupid riding around our park all decked out with all this equipment? Really, all I had in mind when making that silly comment two years hence was a way to relieve my aching arches and have fun waving at the neighbors and friends along the way to our post office.

I remember my granddaughter, Caitlin Miya, encouraging me by saying, "Grandma, go for it! That'll be so cool."

"Soon as I get that bright yellow scooter, I'm gettin' me a cell phone and scootin' all over." I laughed.

Then, I threw in a bit of philosophical advice, "But I'm not having batteries in that cell phone."

"Grandmaaaa, why not?"

"Because cell phones are dangerous. I saw the man who invented cell phones interviewed on TV. He said because of the radiation emitted, they could be causing increased risk of cancer in young people."

Other grandchildren responded in unison, "Grandmaaaa?"

"It's true, and since then I've read that because of this risk, a shield has been developed to help protect users from absorbing the rays."

Well, dear reader, guess what I got for my birthday the following January from Caitlin's mom, Kitty. A used cell phone – without batteries! So, really now, to carry off this joke, all I needed was that yellow scooter, which I knew I needn't worry about, because I would never get it. But...I did! Now,all I needed was courage to ride it.

The first day, without a helmet, I rode it around our circle, about one-twentieth of a mile. My nerves were shot, even at 5 mph. I managed to miss the potholes, but not once could I look up at the neighbors who laughed and yelled, "Dangerous Driver." Trying to show my appreciation to Bill for his thoughtfulness, I even ventured as far as our island post office, about two-twentieth's of a mile – once.

One thing I know for sure, joking around when asking for a gift can be scary, especially if asking for some dangerous, little toy not meant for Grandmas. Never will I be able to wave to my friends or use my no-battery cell phone while riding the beautiful yellow scooter. Why not, you ask? Because believe you me, I'm keepin' one hand on the throttle and the other on the brake.

So please, dear reader, do be careful what you ask for. You might just get it.

Impromptu is truly the
touchstone of wit.
. . . Moliere

Tennis Anyone?

"Love, fifteen, thirty, forty, deuce." Garble! After one tennis lesson, I knew what all that garble meant. Now, I also know that the Wimbledon Jet-Set tennis buffs in England aren't any smarter than us down-home folks here in America. They are just fancier talkers.

Before taking up tennis at 62 in 1988, I actually peeked through our Nettles Island chain-link fence surrounding the tennis court for eight years. I snickered and thought to myself, *I could play better tennis than that with my eyes closed.* Well, dear friends, during my very first lesson I discovered "playing tennis ain't easy."

Determined to win me a trophy like those awarded at our tennis club parties, I contacted the club's tennis coach and former Pro, Mr. Bob Tift. He encouraged me and scheduled private lessons at the local public courts.

During the first pre-lesson warm-up, my friend Louise, another hot-shot hopeful, assured me that all we had to do was hit the ball against the backboard and then, slam it up there again. "Oh, I can do that," I quipped. But, dear friends, she slammed it, I missed. I slammed it, she missed.

After one-half hour of chasing missed balls, not to mention the slightly high ones we sailed clean over the backboard, we questioned whether we would ever get past "love."

Finally, lungs bursting and brows beaded, we pedaled home on our rusty three-speeds. Upon dismounting, I discovered an absolutely awful catastrophe. My arthritic ankles had swelled above my cute little sport socks trimmed in hot pink - the ones that matched the white, cute little short shorts I had rushed out to buy for effect. After all, anyone on the senior tennis circuit knows that a color-coordinated outfit distracts from cellular globs bobbing between fat knees and varicosities here and there.

Then, the lessons began. When our most patient, elderly, tennis pro gently hand-tossed the ball over the net right in front of me, I zinged that sucker right back at him. He smiled approval. Dear friends, the adrenalin was gushing. Things were lookin' up! "Yesiree," I winked at Louise, "We're gonna be tennis players before you know it!"

But, my dear, dear friends, the minute Coach Tift took that Pete Sampras oval of strings in his hand and sliced that little green, fuzzy ball across the net, WHOA! I never even saw that ball.

"You took your eye off the ball, Miss Pearl, the instructor said firmly, shaking his head. "Keep your eye on the ball!" But one thousand balls later, dear friends, that little made-famous-in-Wimbledon, tiny, round devil still zipped by my bifocals, unscathed.

"You gotta run up, step back, turn those shoulders. Right, left, sweep, sweep that ball," dear Mr. Tift barked gently. "Use both hands, keep those knees bent, eye on the ball."

WHEW! I thought that lesson would never end. When it finally did and I glanced down, I could have cried. My cute little pink-trimmed socks had scootched down into my brand new K-Mart tennis shoes.

But I'm not a quitter. dear reader. Not me. So, tennis anyone? I won't mind if you beat me. I look at it this way: Any silver-haired grandma who is gutsy enough to even show up on a tennis court is already a winner.

There's one thing though that for the life of me I cannot understand. Why can't those highcoflutin' folks at Wimbledon just say, "One, two, three, tie, game" and skip all that "love" stuff. In my book, zero is zero!

Confidence is that feeling
by which the mind embarks
on great and honorable
courses with a sure hope
and trust in itself.

. . . Cicero

Three Fig Leaves for Grandma

There is a major catastrophe facing the mature woman today. The bathing suit industry is determined to fully expose us. In Florida, even the sea gulls are embarrassed.

Now, I am what my peers call a modest woman when it comes to sunbathing. But the youngsters, I'm sure, dub me "old fashioned" when they see me in my one-piece Rose Marie swimsuit with a skirt and built-in support for sagging grandmas.

Being a swimmer at our beautiful Silver Lake, and an avid hiker on our high sand dunes, I have always worn what I considered a "decent" suit, one that hides what should be hidden. Indoors, I often wear a cover-up in the presence of members of my family and always in the presence of my Momma. She never wore a bathing suit in her 88 years on God's green earth.

Occasionally, around the cottage on hot steamy days, I have been known to toss the cover-up aside. But I learned my lesson fast when comments from the peanut gallery began to ring out loud and clear. Grandchildren ages 4-10, just noticing feminine shapes and forms, began to question what was hanging over and out of my bathing suit. Precious Caitlin, who never uttered a word to hurt anyone, brought up my sagging chest - not her exact words. Meagan, no doubt wishing she could fly, questioned why God gives only Grandmas bat wings under their biceps.

I waited for one of the others to ask about my thigh-pones or why *only* Santa and I shake like a bowl full of jelly, but Bill beat them to it. "Pearl, you know, you are getting older," he reminded me in his kind, loving way. So, remembering my vows to "cherish, love, and obey," I respected his wishes and promised to never be caught dead or alive clothed in anything other than long sleeves and below-the-knees flowing skirts north of the Mason-Dixon Line. But it wasn't long until that vow was broken.

Forgive me, dear reader, for breaking that vow. I'm sure you know that temperatures sometimes soar in Florida. When we arrived at Nettles Island in October with temperatures hovering around 94 degrees, there was absolutely nothing I could do but ignore the grandchildren's slurs and continue to shock the seagulls. So I went shopping, hoping to find a "decent" grandma bathing suit.

Nice shop, just swimsuits. Racks and racks of swimsuits. All colors, all sizes and for all figures - they advertised. A pretty little blond clerk greeted me at the door and offered to help. "Do you have any little-old-lady bathing suits?" I got right to the point.

Eyeing me up and down and sideways, that well-trained, patient, sweet little thing said what every Grandma wants to hear. "Why, sweetie, you're not old. We have lots of lovely suits for you. Now, let me see." She walked over to a rack of psychedelic, Jamaican prints. Most were two-piece and I swear, if I were a swearer, that those suits were no bigger than half a fig leaf - top and bottom. No stays to hold your boobs up either, and not an ounce of stuffing in the top! One-by-one she slid them by on the endless rack, glancing up now and then, hoping I was still with her.

"I really wouldn't be interested in a two-piece. Do you have any with support up here and with an elastic support to hold in my tummy? You know, a full one-piece with a little more material?" I foolishly rattled on. "Maybe with a swag or a flounce? You know, a 'decent' kind of suit, maybe a Dorothy Lamour sarong type."

Her blue eyes looked straight into mine and with a quizzical look, she said, "No ma'am, we don't carry that brand." Her innocence was comical. "But we do have these lovely one-piece suits," she said, turning to another circular rack.

On and on she slid more and more colorful suits along, stopping often to point out what the youth of today, no doubt, consider a suit's necessary best features. Honestly, they all looked like they were cut up to the armpits and down to the navel. And not a single ruffle on the straps! True! Bewildered, I thanked the pretty little miss and then roamed the store on my own, but no decent suit was to be found. Finally, after two hours, disappointed and very tired, I gave up.

However, dear reader, as I left the store pondering a solution to grandma exposure at the beach, a brilliant idea flashed across my creative mind. Why not capitalize on the swimsuit industry's "flaunt-your-flab" scheme? Design an over-sized tee-shirt line called THREE FIG LEAVES. These would surely cover up all grandmas from Mears to Miami. I'll admit, though, the clever fig-leaf brainstorm was not original - Eve thought of it first.

Wrinkles Are Beautiful

You will never believe this, dear reader, but would I tell a lie on the first day of the 21st Century? I got up this morning, looked in the mirror and counted 64 avenues of corrugation on a face that was like a newborn's ten years ago. Sixty-four wrinkles, mind you. And, that does not include the crows' feet!

All day I puzzled as to what went wrong in the previous decade that put me in such a furrowed state, as well as why women have more wrinkles than men. Analyzing from scalp to chin, the causes proved very interesting.

Take the forehead wrinkles, the ones hidden under a lady's curly bangs. Those are "worry" wrinkles. After all, a mature woman frets and fumes and frowns about everything from what to microwave for dinner to what to wear to her 50th high school class reunion. Men, on the other hand, refuse to get their Fruit-of-the-Looms in a bunch. They like to relax, watch TV and sleep.

You show me a woman who calls her grown children at midnight because she has just thought of a solution to THEIR problem and I'll show you a woman with deep wrinkles. Women are natural problem solvers - hers, his, theirs, the neighbor's, the government's. Dear reader, I like to think a classic furrowed brow depicts a Champion of Causes.

Now, let's move on down to the "mad" wrinkles, the deep crevices between the eyes. No doubt, they made their first appearance when a mom shook her finger at Johnny and then, hoppin' mad, swatted him. But I think I know when mine went from lines to gullies - in the late 90's as I wrangled with pharmacists and doctors who cheat Medicare. One thing for sure, my wrinkles flared like wild fire, when Pretty Boy Clinton defiled MY White House. No woman likes getting mad, but she has to do what has to be done to keep this world good, wrinkles or no wrinkles.

Besides, who would want to be a placid, smooth-faced beauty at 76? Everyone would whisper behind her back that she had had a face lift when in reality, she may have simply spent every afternoon watching "soaps" while sipping mint juleps.

Then, there are those "kissing" wrinkles, little vertical creases on the upper lip, better known as pucker lines. Women are prolific kissers. They kiss mothers, fathers, husbands, babies, and politicians - anybody who puckers up. I'll admit it. I am a kisser. But my lines are much deeper than most. I not only like to kiss, but I am a whistler and whistling requires a constant pucker. Whistlers are noted for being happy people though, and I like being happy.

When I retired - some retirement a Grandma has - oops, that booger "sarcasm" slipped in and rumpled the skin beneath my left cheek and the corner of my whistling, kissing mouth, leaving me with a new wrinkle, No. 65. Go ahead, dear reader, look in the mirror and try talking sarcastically out of the corner of your mouth, like "Oh, no, here she comes again," and you'll understand a "sarcasm" wrinkle.

I just now stood in front of the mirror to test smiling versus crying. Yes, I did! Crying shrivels up the whole face so that wrinkles turn into a dried-up-apple effect. And now that I think about it, I'll bet that crying even twists your heart into wrinkles. Sure feels like it anyway, and, dear reader, wrinkled hearts are hard to smooth out. Let's hope and pray our "crying" wrinkles are few through 2022.

"Smiling" is my favorite wrinkle. Those elongated dimples dance all over your lower cheeks when you smile. And isn't that better than a satiny, stone, face? Besides, there are so many nice people who smile back at you. Personally, I like the warm feeling of a smile, and dimples in any shape are so cute.

So, dear reader, let's bounce into every New Year with a smile and wear our beautiful wrinkles as a badge of accomplishments.

He that is of a merry
heart hath a continual
feast.
Proverbs 15:15

Red Rockers, Rockin!

Several years ago I read a poem titled Warning, written by British poet, Jenny Joseph, which reads "When I am an old woman, I shall wear purple with a red hat which doesn't go and doesn't suit me." I laughed at the picture showing a wrinkled, little old lady and thought, "It would be fun in one's old age to wear a red hat."

Well, guess who has arrived? Wrinkled and needing a boost? Yours truly, Grandma Pearl who has always believed you must make everything a happening and have fun, fun, fun. So, in January 2002, "The Red Rockers" of Nettles Island was born.

Now, dear reader, you might even call our red hatters "The Painted Red Rockers." When I first suggested that we wear red hats to our outdoor activities on the Island, several young-at-heart ladies rushed out to buy red hats. However, they were difficult to find. So, only 5 grandmas, 2 with straw red hats and 3 with red visors, showed up at an outdoor barbecue. "Got a problem," said I.

The following morning, as I peered into my closet and noticed two old straw hats resting there, I thought, why not paint them? So I rushed out to Wal-Mart and purchased an eighty-nine cent spray can of red, fast-dry enamel. Presto, 2 beautiful red straw hats! As the word got around, suddenly red hats were popping up at every outdoor activity, 21 at our next fish fry.

"Time to organize," said Grandma Pearl. At our first breakfast at the Nettles Cafe in early March, 42 women showed up sporting a variety of red hats, several spray painted bright red. Some were ringed with flowers, others trimmed with large, purple chiffon bows. One proud, patriotic grandma trimmed her hat with a red, white, and blue bandanna. There were wide brims, narrow brims, no brims. The oldest red felt was pulled out of mothballs - very chic even at 50 years old. The most creatively trimmed hat was decorated with felt snowmen atop

The following month we traveled by trolley to a luncheon at the Jolly Sailor in Old Town Stuart where 48 women made a scene not to be forgotten. A Stuart News cameraman clicked away the entire time while we red hatters enjoyed the chef's "red hat special." But most importantly, it was evident that these "Red Rockers" of Nettles Island had left their rocking chairs and were enjoying a rocking good time.

Officially, to become a member of our Red Rockers, you must be over 50 years of age and wear a red hat. There are no rules, no committees, no meetings or dues. We are simply elderly women who love to dress up and who enjoy camaraderie. Being a part of such a group is a way to make new friends while having an exciting, exhilarating experience of "painting the town red."

In four years, our numbers at Nettles Island escalated to 250 red hatters during the winter season. Instead of one group of Red Rockers with one reigning Queen, we now have ten groups of 25, each with their own queen. Although they all are still rockin', each group has chosen new, clever names, the latest, Scarlet O'Hatters. With members contributing ideas for outings, there is no limit to the varied activities these vibrant grandmas enjoy. They sip tea in Victorian tea houses, sing and dance on Riverboat Cruises, tour art galleries and historic museums. Albert Schweitzer once said, "In everyone's life, at some time, our inner fire goes out. It is then burst into flame by an encounter with another human being. We should all be thankful for those people who rekindle the inner spirit."

In 2004 a new group, the Cherry Church Belles, numbering 9 was formed in our Mears Methodist Church in Michigan. Ladies from surrounding towns liked the idea of "ringing bells" in red hats and the total jumped to 75. Because of difficulty finding restaurants to accommodate such large groups, again, it was time to split.

Queen Mum Pearl says "Thank you, Red Rockers and Cherry Church Belles, for rekindling the inner spirit of many lonely widows in our groups as well as those you have visited in nursing homes." And yes, "Thank you for making my latter anxious years, health wise, brighter and more blessed."

Dear reader, whether a Red Hatter or not, we must all keep on RINGIN' and ROCKIN'.

Woman is a delightful
musical instrument, of
which love is the bow
and man the artist.
. . . Stendhal

"Forget That Resolution, You Just Broke It!"

It's that time again, dear reader. Time to make those New Year resolutions! In early December 2002, I began jotting down earnest intentions for possible publication in my *Pearls* column. By December 26 I felt certain all ten were ready for the world to read.

However, that very evening several good friends popped in for a surprise visit and shot down my best resolution. Non-stop, pleasant chitchat lasted for about an hour. Then, during the first lull in conversation, I chimed in with, "Wanna hear my New Year's resolutions?"

"Yeah, what are they?" Joe said.

"Number 1, in 2002 I resolve to talk less, and..." He stopped me dead in my flowing expose.

"Well, you can forget Number 1. You just broke it." Har! Har! The room vibrated with belly laughter. Naturally, I didn't proceed with Number 2 and immediately changed the subject. But after our friends were gone, I soothed my ego with, *"Oh, Joe is such a jokester. And besides, he doesn't understand the reason for my resolution."*

In fact, none of the guests knew that one summer, after entertaining six grandchildren for one week, I suffered TMJ - Temporary Mandibular Joint Syndrome, throbbing pain in both joints of the jaw. Who would have thought, dear reader, that a simple thing like telling those kids a few things their parents had failed to teach them would cause such misery? Although my doctor was kind in prescribing a cure, "rest the muscles," in reality he was saying "speak less."

As a child, discussing, quizzing, or just plain chattering on any subject sparked my insatiable eagerness to learn. As an adult, I have always thought that one's ability to communicate verbally was a God-given talent. But I must admit that the older I get the more I realize some talents are better buried.

So, in 2002, having noticed similar symptoms of TMJ, I resolved to weigh my words, which is a wise policy for anyone inclined to speak emptily or trivially at times. But for me, dear reader, that has never been an easy task. Whether expressing feelings for those whom I love, or speaking my mind on issues about which I am deeply concerned, words have often tumbled out unchecked.

Yes, I know that at times I am guilty of verbally over-communicating. Bill, for sixty-two years, has called it "rambling." In response to his much repeated remark, one day I bluntly reminded him that "Rambling certainly is not as serious as tattling or gossiping."

"True," he said," but if you don't have something important to say, don't say it."

"But, there's so much that needs to be said before I die."

"Put it in black and white then," he quipped. "And another thing, you ask people too many questions."

"How else am I going to stay informed?" No answer. Isn't it amazing that no matter how long you live with a quiet, reserved man he never understands a woman's need to look into a stranger's eyes and communicate verbally?

But, dear reader, I do recognize where my doctor, my husband and my friend Joe are coming from. So I am changing this year's resolution to read: "I resolve to diligently work at weeding out of my speech harmful or unnecessary words." More explicitly, let's see, how will I start? Got it! "No more tart comments to our children regarding their weight, beards, dogs or how they waste their money. No more boring my friends about how terrific my grandchildren are - well, at least I'll try to minimize their many accomplishments. And, no more adding my two cents worth to conversations that could possibly hurt another's character or reputation."

Heaven help me in the future to speak words that truthfully inform, praise, uplift, or encourage. And, Heaven help me to do so in short sentences - not paragraphs.

A sharp tongue is the
only edge tool that grows
sharper with constant use.
. . . Washington Irving

Delightful Dilemma

I never dreamed that coming into a lot of money in one's old age could create such frustrating anticipation and indecision. Years ago my Uncle Samuel had promised me a windfall on March 1, 1988. So in 1987 I jotted down in my mind many things I've always wanted but could never afford. Four things at the top of this mental list: Half-and-half for my coffee, real leather Reeboks, rolls and rolls of pretty gift wrap, and at least one new dress a season.

But, dear reader, receiving and dispensing of seemingly unearned monetary gifts is not that simple. No Siree. At Christmastime when I discussed possibilities with our grown-up kids, they promptly threw a monkey wrench into my plans.

"New wrapping paper?" my daughter howled with laughter, no doubt remembering the wrinkled, but darling, Christmas paper with singing angels that I had recycled on her birthday present. "You're lying, Mom. You're too frugal!" She was right, of course. Who in their right mind would throw away perfectly good gift wrap?

"Well, I'm definitely gonna replace my K-Mart Trax with Reeboks now that I'm into tennis," I said.

"Now, Mom, you know you've always made fun of how they make us look pigeon-toed." She was right.

"One thing I am definitely going to indulge in, when I get that extra money, is half-and-half for my coffee. Not just for company. I'll keep it on hand all the time."

"Mom," my nurse daughter-in-law spouted, "that's filled with cholesterol. You can't start using that at 62!" Enough said. Why did I ever mention that upcoming, confounded root of all evil anyway?

"Well, I'm definitely going to buy me a new dress for Spring. I'll walk by the sale racks, not even look at the price tag. Just choose a color to match my eyes, try it on, and hand the clerk my brand new Visa Card."

"Mom, be realistic. You would never pay $75.00 for a new dress when the import you bought at the Palm Beach yard sale for $2.00 fits you so beautifully. You said yourself that after adding the $8.00 beaded belt from Hong Kong, you never felt so elegant." Right again. And,

134

hadn't *everyone* at our Women's Club dance asked where in the world I had found such a beauty?

"Mom," my son Nick rushed in with his great idea, "why not a nice speed boat for the lake?"

Our family discussion on how to spend *my uncle's* money had suddenly turned from "yours" to "mine." At this point I felt the monkey wrench had turned one bolt too many. Needless to say, I dropped the subject, crumpled the list in my mind and postponed making a final decision until I actually had the special gift in my arthritic hand.

On March 3 a long, buff-colored envelope arrived. Bill handed it to me with a joyful, "Congratulations, Mama! I think your Uncle Sam has come through!" Sitting at my typewriter, I eagerly slit the windowed envelope with my fingernail, then, peered down at Uncle Sam's check representing years of hard work and *my* future Social Security. One problem. Now that the prize was here, the delightful dilemma of how to spend it must be faced.

"I've got it!" I screamed silently. "Something I've always dreamed of! Why didn't I think of this before?" Matter settled.

But in an instant, dear reader, when a bead of perspiration plopped from my forehead onto bare tanned legs, a sobering thought shocked me back to reality. "What on earth would I do with a mink hat in Florida?"

Without love and laughter
there is no joy. Live and
love amid laughter.
. . . Horace

Preachin' a Sermon Ain't All That Hard

No doubt, dear reader, in everyone's life there is at least one unforgettable highlight! Not necessarily atop a mountain by the Sea of Galilee, but perhaps atop an Indiana sand dune along the shores of Lake Michigan. Although I was never a Bible scholar, at the age of 23 I was thrust into preaching a sermon on a mount.

The year was 1949. After Bill's junior year at Hope College, he directed a summer Christian camp for children of low-income, Italian immigrant families living on Chicago's West Side. Two other Hope students and I were counselors, responsible for supervising fun and games as well as planning morning devotions.

We were also expected to deliver the Sunday morning sermon if a guest minister should cancel. Usually, counselors knew in advance and had time to prepare. All went well, dear reader, until the last Saturday before camp closing. Late in the afternoon we were alerted that the appointed minister could not come! AND it was my turn to preach the sermon. Not to children, but to 30 buxom Bon Ameche mothers who spoke no English!

After dinner that evening, I anxiously pondered my predicament while sitting in blue jeans on a high sand dune. Watching the blood-red sun dip into Lake Michigan, I suddenly found myself a child again, seated at the feet of our country preacher. He was holding out his big black Bible and proclaiming that the greatest sermon ever preached was Christ's Sermon on the Mount.

"That's it!" I yelled to Heaven. I ran back to our cabin, took out my New Testament and searched until I found the beautiful Beatitudes in Matthew, Chapter 5.

Perfect! An entire sermon in ten short verses! All I had to do was read them. But how was I to get a single word across to these Italian mothers who spoke only Italian?

The next morning I donned my navy blue skirt and white camp shirt. Immediately following Sunday breakfast, I stood, shaking but confident, and dramatically read the Sermon on the Mount, looking up and pausing after each verse. Wish you could have been there, dear reader. The enthusiastic response of these robust women clad in their best, flowered housedresses was almost comical:

"Blessed are the poor in spirit, for theirs is the kingdom of heaven." I expounded. The Bon Ameche's loudly responded, "Si!" Yes!

"Blessed are those who mourn, for they shall be comforted." I lowered my voice. Again, but solemnly, they answered, "Si"

"Blessed are the meek, for they shall inherit the earth." ."Buono!" Good! They cried out.

"Blessed are those who hunger and thirst for righteousness, for they shall be satisfied." "Buono!" I started to relax, even smiled at them.

"Blessed are the merciful, for they shall obtain mercy." "Si! Si!"

"Blessed are the pure in heart, for they shall see God." "Si! Buono!" Yes, Good! They cheered me on as I continued.

"Blessed are the peacemakers, for they shall be called the sons of God." "Ah, Si," they sighed in unison.

"Blessed are those who are persecuted for righteousness' sake, for theirs is the kingdom of heaven." With this promise, the Bon Ameche women seemed a group with a purpose, like they were choosing a champion of causes – in Italian. Feeling victory, I boldly forged ahead.

"Blessed are you," I paused, quickly scanning attentive faces eager to hear more. I raced on, "when men revile you and persecute you and utter all kinds of evil against you falsely on my account". "Buono! Buono!" Good! Good!

On the last verse I raised my voice. "Rejoice and be glad, for your reward is great - great in heaven." "Buono! Buono!" they shouted.

Completely overwhelmed, by their Si's and Buono's, I graciously thanked them. Immediately 30 smiling, high-spirited, sturdy women stood, clapped loudly, and then some reached out to me with a renewed burst of enthusiasm, crying out, "Buono figlia, buono! Buono figlia, buono!"

Much later, I was to learn that those three words meant, "Good, Daughter, Good!" This was truly a highlight in my life, dear reader, helping me to realize that preachin' a sermon ain't all that hard – just read The Beatitudes from Matthew 5.

A Virgin's Story

Dear reader, this strange, true incident took place on a cruise ship somewhere in the Caribbean in January 2003 when I was 77. Truly a night never to be forgotten.

One evening cruisers filed into the theatre to see the Love and Marriage game show. As the curtain went up, Clo, the Cruise Director, swished across the stage in her black, too-tight, evening gown and got the 1500 passengers going with jokes and laughter. Then, she chose 4 couples from the audience to participate and announced that prizes would be given for best answers. Bill and I were selected last as the couple married over 50 years. However, I was not prepared for the embarrassing questions this laughing, buxom hostess asked.

The men were seated on stage, while the wives waited in a soundproof room. The object, of course, was to try and match your husband's answers. Finally, the four wives entered and stood behind their husbands. Questions 1, 2, 3 and 4 were borderline risqué, but the audience roared after each response.

Then, Question #5. "Where is the most unusual place you and your husband ever made whoopee?" the sexy Clo asked. Well, dear reader, you can imagine how flabbergasted this grandma was to be asked such a vulgar question. Didn't faze the other 4 wives though. They giggled and gave shocking answers that matched! No doubt, rehearsed before the show started, I thought..

"On a donkey," the newlywed said. Clo shook with jollity and the audience roared! "Couple #2?" She asked after recovering from the first response. "Up a Tree," quipped the wife married 5 years. Again, the audience roared. Couple #3, married 30 years, simply matched with "in the back seat of our car." My face began to burn like fire and then I broke out with sweat. How could I ever top those answers?

"Now, Pearl," Clo asked respectfully, "what do you think your husband said?" I stammered out, "Jacksonville, Beach?" She screamed into the mike, "ON THE BEACH?" The audience went wild! "No, Maam," I said, reaching for her microphone. "Bill and I were on our honeymoon in our four-dollar-a-week room. Bill was a sailor and I was a virgin." She grabbed the mike, "A VIRGIN?" As she hee-hawed about this unexpected response, the audience was practically rolling in the aisles and the applause deafening. It was a match, but not the end of this unbelievable tale.

The following day many people, young and old, stopped me on deck to ask, "You are Pearl the Virgin, aren't you?" Bill was embarrassed.

Finally, page two. That night, early, Bill and I filed into a row of empty seats to watch the last big show of the cruise. The auditorium was dimly lit. A gentleman in shorts sagged into the seat to my left. Suddenly, he said, "Did you see that Love & Marriage show last night?"

"Uh, yes, we did." I said, never looking at him, afraid of what was coming next.

"Wasn't that little old lady hilarious when Clo asked where she and her husband first made whoopee? Her answers were the best. You know," he continued, almost sadly, never looking at me, "I've been married twice and I never knew a virgin."

Needless to say, dear reader, I could not resist. I turned, looked him in the eye, and with a big smile said, "Well, sir, meet Pearl the Virgin!" All passengers seated around us just howled.

Now, dear reader, you know the rest of the story – and, oh yes, we did win first prize!

Everything is funny as long as
it is happening to someone else.
. . . Will Rogers

Lake of Silver Turning To Gold

"Can you believe," an astonished friend asked me in the summer of 2007, "that a cottage on Silver Lake near Mac Wood's Dune Scooters recently sold for one million dollars?"

Naturally, dear reader, I was as shocked as she. Later, back at the cottage, I contemplated why anyone would pay that for a home on our little silvered lake nestled at the foot of 450 acres of sand?

Maybe they are retirees and sold their permanent home elsewhere, I told myself. *Like us, they probably love watching the beautiful sunsets while providing a place for their grandchildren to swim, water ski, and hike across the dunes to Lake Michigan. Maybe they have young families who come to Silver Lake with dune buggies. With their many garages, they certainly could handle numerous vehicles.* Oh, this contemplating mind of mine!

BUT ONE MILLION DOLLARS? It took a few days to accept the "silver" in Silver Lake turning to "gold." I have noticed over the last few years that nicer homes have sprouted up here and there along the lake shore, but nothing this grandiose. In fact, when we returned from Florida last spring, a gigantic two-story, Louisiana plantation type house had been built on our little dirt road west of the State Park. A very interesting place, indeed, with a hot tub on the front porch overlooking a dune-grass front yard and the lake. The owner invited us in for a tour. We were impressed with his very up-to-date ideas throughout, including a stairway mural with happy children frolicking to the top.

I must admit, dear reader, that viewing this house, which is a $350,000 rental, triggered memories of our original tiny cottage. Rental cottages on Silver Lake in 1966 sold for $7,000. Bill's summer job as a ranger at Silver Lake State Park Campground demanded we find a place to live for three months. We borrowed the $1,000 down payment from his Teachers' Credit Union, and moved into the cabin of three rooms and a tiny bath.

There was no hot water, no shower, no washer and dryer. For seven years I drove eight miles each week to Hart to do laundry. When our five children needed a shower, I squirted a dab of shampoo on their heads, and off they flew to the lake. It was not such a desirable housing situation, but oh the fun we had sailing on silvered waters and hiking on the golden Silver Lake sand dunes.

Our famous resort area with all of its outdoor amenities is changing though. There are fewer boats on the lake, especially large speedboats and small, fast-flying watercraft. In the summer of 2007, I thought perhaps this was due to the exorbitant price of gasoline. But, now I am led to believe that our younger generation is geared up for more land action. It seems they are building or buying very sophisticated, high-powered dune buggies and putting on shows with their wheelies and jumps, unheard of when Bill patrolled the dunes.

Our neighbors of 40 years, the Schippers, recently sold their cottage to son Tim who grew up water skiing with our children. In addition to a beautiful speed boat, he also owns two dune buggies. One is a small, red buggy like many of the hundreds seen skittering across the dunes, but the other one is the "Cadillac" of all dune buggies. He has kindly offered to take Grandma Pearl for a ride in his new power-plus toy. But, believe me, after seeing this photo of his spectacular shenanigans atop one of the sand mountains in that beautiful, purple piece of machinery, I shrank away from his hug and begged off, promising maybe at a later date.

Tim Schipper's dune buggy atop a dune along
the shores of Lake Michigan.

No doubt, dear reader, the little silvered lake area of past years has become a famous, golden outdoor resort. Bigger homes and bigger buggies. But there are still many modest cottages and campgrounds where folks come for memorable family fun!

Freedom

**My Country, Sweet Land of Liberty,
'Tis Of Thee I Sing.**

Top left clockwise. Bill reciting "America"; The Grand Canyon; Hawaii becomes our 49th State; Sunset over Silver Lake Sand Dunes; Snow-capped mountains; "...one nation, under God, with liberty and justice for all."

Faces of Freedom

Summer is the time to travel across America, feel its spaciousness and hear the resounding echo of America's past. It is also a time to watch expressions of awe on faces of tourists from all over the world, who have come to marvel at our oh-so-beautiful land stretching from the Atlantic to the Pacific.

In May, 1990 Bill and I loaded our camper van in Florida and headed west. We traveled along Lady Bird Johnson's wildflower byways, zigzagging from coast to coast drinking in the beauty of our National Parks. Although the kaleidoscopic scenes have now faded somewhat, many faces are still indelibly etched in my mind.

In cotton fields of Alabama and along the levees of Louisiana, faces of laughing black children glowed as they romped hand in hand with laughing white children.

Deep in the bowels of the earth at Carlsbad Caverns in New Mexico, early sightseers scanned the dark mysteries of million-year formations 800 feet underground. North, placid faces of the Acoma Indians, now being educated, expressed satisfaction with their perch atop a Mesa they have inhabited since the year 1300 in this dry, dusty land.

Other faces, like those of Regina and Jurgen Aretz from Germany with whom we picnicked in Billy-the-Kid Country, beamed with amazement after biking across peaked mountains and through cactus-blooming deserts of the once Wild West.

On the rim of our beautiful Grand Canyon, a young Chinese student pursuing a Doctorate in Engineering at UCLA expressed a desire to stay in this land of opportunity. But with a sadness sweeping across his golden face, he stated that he must return to serve his government.

From there, we circled through Canyon Land in Utah. On the brink of Bryce Canyon's dusty-pink, painted fairyland, a young Swedish bookkeeper, steeped in deep thought, struggled to capture all that beauty in poetry. Through thick glasses he squinted up at me and said, "I have no words." Neither did I, dear reader.

At Zion National Park, with its canyons of ancient, massive, wind-whipped temples of grey stone, there were other unforgettable faces. Faces of the host and hostess at the campground radiated with the freedom of their lifestyle. These volunteers spend summers on seemingly holy ground and travel south in winter in their 31' house trailer.

Cruising up the California coast, yes, dear reader, we saluted General Sherman, the largest redwood tree in the world; and, yes, we sat in solitude beneath the misty Bridal Veil Falls at Yosemite. Spring's spray of clear mountain water refreshed the faces of many weary travelers from all over the world.

During our only "big city" experience we warmed our chilled bones in San Francisco with Fisherman Wharf clam chowder. Later we gaily dashed onto a little, red cable car, and then cringed when shelling out $6.00 for a cup of cappuccino atop the famed Fairmont Hotel. But the panoramic view of the Bay area - Alcatraz, boat-filled harbors, clean sea-washed homes, Cannery Row, and many bridges spanning blue, blue waters - was worth the monetary shock.

After crossing the Golden Gate Bridge, we camped in by-the-sea fishing villages in Oregon and Washington. At Glacier National Park winter's blanket was turned back on the Road to the Sun. The snow had, against its will, recently been pushed tight to the winding, sheer-faced mountain wall. Needless to say, the breathtaking views renewed one's faith in God and America. A Japanese tourist, his black eyes reflecting snow-capped mountains, asked and answered his own question, "America, everything, yes?" Neither his clicking camera, nor ours, could capture the grandeur of it all.

There were still four faces we had not seen – faces etched in stone at Mount Rushmore in South Dakota. What a great climax to our 9,000 mile plus dream. At dusk a throng of mixed races crowded into the amphitheater at the foot of the granite mountain for a lighting ceremony. Seated directly in front of us were American Indians. I could not see the chief's face, only the shiny black braids hanging down his broad back.

A Park Ranger told why the great sculptor, Borglum, chose Washington, Jefferson, Lincoln and Teddy Roosevelt as his subjects of freedom. Chills ran down my spine. All through the crowd white handkerchiefs blotted faces of proud men and women. The shoulders of the big Indian began to shake and when the lights came on, silent sobs erupted here and there as Old Glory fluttered in the mountain breeze.

The crowd, with hands over hearts, rose as strains of "land of the free, home of the brave" rang out. Through my own mist I saw young, upturned faces of future leaders all across the theater. But one face, dear reader, will remain with me forever - that of a fresh-faced young girl whose tear-filled eyes seemed glued to the stone-faced leaders of yesterday. Determined and intense!

She could possibly be another Lincoln, I thought. Yes, dear reader, *She could just be America's keeper of freedom - tomorrow.*

LSTs Won the War

A grandma who writes stories occasionally hears tales that spark her patriotic spirit. Such was the case while I sat alone at the Riverside Café in Whitehall, Michigan in the summer of 2001. A casual conversation with two veterans and their wives at a nearby table suddenly turned into an interesting discussion about LSTs. A Mr. Bill Morley from Ohio mentioned that he had served on the LST 621, a US Naval Landing Ship. "Oh, really," I jumped in. "An LST?"

The veterans were surprised that a little old lady knew anything about "landing ships carrying tanks." But Bill, a Navy veteran, and I had recently toured the LST 325 being restored in Mobile, Alabama as a memorial to all LST veterans who in Winston Churchill's words "won the war." The LSTs of World War II were used to discharge men and heavy equipment onto hostile beaches during amphibious landings, including the famous landing at Normandy Beach in France on June 6, 1944. The LST 325 was there. The tale of how the LST 325 arrived in Mobile Bay is an astounding one, indeed.

Aboard, we learned that a crew of 29 "old salts," average age 72, had sailed their 58 year-old, out-of-commission ship over 4,000 miles from Crete, Greece to Mobile, with a stop at Gibraltar and Nassau for repairs. Finally, on January 10, 2001 the famous ship limped up the Mobile River.

On November 11, 2001, President George W. Bush wrote a letter to the USN retired Captain in charge of this restoration, Robert D. Jomlin. Congratulating him and his crew for the successful voyage "home," he then added: "During World War II and the Korean War, the courage and sacrifice of our veterans protected the democratic ideals that make our Nation strong and make this world a better place. I commend your efforts to turn the LST 325 into a living memorial. It will honor your shipmates and those who died while defending freedom. We can mark and remember their loss, but we can never measure the value of the freedom secured by their efforts. Through memorials such as this, a grateful nation remembers their valiant service."

Dear reader, let us remember, as these LST men of WW II remember, the blood shed at Normandy Beach, which was a vital step toward ending Adolph Hitler's march to conquer the world.

Forever
May Old Glory Wave

For many Americans the summer of 1989 will not be remembered as the summer of Chinese revolt, but it will be remembered as the summer a traitor burned our flag. As I watched the news on TV, I flared to Bill, "How dare anyone burn MY flag?" Bill calmed my fury with a hug and these words: "You're my flag waver, aren't you?" *Flag waver?* It seemed as if I had heard those words before. Yes, I had!

Thirteen years earlier on July I, 1976, I had scoured all stores in our Silver Lake area and purchased every available 3 x 5 inch flag. Arriving back home, I poured more than 200 flags out on our kitchen table and proudly announced that we were going to have a birthday party for America. Practically in unison, my mortified teenagers blared, "Mom, you are a flag waver!" Yes, I am!

On the eve of the 4th of July, station wagon loaded with flags and kids, ours and the neighbors', we headed north to Ludington. The public beach was peppered with more than two thousand Bicentennial celebrants waiting for fireworks to be shot out over glimmering Lake Michigan. We found a good viewing spot and spread our blankets in the still warm, golden sand. Looking around at different groups chatting, some lying, some sitting, some standing, I wondered how they would respond to a little white-haired grandma giving them a gift. At that point I almost backed out.

However, a quick glance into the grocery sack full of Stars and Stripes was like a shot of adrenaline. It boosted my courage. As I began passing out flags, winding in and out through the mass of people, eager hands reached out for them. Happy faces beamed in the twilight. "Happy Birthday," I wished each recipient. "But it's not my birthday," many responded. "If you're an American, it's your birthday," I smiled, and they smiled back.

Soon barefoot children scurried through the sand, tugging at my shirt and begging for flags. Before I knew it, a parade of radiant, little patriots, all waving the Red, White, and Blue, had formed behind me.

The crowd, made up of lovers, hippies, grandmas and grandpas, a paraplegic in a wheelchair and many, many children, began to clap and sing "God Bless America." At that moment, dear reader, I thought my heart would burst with love for MY country and MY people. And to think all this was happening because of a simple little flag.

The blood-red sun disappeared seemingly into the Great Lake. In the dark, sack empty, I trudged back to my blanket and lay down. As rocket after rocket shot out with deafening bangs and glorious designs flared against a starry sky, I pondered what our American flag really means. Now, as then, I still feel the same.

Our flag is Betsy Ross who stitched sanctity into every seam and Francis Scott Key who immortalized it by writing The Star Spangled Banner, our National Anthem. Our flag is John Phillip Sousa's Stars and Stripes Forever, its uplifting beat symbolizing hope to the downtrodden and opportunity to the oppressed. Our flag is Frank Bellamy who wrote The Pledge of Allegiance. Our flag is President Dwight Eisenhower. After marching through war-torn countries, he recognized that we are, indeed, a blessed nation and in 1954 added to the pledge the words, "under God." Lastly, let us not forget that our flag represents all those who fought and died that those crimson bars and silver stars might forever freely wave.

So, if I should ever encounter a flag burner, heaven help me to muster courage as great as that of one Barbara Frietchie. When Stonewall Jackson and his rebels rode into Frederick Town, he spotted a lone flag hanging from her attic window. He ordered it shot down, "Fire!" The old woman, fourscore and ten years old, snatched the rent banner from its splintered staff, leaned out on her window sill and shouted: "Shoot, if you must this old gray head, but spare your country's flag."

Barbara Frietchie was a true patriot. I trust, dear reader, that you are a flag waver - not a flag burner.

I pledge allegiance to the flag
of the United States of America
and to the Republic for which It stands,
one nation, under God,
with Liberty and Justice for all.

America's
Lady of Freedom

Many words have been written about famous women, past and present, but I have finally discovered who ranks at the top of the list. She is not Joan of Arc, Queen Victoria, Golda Meier, or even Eleanor Roosevelt. No, she is America's own Lady Liberty who since 1886 has stood as an open door to freedom. Not only for immigrants wishing to be free, but for all of us who love living in a democracy where all people believe in social equality. There are 88,000 web sites on the Statue of Liberty and every year more than four million people gather around her feet and stand in awe to admire the now World Heritage Site in the New York Harbor.

This gigantic statue stands 305 feet tall from the ground to the tip of the torch. Her extended arm is 42 feet high and the tablet she holds is 23 feet seven inches high by 13 feet seven inches wide. Those visitors who wish to climb to the crown must tackle 354 steps. She was given in friendship to the people of the United States by France and is our largest symbol of freedom.

Periodically, the Statue of Liberty has had much attention to her physical well being, including a major reconstruction prior to her 100th birthday. On July 4, 1986 America threw a party for her that will never be forgotten. President Ronald Reagan unveiled Liberty with her new torch and the most spectacular fireworks show ever seen exploded across the sky. With a golden sunset glowing in the background, the President promised that Americans will be "the keepers of the flame of liberty and that we will continue to hold it high for the world to see."

I remember watching this extravaganza on TV and wondering how many of my acquaintances have ever visited the Statue of Liberty. Have they stood at her feet and read the stirring words engraved in a plaque on the pedestal? These words have often been heard in bits and pieces - "Give me your tired, your poor, your huddled masses" - but very seldom heard as a famous sonnet in its entirety, written by a renowned poet, Emma Lazarus.

Several years ago I visited New York City and took the ferry across to Liberty Island. I stood motionless with goose bumps and tears as I read the poem, trying to grasp the full impact of what this Jewish poet, a champion of the poor, was saying to the world. At that time I knew nothing about The Colossus of Rhodes, a statue of Apollo built in 230 B.C. At 120 feet high it was considered one of The Seven Wonders of the World. Now, Lady Liberty is the New World's largest statue. I share with you, dear reader, fourteen lines Emma Lazarus wrote about America's Lady of Freedom:

THE NEW COLOSSUS

Not like the brazen giant of Greek fame,
With conquering limbs astride from land to land;
Here at our sea-washed, sunset gates shall stand
A mighty woman with a torch, whose flame
Is the imprisoned lightning, and her name
Mother of Exiles. From her beacon-hand
Glows worldwide welcome; her mild eyes command
The air-bridged harbor that twin cities frame.
"Keep, ancient lands, your storied pomp!" cries she
With silent lips. "Give me your tired, your poor,
Your huddled masses yearning to breathe free,
The wretched refuse of your teeming shore.
Send these, the homeless, tempest-tosst to me.
I lift my lamp beside the golden door!"

This goddess carrying a torch is not of human flesh, but she stands for the four basic freedoms in America. Dear reader, pause for a moment in gratitude for the freedoms Our Lady represents - Freedom of Speech, Freedom of Worship, Freedom from Want, and Freedom from Fear.

Note:
By the time the Statue was dedicated in 1886, Emma was dying of cancer. In 1903 Georgina Schuyler, a sculptor, had her famous words inscribed on the Lady's base.

A Salute
To An Old Soldier

In late April 1951, an old soldier returned home from the Korean War to a tumultuous welcome. At a ticker-tape parade in New York City, General Douglas Mac Arthur, who had served his country longer than any other past or living person, proudly saluted his fellow Americans. They, in appreciation for his leadership in many wars, ardently cheered for this dedicated General.

A four-square memorial in Norfolk, Virginia now hails America's most decorated soldier, who said, "Old soldiers never die; they just fade away." All loyal Americans should visit this site at some point in their lifetime.

While enrolled in an Elderhostel Program in 1999, Bill and I toured the Douglas Mac Arthur Memorial in Norfolk's old domed City Hall. Many questions as to this Five-Star General's loyalty immediately began to be answered. Every picture, every plaque and every mural in nine galleries testified to his greatness. He was born into a military family, was head of his class at West Point and served his country for 52 years. He also was a man who bowed to kings and conquered emperors.

General Douglas Mac Arthur, after being relieved of his command by President Truman, felt he had been wrongly accused as a warmonger. He said in an address before the National Institute of Social Sciences upon being awarded the Society's Gold Medal:

"If the historian of the future should deem my service worthy of some slight reference, it would be my hope that he mention me not as a Commander engaged in campaigns and battles, even though victorious to American arms, but rather as that one whose sacred duty it became, once the guns were silenced, to carry to the land of our vanquished foe (Japan) the solace and hope and faith of Christian morals. Could I have but a line a century hence crediting a contribution to the advance of peace, I would gladly yield every honor which has been accorded by war."

My admiration for this great soldier, dear reader, was further bolstered as I read his farewell address delivered without text or notes to the Cadet Corps at West Point when he was 82 years old:

"Duty, honor, country. You are the lever which binds together the entire fabric of our national system of defense. This does not mean that you are warmongers. On the contrary, the soldier, above all other people, prays for peace, for he must suffer and bear the deepest wounds and scars of war. In my dreams I hear again the crash of guns, the rattle of musketry, the strange, mournful mutter of the battlefield. But in the evening of my memory, always there echoes and re-echoes: Duty, honor, country. I bid you farewell."

As I walked these historical corridors, there he was, pictured again and again as many remember him. He was wearing the crumpled General's cap and the scarf his mother had knit for him. Douglas Mac Arthur, who died at the age of 84, lives on in Norfolk and the annals of history, dear reader, as "an old soldier who tried to do his duty as God gave him the light to see that duty."

A letter to another great soldier,
George Washington:

Were an energetic and judicious system
to be proposed with your signature,
it would be a circumstance highly honorable
to your fame and doubly entitle you to the
glorious Republican epithet, The Father of
Your Country.
                    . . . Henry Knox, 1787

Soldiers
Unknown But Not Forgotten

Millions go there each year to show respect, but many millions more know nothing about our Nation's most revered monument at Arlington National Cemetery.

Many years ago, wanting our five children, ages 4 to15, to learn and respect the history of American freedom, we planned a Spring Vacation trip to Washington, D. C. A stinging stirring of my soul was felt as we stood at the base of the Tomb of the Unknown Soldier. I remember the two younger children, Kitty and Nick, fidgeting as I read from a brochure some of the facts pertaining to uniformed U.S. Army sentinels who have guarded this monument twenty-four hours a day, 365 days a year, since 1937. Tomb of the Unknowns is a massive, very conspicuous, seventy-nine ton, white marble grave. It honors all brave men and women who have served and died in many wars to preserve our freedom.

After this "Mom" briefing, we slowly made our way around the entire tomb. I'm sure Bill and the children were not as stricken with contained pride, and grief, as I while walking around the giant panels and viewing the carvings and inscriptions. On the front of the Tomb, a large carving depicts a female representing Victory, a male symbolizing Valor, and another Peace. All commemorate the devotion and ultimate sacrifice for the cause of Right.

Of course, our three older boys, Tim, Dan and Jef, who as children played "soldier" with neighbor children, watched in awe as a stately, lone soldier marched across the Tomb. He kept his eyes straight ahead, advanced precisely for 21 steps and then made an about face. He shifted his silent rifle to the other shoulder, hesitated, and made his purposeful return 21 steps back. A twenty-one gun salute is the highest honor given any military or foreign dignitary, and what better tribute for a fallen, unknown comrade?

We lingered for several minutes to observe the very formal, hourly drill when a guard was relieved of duty and replaced with a new, fresh-faced and highly polished sentry. "How come a different soldier?" Our 14-year-old Dan asked. I remember answering the best I could as I wondered at the determined, undeterred march. "Walking at such strict attention, concentrating on his steps and the shifting of his rifle from one shoulder to the other, is very difficult for a long period of time," I simply told my son.

Admiration for these dedicated guards of the Tomb has grown over the years as I have learned of the strict requirements of becoming a member of this highly respected group of soldiers.

Dear reader, believe me, for those chosen to guard this treasured monument, their eternal vigilance is a charge of honor, not intended as a show for the public. Through rain, sleet, snow, heat and cold, night and day these men faithfully and humbly protect that which the Tomb represents – undying bravery.

In the future, if you visit the Tomb of the Unknown Soldier, you will find on the west marble panel a forever memorable, bold inscription that speaks to your heart: HERE RESTS IN HONORED GLORY AN AMERICAN SOLDIER UNKNOWN BUT TO GOD.

Another Not Forgotten

"May one who fought in honor
For the South uncovered stand
And sing by Lincoln's grave.
A soft Kentucky rain was
In his voice, And the Ohio's deeper
Boom was there, with some wild
Accents of old Wabash days,
And winds of Illinois;
And when he spoke he took us
Unaware, with his high courage
And unselfish ways."
.... Maurice Thompson
.... At Lincoln's grave

Bet a Dollar
You Don't Know This!

As many times as a dollar bill has slipped through my fingers, I had never once thought about what all the symbols on that little piece of paper mean. When I heard rumors that Washington might do away with the dollar, out of curiosity I researched our one-dollar bill and came up with some astounding historical facts that sent me to the examining table.

Seeing is believing, dear reader, so right now take one of those greenbacks out of your billfold and follow along as you learn about the U. S. Treasury Seal, the bald eagle, the pyramids, the 13 colonies, and the infamous words, In God We Trust.

First, our seemingly insignificant, common, low-value currency is not made of paper but of a sturdy cotton and linen blend made to withstand constant use.

On the front of the bill, there is George Washington, of course. Take a close look at the U. S. Treasury Seal. The scales represent a balanced budget. In the center, a carpenter's T-square, a tool used for an even cut. Beneath is the Key to the United States Treasury.

Now, take a look at the two circles on the backside, which together comprise the Great Seal of the United States. On the left, notice that the pyramid face is lit, but the western side is dark and that the pyramid is uncapped. Both signify a country unfinished. Inside that capstone, look carefully for the all-seeing eye, an ancient symbol for divinity. Benjamin Franklin, who spearheaded the designing of The Great Seal, believed that with the help of God, Americans could do anything.

Above the pyramid are the Latin words, Annuit Coeptis, meaning "God has favored our undertaking." The words below, Novus Ordo Seclorum, signify "A new order has begun." At the base of the pyramid is the Roman numeral 1776.

There is more, much more, dear reader, which every American should know. In the right-hand circle, is the seal of the President of the United States. The strong bald eagle that can soar above all storms represents a symbol of victory for our country. In the eagle's beak, you can read "E Pluribus Unum," which means "one nation from many people." Above the eagle are thirteen stars representing the thirteen original colonies.

Notice that the Eagle holds in his talons an olive branch and arrows. Peace in one hand and a determination to fight in the other in case that peace is threatened.

Most Americans know, dear reader, there were 13 original colonies, but think about this: There were 13 signers of the Declaration of Independence, there are 13 stripes on our flag, 13 steps on the pyramid, 13 letters in the Latin above, 13 stars above the eagle, 13 plumes of feathers on each span of his wing, 13 bars on the shield, 13 leaves on the olive branch, 13 fruits, and if you look closely, 13 arrows. So never believe that the number 13 is unlucky. America is the richest, greatest, nation on earth who tells the world in bold letters on its One Dollar Bill that it is In God We Trust.

Now, dear reader, you also know what is on the Dollar Bill. Do your children know? Your grandchildren? Your children's teachers? Your friends?

Every true patriot upholds what those symbols stand for and at every opportunity should point them out to anyone who will listen.

A Nation's Strength

Is it the sword? Ask the red dust
Of empires passed away;
The blood has turned their stones to rust,
Their glory to decay.

It is not gold. Its kingdoms grand
Go down in battle shock;
Its shafts are laid on sinking sand,
Not on abiding rock.

Not gold but only men can make
A people great and strong;
Men who for truth and honor's sake
Stand fast and suffer long.
. . . Ralph Waldo Emerson

Top: Long may Old Glory Wave. Left clockwise: Betsy Ross; Freedom of Worship; A Cherokee Papoose in Tragedy & Triumph; George Washington, Father of our Country; Bet a Dollar You Don't Know This!

"One Nation Under God"

Perhaps most people know that it was during President Dwight D. Eisenhower's term in office in 1954 that the Pledge of Allegiance to our flag was officially changed to 31 words. After the words "one nation," the words "under God," were added." But what most people don't know is that the Reverend George Macpherson Docherty, pastor of the Washington, D. C. Presbyterian Church, first proposed adding "God" to the Pledge in a Sunday sermon. President Eisenhower was sitting in the front pew of the 1400 seat sanctuary where Lincoln and many successors had sat. He considered the Reverend's suggestion and presented the idea to Congress. Four months later "under God" was added and remains after 53 years.

Looking back to the 1930s when children were taught both at home and in school to respect "their flag," I remember Momma saying, "Pearl, stand up straight and be proud when you recite The Pledge at school because God has placed us in this great land of the free." And so I did stand up straight, with my little hand over my heart, every morning at Charles Russell Elementary School in Ashland, Kentucky. The entire school of children, I dare say more than 100, ages 6 through 12, gathered with teachers around the flag pole in heat or cold and recited The Pledge, "one nation, indivisible, with liberty and justice for all."

Evidently, dear reader, I was born a natural "flag waver." At ten years old on bright, cold mornings when Old Glory fluttered against the blue, blue sky in the school yard, my heart fluttered right along with her. I remember wondering why we black-stockinged children were blessed to live in Momma's and God's land of the free.

Eighteen years later Reverend Doherty's idea of adding God to The Pledge flourished, even amidst much controversy in the courts and Congress. In his sermon, which was later printed in the Congressional Record, he logically presented to the parishioners that reciting the Pledge didn't influence nonbelievers to profess a faith in God. He said that anyone reciting The Pledge is "pledging allegiance to a state, which through its founders, laws and culture, does as a matter of fact believe in the existence of God." Later, he emphasized that "Without this phrase, 'under God,' the Pledge of Allegiance to the Flag might have been recited with similar sincerity by Muscovite children at the beginning of their school day."

Certainly, dear reader, because this nation was built on faith in God, the words "under God" should remain in our Pledge of Allegiance.

Over the years I, like Momma, have tried to instill in my five children and ten grandchildren respect and love for their flag. Bill and I have encouraged patriotism by giving married children a special anniversary gift. Instead of dinner out or a gift of money, we have presented them with a flagpole and a nylon flag for their yard. Now, they, in turn, can teach their grandchildren the Pledge and the meaning of the words "one nation, under God."

In the future, dear reader, when you pledge your allegiance, be sure to stand up straight – like Momma said - with your hand over your heart, as you watch the Red, White and Blue flutter against that blue, blue sky.

Wouldn't it be a pity if someone said that the words "under God" was a prayer, and that our schools would eliminate our Pledge of Allegiance?
. . . Red Skeleton

Old Timey Schools

Two miles along a frozen road,
Twern't far at all to trod.
The lacy frost on holly leaves
Cheered even sleeping sod.

We'd rally 'round Old Glory,
Our hearts aglow with pride,
Then promise to uphold our land,
And by its laws abide.

The children answered clanging bell,
Afire to do their best,
In readin', writin', 'rithmetic,
Foundations teachers stressed.

Geography and history,
Seemed things we could not use,
But spelling bees taught diligence
In life, win or lose.

Old-timey schools were different.
Don't know, but I suspect
Because of daring discipline,
Children showed respect.

They Are Dying,
One Thousand a Day

Every November 11, Veteran's Day, Americans should pause in remembrance of the still living brave men who served their country in World War II and who are now dying at the rate of one thousand a day.

In the year 2000 Bill and I attended an outdoor patriotic rally of 300 retired Senior Citizens on Nettles Island. Three veterans told stories of how they had won a Purple Heart during combat in WW II. These men in their late 70's were beginning to show physical signs of aging. But all were proud to have fought to make America the leader of the free world. They too, I'm sure, believed that WW II was "the war that was to end all wars."

Sixteen and one-half million Americans took part in WW II - 407,000 of them died in service to their country, more than 292,000 in battle. Those veterans who are still with us will soon be deceased, honored perhaps once a year with a small flag placed on their graves on Memorial Day.

This poem, written by a WW II veteran friend, Reynolds Smith, recalls very well that most critical time in America's history when freedom and democracy were staunchly upheld:

One Thousand A Day

A generation of the bravest is fading away,
They are passing on, One Thousand a Day.
Those men and women who answered the call,
When it seemed sure our freedoms would fall.

In World War II, with mad men in charge,
The future looked bleak and disaster loomed large.
From every city, hamlet, and farm,
Patriots responded, fearless to harm.

They said, "Here I am. What can I do?"
Answering the wave of the Red, White, and Blue.
Sons and daughters signed up on the spot,
Agreeing to serve, whatever their lot.

Mothers and fathers also answered the call,
To protect our freedoms, so precious to all.
Their normal life was put on hold,
As they donned uniforms bright and bold.

With the future uncertain, no one knew when,
Or if, they would return to their families again.
The training was rugged, but each did their best,
Results showed the USA passed the test.

Battles raged, and thousands would die,
Deep in steamy jungles or high in deadly skies.
Upon hostile beaches and across desert sand,
Our forces sacrificed to protect our land.

The Navy manned a mighty fleet,
Foot soldiers trudged against damning heat.
War, not a glamorous game with parades and ringing bell,
War, fellow Americans, is hell!

Much is owed those who fought with pride,
Some told their stories, some kept all inside.
Future generations will come and go,
How many will know the facts, the ones that we know?

A monument is being built, so long overdue,
To honor all veterans of World War II.
So, God of us all, give eternal peace, we pray,
To the one thousand souls who left us today.

In honor, dear reader, of those who have served this great country,
let us not fail to salute them as they pass by in our parades on Veterans
Day. They, along with those one thousand a day who passed on before
them, have covered us with the very warm blanket of freedom we live
under - every day.

A Future Patriot
May Be Watching You

She was there! Seated right next to a future patriot at the Asparagus Festival parade in Shelby, Michigan! That little, old, white-haired lady clad in red shorts and a white blouse was none other than Grandma Pearl. My bright red sun umbrella matched perfectly the red, white and blue 11 x 17 inch flag that fluttered in the breeze. Bill thought the flag a little unnecessary, but he went along with my shenanigans, didn't even complain when my red umbrella occasionally tangled with his common black one.

A little boy and I became fast friends when he looked up from his small canvas chair and asked "Why did you bring a flag to the parade?" To which I replied, "Because my flag shows that I love America." He then said, "Can I try it?" Reaching for the flag, he scooted his chair closer in the shade of my umbrella. At that moment, dear reader, another patriot was born.

Looking back, I remember the exact month and year I became a flag waver. It was January 1942, just before my 16th birthday. America had declared war against the Japanese. On that particular day, a soldier friend from the mountains stopped in to say goodbye. He was only 17 and had quit school to join the Infantry. Marvin Newsome looked so handsome in his khaki winter uniform and before he left our dusty holler I had fallen for this soldier who gave me my first kiss. When I went to the train station in Ashland, Kentucky to see him off, I proudly waved a little 4 x 6 inch American flag - like the one I sadly placed on his hillside grave when his body was shipped home from France a few months later.

Now, in honor of Marvin, as well as cousins and high school friends who died in the 2nd World War, I still proudly wave Old Glory at parades. I have even been known to lead a parade of marching little patriots through Silver Lake State Park on the Fourth of July.

Anyone who drives by our cottage on the Fourth will see, not just one, large flag flying atop a 20' flagpole, but many, many smaller flags bordering our "happy walk." Occasionally, interested tourists and their children, strolling past our lakeside cottage, are invited in to view many more Stars and Stripes. Inside, an antique, waving, metal flag hangs on our living room wall. Another small one is bravely held by a tall, wooden Uncle Sam figure by the fireplace. And, yes, on an end table, a shriveled, apple-faced, dear Betsy Ross proudly stitches America's first flag in 1776. And there's more.

In the dining room flags grace antique jugs, each making their statement to family and friends who visit. All in all, on the 4th of July I display 41 flags in one way or another, thrilled that our flag still symbolizes peace, honor, truth and justice in the greatest country in the world – the United States of America.

Actually, Independence Day is only one of many days a year that Americans should fly the Stars and Stripes. Our country's flag can be flown, with pride, on any National Holiday: New Year's Day, Jan. 1 ~ Martin Luther King Day, Jan. 15 ~ Inauguration Day, Jan. 20 ~ Lincoln's Birthday, Feb. 12 ~ Washington's Birthday, 3rd Monday in Feb. ~ Easter Sunday ~ Mother's Day, 2nd Sunday in May ~ Armed Forces Day, 3rd Saturday in May ~ Memorial Day, the last Monday in May ~ Flag Day, June 14 ~ Independence Day, July 4 ~ Labor Day, 1st Monday in Sept. ~ Constitution Day, Sept. 17 ~ Columbus Day, 2nd Monday in Oct. ~ Navy Day, Oct. 27 ~ Veteran's Day, Nov. 11 ~ Thanksgiving Day, 4th Thursday in Nov. ~ Christmas Day, December 25.

Remember the little boy at the parade, the new patriot? His name is Austin Charles Leo Boundy, now the proud owner of my flag. I can still see him smiling amidst the dispersing crowd as he and his parents walked to their car. The Red, White, and Blue stood out as he waved it high above his head. When you join other flag wavers at next year's Fourth of July Parade, dear reader, why not take along an extra flag for the young, future patriot who may just be watching you?

Conscience is the inner voice
that warns us that somebody
may be looking.
. . . Henry Louis Mencken

America's
Paradise on Earth

Dear reader, if you would like to give someone a special Christmas, anniversary or birthday gift this year, do consider giving them a cruise around the Hawaiian Islands where "Aloha" is the language of love.

In 1998 I booked a Heritage Cruise for the third week in September. Twenty friends from Nettles Island joined Bill and me in celebration of Hawaii's Annual Aloha Festival throughout all the Islands. On every lush island young girls, crowned with wreaths of flowers, danced in grass skirts while singing in their native tongue. Grandmothers, living legends of hula grace, strummed ukuleles and swayed like gentle breezes on mist-covered mountains.

Our group flew from West Palm to Honolulu and spent three nights in a beautiful hotel overlooking Waikiki Beach. One afternoon we challenged the surf in outrigger canoes, just like the natives. The second day we rode a trolley to the historic district to view Hawaii's first King, Kamehameha, in all his bronzed glory. The last day on Oahu, we took a bus to Pearl Harbor. It was a most memorable, but rather sad occasion, as many visitors wept while reliving December 7, 1942. On that day the Japanese had bombed the Battleship Arizona, killing 3,000 American service men.

Aboard the cruise ship, the S. S. Independence, all passengers were greeted with "aloha" smiles and beautiful, fresh orchid leis. Soft music accompanied Hawaiian folklore and we were all simply mesmerized by this introduction to our beautiful 50th State.

During the week of cruising, several in our group learned to play the ukulele or other island instruments. Some took hula lessons and others the art of lei making with fresh flowers.

One evening Bill and I joined 50 other couples in a lovely renewal of wedding vows ceremony in which we re-pledged our love for each other - Hawaiian style. Since we always renewed our vows when the opportunity arose, Bill joked later to our friends "This is the fifth time I've repeated these wedding vows. I must be in a rut, because it is always to the same woman."

Another highlight for us on this Heritage Cruise was the Fifties Night Jitterbug Contest. I dressed up in a pink sweetheart blouse and a white, flowing skirt trimmed with a sequined pink poodle. Bill double cuffed his Dockers and tucked a fake carton of cigarettes in one rolled-up sleeve of his white tee shirt. Competing against thirty-year olds, we at 72 and 73 jitterbugged ourselves, dear reader, into a state of exhaustion, but it was worth it - we won 1st place.

Shore excursions offered breath-taking scenery of each island. On Kauai, the Garden Island, we experienced Waimea Canyon with spectacular views of lush cliffs and beautiful, plunging waterfalls.

Unique Maui dazzled us with its array of changing climate and mountain gorges filled with abundant plant life. By tram we toured verdant fields of pineapple, sugarcane, mango, guava, coffee and flowering ginger. Of course, the samples were mouth watering!

Then, there was the Big Island of Hawaii that presented striking differences geographically. On Hilo, lilies, bromeliads and orchids grew wild. Just a few miles beyond we were awe-inspired by the arid, desert-like volcanic landscape.

One afternoon Bill was able to realize his dream of soaring by helicopter over Kilauea, the world's most active volcano. That night all passengers gathered on deck to watch fiery lava flowing down the mountain to the sea through windowed volcanic tunnels.

At Kona, we picked coffee beans and sipped complimentary Kona Coffee that sells for $19.00 a pound. And, dear reader, the presence of missionaries who brought civilization and Christianity to this pagan land could surely be felt as we viewed murals of their labor in St. Benedict's Painted Church high on a mountain overlooking the Gold Coast of Kona.

On the last morning of our cruise, during a farewell ceremony, we tossed our leis overboard. It was a chilling sight never to be forgotten as 600 colorful leis solemnly floated toward Pearl Harbor and the S. S. Arizona. While the band played "Aloha Oe," the cruise director summed up the righteous meaning of "Aloha": "When a person lives in the spirit of love, he lives in the spirit of God."

This island-by-island recollection, dear reader, only partially sums up our beautiful State of Hawaii, truly America's Paradise on Earth.

Community Treasure Chests

Never had I been so thrilled with a fresh-dug hole in the ground as when we returned to Michigan in May of 2003! The city of Hart, our County Seat, had finally begun to build a much needed, larger and updated public library.

The enthusiasm and financial support of all those involved in bringing this long-time-coming project to fruition was proof of what foresight, planning, and positive thinking can accomplish. Although the city's financial goal for completion had not been met, the substantial amount already raised, plus pledges from its citizens, assured all that the I.4 million-dollar "treasure" would open by the beginning of the New Year 2004. And it did!

To me, the greatest gift a community can give its citizens is an institution where access to knowledge is free. Whatever the cost to build and maintain a library, the price is cheap compared to that of an ignorant nation.

Many folks do not hesitate to applaud the local library and credit them with their personal love for reading. Many of America's very elite have let it be known that no matter how wealthy one is, money cannot provide a citizen with the wealth of information available at the local library. It is a fact that the wisdom of a civilized nation can be measured by respect and preservation of libraries, which hold the key to knowledge of all that we are, all that we were and all that we can become.

Older Americans know that Benjamin Franklin was a printer, inventor, and renowned statesman. He also was a librarian. In fact, because of his leadership among scholars and his interest in helping his community, he is considered the "father" of our first American library. Books were very expensive in his day, so not everyone was able to afford them. He and his printer friends actually pooled their money to purchase books and at his suggestion opened a lending library in 1731 that was open to the public. Other towns began to imitate this library system and reading became fashionable, even among the less educated.

However, dear reader, two hundred years later in 1931, when I was five years old, the Appalachian mountain people still knew nothing of libraries. Momma's most treasured piece of furniture in her "front" room was an oak, oval "library" table. On that table was a single book, the Bible. That big, black Book was the only book I ever remember seeing my Momma read.

One Christmas my fourth grade teacher gave me a book of fairy tales, which I placed every night on that special library table by Momma's Bible. When a teenager living in Ashland, Kentucky, I learned that the wealthy had not only library tables with many books on the bottom shelf, but library "rooms" with tall shelves of books in their homes. But, our high school had no library and if our community had one, I was not aware of it.

After graduation in 1944, I left Kentucky, moved to Oklahoma City to live with my sister, and one year later married Bill, a Navy Air Force cadet. After the end of WW II, he enrolled in Hope College in Holland, Michigan. There I discovered the Public Library where even a child could travel to far-away places or identify with heroes out to save the world. Later, when our children were in elementary school, I would load all five into our station wagon and once a week cart them off to that magical place, the library. Each was allowed to check out 5 books and before the books were due back, the older children had read all 25. And so had I! That was their introduction, and mine, to a love for reading.

One of the greatest monetary gifts an adult can give to his community, dear reader, is that which helps to update a present public library or to build a new facility for use by young and old alike.

One of the greatest material gifts a young child can receive is a library card which introduces him to a life-long world of wonder and knowledge.

Dreams, books, are each a world;
And books, we know, are a
substantial world, both pure and good.
Round these, with tendrils strong as
flesh and blood, our pastime and our
happiness will grow.
. . . William Wordsworth

Moms
March for Mankind

Mother's Day, May 14, 2000 will go down in history as the day Moms from all across America marched from the Washington Monument to the Capitol to alert Congress that the killing of our children by guns must be stopped.

It has been said that "what needs desperately to be done is often left undone when good people simply do nothing." So, moms, children, and grand moms, 750,000 strong, flew in or traveled by bus to join the historic "Million Mom March." Grandma Pearl was one of those moms who arrived in Washington exhausted after a 14 hour Friday night bus ride. But after a night of rest, spirits soared and all moms were determined to make a difference in this world of gun violence.

For me the need for "banning" handguns was brought to light in September of 1999 while we were vacationing in Austria. At an outdoor festival, a middle-aged German gentleman asked if his party of four could join us at our picnic table. He then said jokingly, "I promise we won't shoot you." Everyone laughed, but after seated, he then seriously questioned why so many children in America were being shot - an embarrassing moment, indeed. When I asked what Germany's policy on gun ownership was, he stated that only law enforcement personnel are allowed to own handguns, now a common policy in many countries.

Staggering statistics show that there are 70 million handguns in our country and until we view handgun ownership as dangerous behavior, the killings will not stop. Twelve children are killed with a gun every day and 9 out of 10 murders of children worldwide occur in the United States.

When I first read about the "Million Mom March," I knew, even at 74, as a mother of five children and grandmother of ten, I must be one in that million. For three days I tried to think of something poetic, clever, and with a strong message for my poster. But nothing clicked until one morning I awoke at 4 a.m. and the words of the 6th Commandment flashed in the dark - "Thou shalt not kill." That was it!

On Sunday, the day of the Moms March, the red poster with its bold, white-lettered message twice filled the many large TV Screens on the

Grand Washington Mall. Many other posters displayed pictures of murdered children. As I scanned the sea of faces, I thanked God for loving Moms who care.

Along with thousands, I wept when the mother of little Kayla, shot down by another six- year-old, spoke on the Million Mom March stage. I wept along with an American Indian mother who told of one son being murdered and another badly injured by a handgun. I also wept when a rabbi challenged our country to "love one another."

Thousands cheered when a nine-year-old little black girl in a long white dress marched back and forth, back and forth across that huge stage and for 5 minutes begged Congress to save America's children from fear and death. One victimized Mom shouted into a microphone, "Are Moms more powerful than the NRA?" Again, the crowd roared a resounding "YES."

And so, dear reader, I salute the multitude of Moms who sacrificed a comfortable, frilly day at home honoring them. Instead, on Mother's Day, they were in D.C. marching - not for glory but for children still living in America's world of gun chaos.

The deed is everything,
The glory naught.
. . . Goethe

A Dime's Worth of Silver

This is a Christmas story, dear reader, of homesickness and love in wartime. It is also a story of a seemingly insignificant but unforgettable Christmas gift.

On December 25, 1944, two Navy Air Force cadets and two eighteen-year-old gals, each wearing shiny nylons and high heels, bustled around in an unfamiliar kitchen in Oklahoma City. Barbara and Cliff were married, but Bill and I were new sweethearts of four months. Teachers of our adult Sunday school class, Mr. and Mrs. Floyd Bulis, whose only son was fighting overseas, had adopted us as their war-time children and invited us by phone to spend Christmas in their home.

"You will have the entire house to yourselves," they said, "because our daughter-in-law needs us." We four young people, who were experiencing our first Christmas away from home, were excited about making our own Christmas dinner, but a great surprise awaited us when we entered their house that afternoon.

The back-home smell of roast turkey greeted us as we opened the unlocked door. In the oven, sugary sweet potatoes bubbled a welcome. On the kitchen counter cranberry relish, fresh ground, winked at us through a glistening glass bowl. Beside it lay a note: "Turkey will be done at 4:00." No doubt, knowing we were novices at preparing a Christmas dinner, Mrs. Bulis had also left explicit instructions on how to cook the fresh string beans, already snipped, how to bake the rising, home-made dinner rolls and how to whip cream for the already baked pumpkin pie.

Like children playing house, we laughed, chatted and sang along with carols coming from a small kitchen radio. Together, we set the table with fine china and red poinsettia napkins. The golden turkey, flanked by two flaming red candles, looked elegant as we sat down to our first Christmas dinner away from family. Holding hands across the table, we gave thanks for the Bulises and the special dinner they had prepared for us - all practically strangers to them. I remember thinking, as I glanced at Bill, *spending Christmas with a sweetheart is perfect.*

Then, strains of *Silent Night* drifted through the dining room door. This, dear reader, triggered a longing for Momma and my Kentucky home. Tears sprang like a gushing spring into my eyes. To avoid spoiling Christmas for my friends, I ran to the nearest bedroom, fell upon the bed and sobbed. Soon the others, also feeling pangs of homesickness, joined me. Together we blubbered thoughts of family, hugged, and hugged some more, then laughed our way back to a cold, but merry, feast. As I look back, no pumpkin pie, not even Momma's, has ever tasted better than Mrs. Bulis's pie topped with my first dollop of whipped cream.

After making the kitchen "shipshape," the four of us gathered around a six-foot tree to exchange our meager gifts. None had much money, of course. Like all Seamen 1/c, Bill's salary was $66.00 per month and this was spent mostly on weekend "courting" excursions. Neither he nor I remember my present to him, but I shall never forget, dear reader, the "dime" he gave me on our first Christmas so long ago.

From fresh, pine-scented branches laden with red and gold antique ornaments, Bill pulled a tiny package, the size of a silver dollar. The wrapping was crumpled white tissue paper, bowed with a thin piece of red ribbon. The light in his hazel eyes danced with pride as he presented the gift and whispered, "I made it for you in the craft shop at the base." Beneath the folds of the tissue paper I found his unforgettable gift - a silver dime head molded into a clear plastic heart. A thin, black, velvet ribbon ran through a tiny ring at the top. When with great tenderness my sweetheart placed it around my neck, Christmas was transformed into a beautiful, happy moment.

War seemed far, far away. Melancholy thoughts of Momma and my girlhood home vanished. Love, dear reader, presented in the form of a dime's worth of silver, transcended all my expectations and has prevailed for 62 years - years not always *silent, calm, and bright,* but certainly blessed.

There are certain fastnesses within our soul
that lie buried so deep that love alone
dares venture down; and it returns laden with
undreamed-of jewels, whose luster can only
be seen as they pass from our open hand to
the hand of the one we love.
. . . Maurice Maeterlinck

9/11

September 11, 2001 - The day a peaceful nation was battered. A day thousands died and family hearts were broken. A day when America was brought to its knees and cried out for help from Almighty God. 9/11 - A day America will never forget!

At 8:45 a.m. I sat sipping my coffee in our living room while watching Good Morning America on TV. Suddenly the program was interrupted by newscaster Peter Jennings appearing with a news flash - THE WORLD TRADE CENTER IN MANHATTAN IS ON FIRE. Not realizing the magnitude of such a disaster, I was not shaken or stunned, thinking everything would soon be under control. However, the fire raged on and smoke billowed across Manhattan's skyline. Peter, in shock, announced that a plane had hit one tower, possibly an act of terrorism. Still, I remained calm. Then, 18 minutes later, the second plane shot through the other tower. I was horrified as I witnessed the fiery scenario of destruction and eminent death en masse.

Like most Americans, questions began popping into my mind: "What happened to our national security?" "Who is this enemy who hates America and attacks freedom-loving people with such bloody symbolism?" "Will we as a nation 'under God' strike back with a vengeance that will bring about more destruction and death?"

After a grueling day of trying to grasp the meaning of this reign of terror, I lay down upon my bed and prayed fervently for God's comfort to the living victims. And, I prayed for the souls of those who had died so unexpectedly. Later I read the quote of a counseling priest to NYC firemen, "If you want to make God laugh, tell Him what you're doing tomorrow." Sometimes, dear reader, there is no tomorrow.

September 12, 4:00 a.m. Continued grief awakened me - grief accompanied by tears that had trickled down onto my pillow. Feeling distraught because of my helplessness in this time of our country's most devastating tragedy, I vowed to in some way show my love and concern. Shortly, with the first light of dawn, I glanced out my bedroom window and streaks of a sunrise glowed across a patch of blue, a positive sign to me that beyond those mountainous clouds of smoke and despair in New York, God in all his glory was truly marching on.

I could not be there at the smoldering towers to hug and cry with families and friends of the dead. I could not be there to dig and search for possible survivors. Because of anemia, I could not even give a pint of blood to save the injured. All I could do was contribute to the Red Cross to help in their monumental efforts to aid what was now referred to as the "war effort." In a *Pearls* column one week later, I admonished my readers to remind their children and grandchildren that the darkness and evil that had struck our nation on 9/11 must be met with love and integrity – not with hatred of the innocent.

And yes, I did pray as our nation's leaders joined other world leaders in planning to eradicate terrorism that they would not rely upon their own judgment, but would look to God for guidance.

Sept. 13. We drove to our son's in Holland, Michigan. Flags everywhere! Flags flew at half-mast in both yards of residential homes and businesses. Flags fluttered on extended aluminum poles on many porches. Flags waved across front pages of powerful newspapers. Many homes had paper, page-sized flags taped in their front windows. These colorful flags had been furnished by the Holland Sentinel, enough to cover every home in the area that did not own a flag. What an outpouring of patriotism! This was a day to stand up and be proud of all fellow Americans. That day I did not cry, but burst with pride.

September 14. A day of honor and remembrance. A day of prayer at the National Cathedral in Washington. As I watched this ceremony on TV, hundreds bowed and wept. And yes, I too bowed and wept. There were many monumental statements from men of distinction, but the invocation by Dean Nathan Baxter stirred my very soul. He prayed for President Bush and his national security team as they plotted retaliation. And, he prayed that America would not become the evil we deplore.

On September 11, 2007, the war in Iraq was still raging with our heroes and innocent people dying by the thousands. Could it be, dear reader, that our nation "has" become the evil we deplore?

Ponderings of Painted Post

Tis not the understanding or poring
upon books that makes a man wise
or serviceable, but the knowing of
the true nature of things.
       . . . April 8, 1728
              New England Journal

Learning, without books, about American pioneers and Indians can be exciting and invigorating when your day ends with a lively little Honkytonk Stomp.

In September, 1992, Bill and I powwowed with forty-five retirees from many states at an Elderhostel in Painted Post, New York. The unique small town of Painted Post is so named for an actual post on which Native Americans recorded their struggles. For five days at Watson Homestead, a retreat center nestled in the beautiful southern tier of New York State, we experienced early frontier farming during our nation's first century, as well as the life and death of the Iroquois Indian in lands surrounding Painted Post.

This was our first Elderhostel, a worldwide program for senior citizens. The instructors were experts in their fields and because there was no homework, no term papers or exams, note taking was not necessary. The entire learning experience was one of fun and relaxation.

Watson Homestead is a very popular Elderhostel site because of its spacious motel-like rooms and delicious meals. We attended two classes in the morning. After lunch we "boot scooted" in round, square or line dancing classes. Evenings were filled with special entertainment and socializing. For talent night, believe it or not, dear reader, I didn't do my holler hoedown or yodel because Bill threatened to leave. Instead, our Michigan "Painted Post Sextet" did an original, song-and-line-dance routine which triggered whoops of laughter. During free time in the lands of Painted Post, we visited the Corning Glass Museum and explored magnificent landscapes of the American frontier through an exhibit of Western art at the Rockwell Museum. One exceptionally interesting, off-site activity was a bus trip to a restored 18th century Inn where travelers slept on rope-supported feather beds, several beds to a room. Since all points of interest in and around Painted Post could not be covered in one week, the day of departure we visited Mark Twain's study at Elmira where he wrote *Huckleberry Finn*. Naturally, we posed for pictures on the steps. Just as the shutter clicked, the thought of treading where a great American author once tread shot tingles down my spine.

To wind up our Elderhostel experience, we hiked in Watkins Glen State Park, which has to be New York's most spectacular scenic area. In awe, we spiraled down the mountain, 832 steps, listening to the singing roar of nineteen waterfalls plunging into a deep, twisting gorge carved by time. Pausing there, in that cathedral of ancient trees, I pondered our week's tales of the lands of Painted Post.

No doubt, dear reader, the Red Man knew the true nature of things. He said, "The Great Spirit owns the land." And, "We, unlike the White Man, ask for nothing, only give thanks for what we have."

Note:
Elderhostel catalogs of courses offered in both the U.S. and abroad can be obtained by writing to: Elderhostel, 75 Federal Street, Boston, MA. 02110

Scenes from the 1998 Musical Production Tragedy and Triumph, written and directed by Pearl Flaherty. Top four scenes from the Tragedy and two bottom scenes from the Triumph in the Red Hatchet Casino.

Tragedy and Triumph

As the curtain came down on the final performance, a patron approached me and asked, "Pearl, why did you choose to tell this moving story of The Trail of Tears?" My reply, "Because that awful truth in American history needs to be told again and again – and, because I am a Cherokee."

After two years of research, I had finally written and rewritten my second stage production, Tragedy and Triumph, for our non-professional theater group in Florida. Tragedy, Act I, depicted removal of the Indians from their homes in the Carolinas and the aftermath when more than 4,000 died en route to Oklahoma. Triumph, Act II, portrayed Native Americans building casinos on reclaimed land. In preparation for this musical extravaganza, I searched for months for appropriate Indian music. I listened to voices of live Cherokees on historical tapes and videos. Hours and hours were spent collecting feathers for all cast members along Lake Michigan's shore.

However, one of the most overwhelming aspects of producing Tragedy and Triumph was cheaply costuming 66 amateur cast members. For two summers I hit yard sale after yard sale throughout Michigan. Bill fretted and fumed at summer's end as he pushed and shoved boxes and bags of my great Indian "finds" as well as gamblers' black Stetsons into our Buick LeSabre for our trek to Florida.

A production of such magnitude is a tremendous challenge for all involved. I hope the following anecdotes, dear reader, will give you some insight as to what went into finalizing this true tale of tears - and laughter.

From the base of dead fronds of a palm tree, One Feather, my Bill, carved five Indian masks for a two-minute song, "I'm an Indian too."

During the summer a cast member's son, with a hidden recorder, taped sounds of bells clanging and coins clinking in a Connecticut Indian casino. This tape was used very effectively in the second act when gamblers played the slots, which were designed by Ed Green, our props man.

Gordon Sawyer, a Canadian member, spent many hours in Ontario sawing and assembling twenty red and white hatchets wielded by the savages and Cherokees alike. One Feather created his own costume from a pair of orange pajamas found at a yard sale for twenty-five cents.

Please notice on the pictorial page 177, dear reader, the 500 feathers majestically adorning the human Eagle. They were donated by the BilMar Turkey Farm in Zeeland, Michigan. "Fresh" from live turkeys, they still had bits of meat attached, which had to be stripped from each feather. Then, all 500 were soaked in Clorox for one week. For several days thereafter, they were spread each morning in the sun to dry and each evening taken into the garage for protection from raccoons.

When I asked a lady at one yard sale if she had anything that could be used in an Indian show, she pointed out a "real" beaver fur coat which had been stored in her barn for many years. She begged me to take it off her hands for twenty-five cents. Twenty-five cents! A great coat, indeed, for the English fur trader who sang the Indian Love Call to Pretty Red Wing.

Grey Wolf's costume was fashioned from a pair of used, earth tone, lady's size sixteen Dockers and the papoose was clothed in a colorful, pillowcase of Indian design from a Frankenmuth, Michigan yard sale.

When we arrived in Florida, Bill and I scoured the ocean beach many times in search of special, white shells, with tiny holes. During the four performances, eight Corn Dancers, wearing their shell, ankle "rattles", chanted and danced on our Nettles Island stage.

During research on this monumental undertaking, we visited Capitols of the Eastern Band of Cherokees in Cherokee, N. C. and the Western Band in Tahlequah, Oklahoma. Today, there are more than 308,000 Cherokees enrolled in these two bands.

While in Tahlequah, I was proud to learn that my grandmother, Mary Jones Henson, was listed in the 1920 Cherokee Census. This in itself was a triumph and urged me on to tell that which must continue to be told, dear reader, to your children and their children's children.

Walk on a rainbow trail;
Walk on a trail of song,
and all about you will be Beauty.
There is a way out of every dark mist,
over a rainbow trail.
. . . A Navajo Song

A Message from Chief Seattle

Every part of this earth is sacred to the red man. Every shining pine needle. Every grain of sand upon the shore. Every mist in the dark woods. Every meadow and humming insect. All are holy in the memory of our people.

The sap which courses through the trees is as the blood that flows in my veins. We are part of the earth and it is part of us. The perfumed flowers are our sisters. The bear, the deer, the great eagle – they are our brothers. The rocky deserts, the meadows, the wild ponies. All belong to the same family.

In every stream I hear the voice of my ancestors. The shining water in the rivers is not simply water, but the blood of my grandfather's grandfather. In the water's murmur I hear the voice of my great-great grandmother. Rivers and streams are related to us; they quench our thirst. They carry our canoes and feed our children. You must protect our rivers as they are our brothers.

My grandfather told me that the air is precious. All things share the same breath. The wind that gave my grandfather his first breath also received his last sigh. You must keep the land and air apart and sacred, as a place where one can go to taste the wind that is sweetened by the meadow's flowers.

This the red man knows. The earth does not belong to you or me. We belong to the earth. All things are connected like the blood that unites us. We did not weave the web of life; we are merely a strand in it. Whatever we do to the web, we do to ourselves. My people love this earth as a newborn loves its mother's heartbeat.

Hear my voice and the voice of those gone before us:

Teach your children what we have taught our children that the earth is our mother. Teach them to love the earth as we have loved it. And, teach them that they must preserve our land and the air and the rivers – for their children's children.

Places with Soul

"...a past of plank and nail
and slowness...then the scaffolds
drop, affirming it a soul."
   . . . Emily Dickinson

Museums are not boring. Neither are ancient trails waiting to be trod, nor historic homes depicting the lives of famous Americans, and others, of a by-gone era. These memorable places can stir the inner being of young and old alike. They are, indeed, places with soul.

Beginning in August 1990, Bill and I camped in our mini-van across New York, Massachusetts, and up the coast of Maine en route to Nova Scotia. Along the way, dear reader, we searched for and found vibrations of the past that brought true enlightenment.

At the Corning Glass Center in southern New York, Russian ornate glassware dating from the 14th Century glowed with innate talent. Throughout the museum, perfection, beauty, and grace glowed through each piece, whether a French paperweight, a Bohemian wine glass or early American lead crystal candlesticks. All heralded the fine art of glassmaking.

In the Norman Rockwell Museum in Stockbridge, this prolific illustrator, through his original paintings, ushered us through WW I, the civil rights struggle, and man's first step on the moon. Each painting was brushed with love, faith, and hope in the common man. When I viewed the tousled little fisherman abandoning his pole for a pig-tailed charmer, a breath of warmth crept into my very soul.

Then, we meandered through the rolling hills of Massachusetts, stopping in Amherst at the Emily Dickinson Homestead. As I read original poems and letters jotted on scraps of yellowed paper, I could almost hear the scratch of her pen. And as I peered out her upstairs bedroom window, I could, it seemed, smell the sweet aroma of the gingerbread she lowered in a little basket more than 100 years ago to laughing children below.

Although it was raining, I strolled through gardens where gigantic, cultivated Queen Anne's Lace blossomed, testifying to Emily's love of flowers. This house and its surroundings still throb with a life long ended.

Making our way up the coast to Kennebunkport, Maine, we saw President George Bush's home on Walker Point and took a short nostalgic trip through Maine woodlands. At the Trolley Museum bells clanged and whistles blew as a volunteer conductor called out, "All aboard." Another volunteer, definitely loving his hobby, later guided us through three car barns of old-time trolleys collected from around the world. Interesting and exhilarating!

At Acadia National Park we drove to the top of stone-roofed Cadillac Mountain, the highest point on the Atlantic Seaboard. Numerous islands could be seen lounging in the ocean's serene waters. Along Maine's rocky shores, hundreds of land fingers clutched at fishing villages and sailing harbors. On this calm day, gentle soulful waves slapped at natural, stony seawalls protecting the coastal land.

After a night of camping at Bass Harbor, we hiked along Ship Harbor Trail where blackberries glistened with wild sweetness and spires of spruce swayed to the "whisper of a gray ocean upon the rock."

One week into the journey to places with soul, dear reader, we reached Lubec, Maine. Here on Bobscook Bay, we dug our first clams and under a purple sunset cooked our first lobsters over an open fire. When Franklin Delano Roosevelt was a child, he sailed these waters with his father. FDR and Eleanor's honeymoon cottage, Campobello, is now an International Landmark and in each of the 34 rooms, the immortal fame of a great leader lives on.

Beyond our venture to American places with soul, we traveled to Nova Scotia. En route we stopped in Moncton, New Brunswick, to experience the Tidal Bore. When we arrived at the Information Center, I, hearing of this for the first time, excitedly asked, "Where can we see the ten-foot wall of water when the tide comes in?"

A sweet, young miss replied, "The significance of the tidal bore is not in the height of the wave, ma'am. Today it might be only six inches. The significance is in the empty Peticodiac River flooding in an hour when the tide funnels in from the Bay of Fundy."

"Oh," a disappointed I said. She was right - six inches that day! But fortunately, while waiting for the "big wave," we toured the Acadian Museum on the University of Moncton campus. Our student guide gave an excellent presentation on the history and culture of the gentle French Acadians. The burning of their homes and deportation by the British in 1775 was a sad time for the warm, music-loving people. However, many settled in the maritime region, so their courage and fervor live on through their descendants.

Eventually, a ferry at Cape Tormentine carried us to Prince Edward Island, Canada's smallest province. On this island cradled by gentle waves, quiet country roads connect a colorful mosaic of farmland and harbor. The tallest towers are those of pretty Malpeque Bay and from here each day we traveled to once-in-a-lifetime points of interest.

One outstanding attraction, dear reader, was "Woodleigh." On several acres Col. E. W. Johnstone labored sixty years, creating with natural stone many scaled-down models of famous historic British structures. We marveled at the century-old stained glass windows in York Minister and the magnificent dome of St. Paul's Cathedral. Also, on the grounds lay Robert Burns' and William Shakespeare's thatched roof birthplaces. We climbed the Tower of London, which took five years to build, and heard screams of the soon-to-be beheaded. All of these replicas speak boldly of a highly spirited time in British history – yes, places with soul.

Just south of Cavendish, Prince Edward Island's resort area, Green Gables still stands as it was when immortalized by novelist Lucy Maud Montgomery at the turn of the century. We toured the house and peered through those gabled windows where she pictured her beloved Anne romping in green pastures dotted with wildflowers. Later we attended the "Anne of Green Gables" musical at the Charlottetown Festival. There, we laughed, cried, and cheered as Anne sang and danced her way into our hearts.

Finally, on September 2 we boarded the Woods Island Ferry to our destination, Nova Scotia. After a day of tennis, laundry and rest, we began the famous drive around Cape Breton. In Baddeck we spent two hours at the Alexander Graham Bell Museum. Exhibits and films traced this genius' life from his birth in 1847 in Scotland, to his extraordinary achievements in North America - medicine, genetics, aeronautics, marine engineering and the teaching of the deaf. The telephone, of course, which he gave to the world, still speaks for itself.

Just beyond Baddeck at Cheticamp, we took the unforgettable Cabot Trail, 106 miles long, around Cape Breton Highlands. The scenery was breathtaking. Mountains dove to the sea and then shot up again. Rugged, rocky coves jutted into the highway, offering sublime views of land and sea.

One thing Bill and I certainly agreed on, this was a beautiful ending to a 2,000-mile journey to places with soul.

Is There Another Abe Out There?

Above the mantle in our Silver Lake cottage hang many historical treasures, including a white, square tile etched with the Gettysburg Address. Beside the tile hangs a die-cast pewter profile of the Great Emancipator, Abraham Lincoln.

That Abe has a place of honor in our home is not because he hailed from Kentucky. I have always admired this compassionate, humanitarian President for his profound writings that have waxed true well into the 21st century.

Eloquent statements of this humble, great man while leading this nation from 1861 to 1865 flowed onto paper as wise words never to be forgotten. Fragments of his most famous writings have sold for sums that made auction history, often well over a million dollars.

In 1989 Bill and I visited Abe Lincoln's log cabin birthplace in Hodgenville, Kentucky. I spotted in the gift shop a framed, parchment page of Lincoln's quotes titled Ten Cannots. These cannots are as true today as when spoken in 1862:

You cannot bring about prosperity by discouraging thrift.
You cannot help small men by tearing down big men.
You cannot strengthen the weak by weakening the strong.
You cannot lift the wage earner by pulling down the wage payer.
You cannot help the poor man by destroying the rich.
You cannot stay out of trouble by spending more than your income.
You cannot further the brotherhood of man by inciting class hatred.
You cannot establish security on borrowed money.
You cannot build character and courage by taking away man's initiative and independence.
You cannot help men permanently by doing for them what they could and should do for themselves.

Over the years Abe's words have reverberated throughout the world, often finding their way into speeches of historic scholars and presidential hopefuls. Our 16th President of the United States was truly dedicated to a government "by the people, for the people."

Let us pray, dear reader, that one day a future president will emerge, not as a mere politician but as an "Honest Abe" who will serve our country with lasting honor.

"From these honored dead we take increased devotion to that cause for which they gave the last full measure of devotion—that we here highly resolve that these men shall not have died in vain—that this nation, under God, shall have a new birth of freedom—and that government of the people, by the people, for the people, shall not perish from the earth."

. . . Abraham Lincoln

Is Freedom Worth Saving?

Many presidential inaugural speeches ring of hope for liberty and freedom throughout the world. Often dynamic excerpts from speeches by past presidents are used to challenge Americans to try harder, aim higher, and fight 'til the finish to hold on to the principles on which America was founded.

In January, 1941 President Franklin Delano Roosevelt delivered a most memorable, inspirational speech. He too spoke of freedom, not just for our country but for the world.

Recently when I read this dynamic, historical, hopeful key to an understanding of life, it brought back memories of my Daddy sitting, ears glued to a floor-model radio. He demanded that my brother and I listen to every word. Perhaps it was Roosevelt's oratory that influenced my thinking on patriotism and world peace, even at the age of fifteen. Now 82, this Grandma sincerely believes, dear reader, President Roosevelt's speech is worth repeating:

"In future days, which we seek to make secure, we look forward to a world founded upon four essential human freedoms. The first is freedom of speech and expression - everywhere in the world. The second is freedom of every person to worship God in his own way - everywhere in the world. The third is freedom from want, which, translated into world terms, means economic understanding that will secure to every nation a healthy peacetime life for its inhabitants - everywhere in the world. The fourth is freedom from fear, which, translated into world terms, means a worldwide reduction of armaments to such a point and in such a thorough fashion that no nation will be in a position to commit an act of physical aggression against any neighbor - anywhere in the world. That is no vision of a distant millennium. It is a definite basis for a kind of world attainable in our own time and generation."

While we the people of the United States of America do realize, somewhat, the price paid for freedom in the world, we also are deeply concerned about many social and moral changes in our society right here at home. Is our freedom worth fighting for if we live in a society where abortion is legal and gay marriages are acceptable? Is our freedom worth fighting for if divorce is ripping our families apart? Most importantly, is our freedom worth fighting for when "God" is being removed from public documents?

Neither we the people, nor our government in quest for world freedom should ignore the important fundamentals on which America was founded.

As President Roosevelt said in his inaugural address on March 4, 1933, "This is preeminently the time to speak the truth, the whole truth, frankly and boldly. We must not shrink from honestly facing conditions in our country today."

Freedom in America is precious, dear reader, and indeed worth saving. But to keep it so, we must each do our part to uphold our moral and spiritual values.

AMERICA

My country 'tis of thee,
Sweet land of Liberty
  Of thee I sing;
Land where my fathers died,
Land of the pilgrim's pride
From every mountain-side
  Let Freedom ring.

My native country, thee,
Land of the noble free,
  Thy name I love.
I love thy rocks and rills,
Thy woods and templed hills
My heart with rapture thrills
  Like that above.

Let music swell the breeze,
And ring from all the trees,
  Sweet freedom's song,
Let mortal tongues awake,
Let all that breathe partake,
Let rocks their silence break,
  The sound prolong

Our father's God to Thee,
Author of Liberty,
  To Thee we sing,
Long may our land be bright
With Freedom's holy light,
Protect us by Thy might,
  Great God, our King.

. . . Samuel Frances Smith

Top left, clockwise: Earthly Billboards, a message from God; Great granddaughter, Kelsey; Additions to our family, Kathryn & Rob; Granddaughter Angela weds Kyle Gruppen; Grandma's Wish book; Family Reunion at Silver Lake, 1992.

Faith

**God is our refuge and strength,
a very present help in trouble.
. . . Psalm 46:1**

O God,

Thou hast taught me
from my youth: and
hitherto I have declared
Thy wondrous works.

Now when I am old and
greyheaded, forsake me
not, until I have showed
thy strength unto this
generation and thy power
to everyone that is to
come.
. . . Psalm 71:17-18.

Goin' to the Meetin' House

The meetin' house in the bottom
Was really God's house, you know,
One heard good words to live by,
Sometimes you'd catch a beau.

The Sunday School Convention
Was an all-day, happy affair.
Good gospel singin' and a picnic
Made folks glad to be there.

I liked goin' to the meetin' house;
Momma prayed out loud for me,
So I growed up knowin' for sure
God-fearin' was what I'd be.

At the meetin' house in the bottom
Every night "Hallelujahs" rolled,
Goin' to the meetin' house
Renewed one's very soul.

Our Meetin' House in Mears, Michigan.

Earthly Billboards
With a Heavenly Message

All across our country, billboard messages, signed "God", have appeared along major highways. Reportedly, the bold white letters on a stark, black background shook up many travelers.

I remember seeing the first billboard in 1999 along a Michigan highway. Friends also began to notice. Once I was asked, "Pearl, have you seen the 'God' billboards? Some of them are so funny, but all make you think. Wonder who is behind all this?" I was, indeed, curious myself and became more so as we traveled south that winter and saw numerous other signs. I jotted down some of the jolting messages and for several months puzzled over who dared to express his faith in that manner.

In Florida a high school student posted one of the quotes, "We need to talk...God." He was immediately required to remove it, which caused an uprising of parents and "freedom-of-speech" supporters. It was then that I began to search the Internet for the origin of the billboards. I simply typed in "God," and a wealth of information on God immediately appeared on the screen, but not what I was searching for. Finally, the answer came when I typed in "billboard." Up came "God Speaks" and an amazing story of how it all started. Here, with God Speaks, Inc. permission, I relate this phenomenon to you:

An anonymous donor from the Miami area, working with an advertising agency, began a campaign to subtly tell people of all walks of life and faith that God is not dead - that He still speaks. And it worked!

The thoughtful, short, and occasionally humorous reminders from "God" continued to appear, dear reader, on 10,000 billboards in over 200 cities. Special news reports from NBC, CBS, ABC, and CNN also spread the word. Here is what "God" was saying in black and white all across our country:

Tell the kids I love them...God
Let's meet at my house Sunday before the game...God
C'mon over and bring the kids...God
What part of "Thou shalt not" didn't you understand? ...God*
We need to talk...God
Loved the wedding, now invite me into the marriage...God
Keep using my name in vain, I'll make rush hour longer...God
That "Love Thy Neighbor" thing - I meant it...God
Will the road you're on get to my place?...God
Follow me...God
My way is the highway...God
Need directions? ...God
Do you have any idea where you're going? ...God
Don't make me come down there!!! ...God

These startling messages have spread like wildfire into the hearts of millions in both this country and around the world. Response from "listeners" has been phenomenal. E-mails have flooded in saying these age-old reminders of love and hope have touched them deeply.

Sure makes one sit up and take notice, dear reader.

Because I love you, I'm waiting
for your call. I want to help you
in your time of trouble and
celebrate with you in your time
of joy. Please don't forget I'm
always here for you and that I.
am the Way. But it's all up to you.
Please give me a call.

Your friend, God
. . . Anonymous

Midnight Hours of the Soul

When the phone rang at five in the morning on February 19, 2000, the sobs on the line told me that something terrible was wrong. And it was. Our grandson, Shawn, had hit a bridge abutment and was in the trauma unit of Sparrow Hospital in Lansing, Michigan. He had multiple fractures, but his severe head injuries were the most life threatening. The right side of his face was crushed and he lay in a deep coma, gasping for breath. A priest came to give last rights.

What does a Grandma do? Knowing that "all things work together for good to those who love God," on my bed, in total darkness, I prayed not for his life but for his soul. Suddenly, a very white, angelic vision of Shawn as a child appeared before my closed eyes. He was *looking* heavenward toward a bright shining path, but he was not *walking* toward it. This positive, uplifting sign helped me make it through the night.

By phone I alerted our friends, relatives, and churches from Florida to Maine, Michigan to Japan. Thousands began to pray for him, his wife and precious six-month-old baby girl, and his parents. Our children discouraged our flying back to Michigan, so during this time we waited and cried and prayed. Five days after the accident, I wrote this letter to Shawn, hoping he could feel my love for him and would strive to hang on to life:

Dear Shawn,

This is Grandma Flaherty in Florida. Since we are not there by your bedside, we want you to know we are praying for you night and day. We know God is listening because right after your accident, in my very first prayer, a vision of you smiling your little-boy smile appeared. Now, with all that Flaherty spirit of determination, you must strive to come back to Sara, little Kelsey, your Mom and Dad, Grandma and Grandpa and all of those who love you so much.

Remember, please remember, Shawn, GOD LOVES YOU AND HE WILL HELP YOU THROUGH THIS. I am waiting for you to put your arm around my shoulder, and say, "Yep, Grandma, I know what you're saying," like you always have. Please, Shawnee, with all your strength fight to come back to us.

Love, Grandma Flaherty

The letter was read to him. Whether or not he heard, dear reader, we will never know as he was in a coma for 5 weeks. During this time, surgeons repaired facial bones, including his left eye socket, both jaws and nose, as well as a broken ankle, wrist and femur. For the rest of his life his body will be held together with 136 titanium screws, 53 in his face alone.

A few days after Shawn regained consciousness, a most tragic and heartbreaking aftermath of this accident surfaced. Not knowing what doctors had suspected, he began to beg his parents to take the goggles off his eyes - but there were none to take off. Shawn had lost his sight! Totally in the left eye and he had only a slit of foggy peripheral vision in the right. But he lived!

During his six months in rehab, Shawn learned to chew, he learned to walk with a white cane and, yes, he learned to accept his future life of darkness in which he would never watch a seagull take flight or see his baby daughter smile. Indeed, a tragic price to pay for driving under the influence of alcohol.

Hopefully, dear reader, you will never have to experience midnight hours of the soul. Please pass this "Pearl of the Heart" on to your children, and theirs. Maybe it will help to save them from a life of darkness.

Grandma's Wish Book

It seems like yesterday. The memory is so clear. In October, 1988, while helping to care for our newborn twin granddaughters, Meagan Pearl and Caitlin Mia, I searched through numerous catalogs for just the right treasure to give them for their first Christmas. But everything, dear reader, seemed so "plastic", so temporary.

Finally, giving up, I leaned back in my rocker and with closed eyes let beautiful thoughts wander back to September 18. At 4:45 a.m. I had stood by the hospital, newborn nursery table and watched two naked, pink, little preemie granddaughters, just 15 minutes out of their mother's womb, flail and wail their way into the world - and into my heart.

As I rocked and thought about their miraculous births, an idea for a lasting gift flashed through my mind. Why not give them a book of wishes to grow on? Thus began the first jottings in their Grandma's Wish Book.

While changing diaper after diaper, spindly newborn legs prompted me to wish for strong legs that would not only one day dance merrily at Christmastime, but could also walk a far piece for a stranger in need.

Whenever I bathed their scrawny little bodies, I traced with my fingertips their flat, mashed tiny ears and wished for them clear sounds of church bells across the snow as well as a yearning to know why and for whom they tolled.

Once when I cooed "precious baby," Caitlin peered up at me with beautiful, dark, crossed eyes. I whispered, "May you both, dear Caitlin, have bright vision to enjoy the glitter of Christmas. And may you, with compassion I pray, recognize a tear shed in despair."

The first time sweet little Meagan grasped my index finger, I longed for inherited nimbleness for both - perhaps to finger Jingle Bells on a flute, to crochet a Christmas stocking, or to pen a poem as their gift to others.

How beautiful were their button noses, rosebud mouths and perfectly shaped little heads. As I observed them, I jotted down a wish for keen senses to savor spicy gingerbread baking on Christmas Eve, along with a wish for the mental ability to choose that which is virtuous. Rocking, feeling their fast, little beats of life against my breast, I wished most of all for kind and loving hearts that would help to bring joy to the world.

As I write this *Pearl*, dear reader, it is now Christmastime, 2006. Meagan Pearl and Caitlin Mia are intelligent, healthy, beautiful and talented young ladies. I pause to thank God that those wishes jotted in Grandma's Wish Book eighteen years ago have gradually been granted. Yes, they do enjoy the glitter of Christmas. But they also light up the world by serving others. What more could a grandma wish for?

A Child is Born

"I was so glad I was there, just to be there and to share that wonderful moment with the children. And when I saw that baby, well the way I felt was unbelievable.

When I first saw each grandchild, I was bursting with pride. A feeling never felt before...to see your own child produce another child and to know that it came through you.

It was a wonder. It was a spiritual experience. Just as if you would sit there and look at a flower for a long time. That kind of a feeling, a religious feeling."

. . . Anonymous

Oh, Who Can Make a Dad?

Perhaps you, dear reader, learned a little ditty of a song in Sunday school titled, Oh Who Can Make a Flower, I'm Sure I Can't, Can You? There were many verses that spoke of other miracles that children could see in their daily lives – the sun, the moon, the stars. In a class that I taught, the Sunday before Father's Day we would add an extra verse, all joyfully singing out "Oh who can make a Dad, I'm sure I can't, can you? Oh, who can make a Dad, no one but God 'tis true."

When children become adults, they begin to realize how special Dad is. Over the years Bill has received many cards and hand-written notes from our children thanking him for constant love and guidance as well as for camping trips in the wilds. A personal, happy remembrance is the very best Father's Day present any dad can receive. Sometimes these evoke tears of joy when a dad recalls the best years of his life. Below, I share with you, dear reader, excerpts from humorous cards and touching notes that Bill has received in the past for Father's Day:

Jef, at age 32, 1984: "Dad's Day is here and I want to take time to think of quality times we've shared – eating tailgate suppers while deer hunting, tenting on Swan Creek backwaters, and pheasant hunting on Van Dam's farm with my 25 lb. bow, just to name a few. You know, Dad, not all of us could develop organization in that part of our brain to 'get' Math, but you helped me develop in so many other ways as to not make that seem so important...Thanks for being a great Dad and grandfather for our girls Angie and Necia. Love, "Charley" - Bill's little-boy nickname for Jef.

Dan, at age 48, 1998: "Dad, you provided me with a snow shovel in Winter, a rake for the birch leaves in the Fall, a mower for the grass in the Spring, and a paint brush for the garage in the Summer. Thanks for being a wise provider, Dad. Love, Dan."

Kitty, Daddy's precious little girl at age 37, 1995: "Dad, thanks for being the best Dad that God could give anyone. You are the first man who held me and the first man I gave my heart to. All that you have taught me I have tried to instill in Eric, Meagan and Caitlin. They still talk about lunch on the "hobo" stove you made, and Eric wants a tent for Christmas, like the one he slept in on the beach at Silver Lake. You are a wonderful example of what all Dads should be and I love and respect you more than you will ever know. All my love, Fuzzy Lou" - Bill's nickname for Baby Kitty with fuzzy hair.

Nick, at age 31, 1991: A thank you note in response to a monetary gift to the children. "Dad, it is hard to put into words the thanks that both you and Mom deserve for such a generous gift to us kids. I remember well you biking off to work every morning while we kids were 'funning' at Silver Lake. It makes me wonder if we deserve now to be paid for that. Both of you worked hard all your lives so that five kids could go on family vacations, have decent clothes, have a good place to live and have a beautiful vacation home on the lake too. Dad, I just hope one half of your insight, guts, and determination rubbed off on me. With love, Your Baby Boy, Nick – P. S. I don't want to read about this in Mom's 'Pearls' column! HA!"

Tim, at age 47, 1997: The card that Tim, our oldest son, chose for his Dad for this particular year was the one that prompted this tribute to Bill, and all dads on Father's Day. "Only God can make a gentle, loving Dad, one who laughs and plays with his children, one who is there to guide them along their way. I love you Dad. Tim."

Perhaps, dear reader, when Tim chose this card for his Dad, he was remembering that ditty-of-a-song he learned as a child in Sunday school: "Oh, who can make a Dad, I'm sure I can't, can you? Oh, who can make a Dad, no one but God 'tis true."

Give a little love to a child, and
you get a great deal back.
. . . John Ruskin

Who Really Stole Christmas?

It's shocking. It's scary. It's sad. The Christ in Christmas, for many, has disappeared and few seem to know where to look for, or how to recapture Him. In a recent poll asking what makes Christmas important to them, only one third of adults surveyed said the birth of Christ.

The birthday of the Christ Child has been twisted into a secular holiday. The questions tumbling around in my mind are: When did America's disinterest in the real meaning of Christmas begin? Who are the culprits who have gradually stolen Christmas?

Looking back, perhaps it was Uncle Sam in WWII who stole Christmas. He called fathers into battle and mothers into the work force, often leaving fatherless children and weary mothers with less time for Christian training and worship.

Or was "she" the robber? Atheist Madelyn Murray O'Hair was instrumental in removing prayer from the schools, which eventually silenced the reading and reenactment of the Christmas story. For many children, the schoolroom was the only place where the Babe in the Manger came alive. I remember, as a child, how thrilled I was to follow the Star to Bethlehem in the school Christmas pageant. Every child knew what we were searching for and where to find Him.

As I ponder the stealing of Christmas, I think of Evangelist Jimmy Baker. Perhaps he is responsible for the missing Christ in Christmas. Many people, especially young people, often lose trust in the teachings of Christian leaders who are involved in fraudulent deeds.

In the 1990's, church attendance for ages 18 to 34 dropped drastically. Most young parents today are not even looking for the real meaning of Christmas and "sleep in" on their holidays off. Neither they nor their children ever hear the "Song in the Air" that heralds the birthday of a King.

Then, there's Walt Disney. Could the famed creator of Mickey Mouse possibly have had a big part in stealing Christmas? Family Yuletide celebrations at a Disney theme park often take preference over a candlelight service in a sanctuary where the Christ Child can be found.

A few years ago we were at Disney World on Christmas Eve. Thousands wound their way from one attraction to another. Occasionally they stopped to admire the gold and glitter surrounding them. Arms of a towering Christmas tree majestically held giant shiny balls. Endless strings of lights twinkled on endless strands of garlands. Bands marched. Drummers drummed. Minnie sang "Santa Claus is coming to Town," and Mickey pranced and waved to the throng of families watching, listening, searching.

At days end, we boarded the monorail for a ride back to the parking lot. While reflecting on the day, I overheard a mother say to her child, "Melissa, did you like Mickey and all the pretty Christmas decorations?" The weary little girl leaned her curly blonde head against her mother. Then, half crying, she said, "Uh-huh, but I didn't see no Baby Jesus." Indeed, she had not. There in that land of fantasy I began to suspect that America was losing the spiritual significance of the holiest of days.

And now, can it be that the toy industry, with their sexy dolls and violent, smashing, crime-related toys, has had a major part in stealing Christmas? All stores where toys are sold are bulging at the seams with toys, toys, toys - all aimed at satisfying frantic shoppers who are unaware that perhaps a thief lurks in every aisle.

But, dear reader, it is up to each of us to analyze WHY we celebrate Christmas. A few years ago, when our six youngest grandchildren opened their gifts from Bill and me, we were happily surprised that the gift they seemed to treasure most was a tiny porcelain nativity we had wrapped for them. Hopefully, for years to come this will be a reminder that they, and their children, must strive to keep Christ in Christmas and know in their hearts that CHRIST means Savior of the world.

All your children shall be
taught of the Lord; and great
shall be the peace of your children
. . . Isaiah 54:13

Children
Crying in the Wilderness

I wept when I saw two beautiful, flawless, blank faces in the news. Two children, 12 and 13, shackled, handcuffed, and wearing prisoner's gray, appeared before a judge in Florida for killing their father's live-in girlfriend. These children were crying out in a wilderness of frustration for a parent's love, in this case their father's love.

The number of close-knit families in America declined drastically in the last half of the 20th Century. Due to the effects of separation, divorce and often abandonment, trust of the innocent child was destroyed. Why is it, dear reader, that many parents ignore their conscience, that God-given, built-in compulsion to do right, not wrong? The protective veil of marriage has been severely rent, leaving over four million children in our country without the love and security of both a mother and a father who care about them.

It's time that parents listen to their children's cries for help - cries for a home life without alcohol, drugs and guns. Such stress often ends in murdering a member of one's own family. Children are crying for discipline and spiritual guidance, something and someone a child can count on. Yes, and there are cries for moral values in the home, in the schools, and in our government.

Who would have ever thought, dear reader, that in less than a month from the time that I saw those children in chains, two of my own would be crying out for their father's love?

The year 1998 was a most devastating time in their lives and my own. I experienced months of heart-wrenching phone calls and long, sleepless nights. For the first time in my 72 years on this earth I came to realize the true meaning of "heartbreak." Often at night, uncontrollable sobs choked me so that my breathing came in gasps and I truly feared that my heart would fail to beat.

The unbelievable scenario began when our youngest son, 40, and his wife separated. Naturally, I was deeply concerned for their two beautiful daughters, ages 12 and 13.

After two years of prayerful petitions for their reconciliation, I came to realize that this was not to be. One night, like a bright light in the dark,

God shook me and said, "The burden is too heavy, I will carry it for you." It was time to let go, and I did. But concern for the children continued to trouble my soul.

A year passed. Both girls still questioned why their family was no longer a family. The 13 year-old not only was concerned about her Mom, Dad and sister, but about her friends and the evil upheaval in the whole of our society. This was indeed a great burden for a child. With her permission, I quote chilling excerpts from my disturbed granddaughter's hand-printed letter to me:

"Grandma, over the summer I would rollerblade downtown to hang out with my friends. When they started to swear, I wanted to leave so bad, but felt that if I did I wouldn't fit in.

Finally, Mom stopped allowing me to go there and I was glad. The kids down there have parents who don't care where they are or what they are doing.

Grandma, on the news, just 45 minutes ago a car with a baby inside was stolen in Grand Rapids at a gas station. It's so sad. Why would anyone want to take a baby from its mother? It's terrible nowadays, isn't it? America is failing and President Clinton is not a good example anymore. But, Grandma, we still have to pray and believe that America will find God, even if there doesn't seem to be much hope."

Fortunately, unlike many children of today's fractured families, this granddaughter had faith in the One who helped her bear her burden. It is my fervent prayer, dear reader, that Erin's generation will be the one to turn America around so there will be fewer children crying in the wilderness.

Let the children come to me;
and forbid them not; for of
such is the kingdom of God.
. . . Mark 10:14

America Cries for Momma

She looketh well to the ways
of her household and eateth
not the bread of idleness.
. . . Proverbs 31:27

At the end of the 20th Century, startling statistics shook America. A 1999 survey showed that 62% of American women held jobs outside the home compared to 9% in 1920. Now, the big question puzzling both professionals and parents arose: Is the absence of mothers in the home causing disintegration of the American family?

No doubt, we have become a society where the center pole in the circus of family life is missing. Many working mothers lack time or stamina to provide the love and guidance that children need in their growing and learning years. Neglected children have become ill mannered and morally and spiritually depraved.

With the economic explosion in the 1990's American families began to want more - bigger homes, multiple cars, and a luxurious lifestyle. All of this was possible because more and more mothers had entered the work force.

When I was growing up, the average family did not have all of these "things." A mother's primary responsibility was to care for the children while the father worked to feed and clothe them all. There was no extra money for "eating out" and extended vacations were unheard of.

Although Momma did occasionally scrub floors in homes of the rich to help feed and clothe us when Daddy suffered a debilitating illness, she firmly believed a mother's place was in the home. She had no dresses of silk or strands of pearls. Like my grandmothers before her, "Strength and Honor" were her clothing. In reality, she was a jewel shining with moral beauty.

During Momma's "down time" she rested on the front porch. Often I would climb into the swing with her and while swinging back and forth, she would sing her favorite hymns. No doubt, the words of those great hymns instilled in me the need for an unshakeable faith in my Creator.

Now we are well into the 21st Century. America is, indeed, dear reader, crying for Momma. Let us hope and pray that priorities in today's working society will change so that mothers can respond to those cries and "look to the ways of her household" – first.

Momma's Apron

Momma's apron was oh so lovely.
Fields of flowers dressed its meadow.
Like helping hands it wrapped around,
Hugging plumpness like a shadow.

Speckled with frothy frosting
At cake-bakin' time each week.
Dancing daisies and winking violets
Pressed kisses upon my cheeks.

Quickly bunched at the bottom,
'Twas a perfect pouch-like sack,
For scattering corn to cacklers
Scratching hungrily out back.

Her apron shuttled shivering chicks
To a cozy kitchen corner
Where our old-timey cook stove
Warmed fuzzy, chirping charmers.

The pretty flowered apron bulged
At egg-gatherin' time each day
And at churnin' time on the porch,
It flipped pesky flies away.

A thirsty, handy handkerchief,
Momma's apron dried my tears.
Threadbare, it shined our painted floors,
Refusing death with floral cheers.

Oh, dear Momma, I wish I knew
Why Mommas with meadowed aprons
Are now, too few.

Three Little Words

In early March 2001, I walked into a pharmacy hoping to quickly pick up a few greeting cards, pretty ones extolling the true joy of Easter. But after one hour of searching, it was very clear that Easter, like Christmas, had become a commercial "Ho-Ho-Ho."

On one long display rack, more than 300 "Happy Easter" cards were displayed. Bunnies of all sorts topped the list of greetings. Brown bunnies, pink bunnies, white bunnies. Frisky and smiling, they happily hopped through meadows across many colorful cards. Some bunnies carried baskets of colored eggs. One card, displaying a dark chocolate bunny, disgustingly spoke of chocolate eggs being like "bunny droppings."

A weird card, hiding amongst the bunny cards, caught my eye. A sinister-looking black cat sat licking his chops. Inside, I read the cynical words, "I ate the Easter bunny. But have a Happy Easter anyway."

On this endless rack of cards were also many frolicking, yellow, fuzzy chicks aiming to chirp their way into spring and hopefully into happy, human hearts.

Of course, there were numerous pretty, pastel, egg-shaped cards. Some were beribboned and others tinted in rainbow colors. Most were certainly eye appealing, many decorated with zigzags filled with an artist's version of tiny wild flowers.

Then, there were humorous, jellybean cards, gosling cards and duck cards. Several nostalgic ones burst with sunshine, budding trees, or Easter lilies heralding Spring and wishing someone - nieces, nephews, brothers, sisters, mothers, fathers, grandmothers - a Happy Easter. Although many of the greetings were poetic, most were shallow and failed to mention why we celebrate Easter.

The shocking part was that only one greeting card depicted a church scene and more shocking, three, yes three, out of 300 plus cards displayed the symbol of a cross.

One hour into scanning the racks, I thought I had finally found the perfect Easter card. Words splashed across a beautiful, pastel card jumped out at me: "Three Little Words Everyone Longs to Hear." When

I opened the card, little chocolate bunnies hopped here and there. Then, I read these three words: "Chocolate Isn't Fattening."

Finally, I left the store empty handed, came home and designed and hand-colored my own Easter cards. No doubt, dear reader, the greeting card industry has failed those people who rejoice on this Holy day. The three little words millions still want to hear on Easter are: HE IS RISEN.

Why Easter Eggs?

Pretty colored eggs nestled in a child's Easter basket are symbols of celebration. Whether brightly tinted with water colors or creatively trimmed with gold and silver braid, Easter eggs represent an awakening in the spring. Spring - the time when satin violets wink through the bleak blankets of winter and golden daffodils nod a "good morning" to the goddess of dawn, Easter.

Easter eggs are also a symbol of light. Gaily colored eggs are hidden by an unknown Easter Bunny in the damp, dark woods. The brightness and joy, when found, are surpassed only by a glorious Easter morning sunrise bringing a new day, a new season, and a new hope to all.

Likewise, Easter eggs are a symbol of giving. Brightly woven baskets are filled with chocolate bunnies and rainbow-colored candy eggs, topped with a big shiny, pink or yellow ribbon. All baskets are filled with love for someone special. Mom's reward is the sound of her child's squeals of delight when he or she peels back the pink cellophane and marvels at the beauty and goodness that clothes an Easter egg.

The legend of the Easter egg is best summed up in this Ukrainian Folk Tale:

"One day a poor peddler went to the marketplace to sell a basket of eggs. He came upon a crowd mocking a man who staggered with a heavy cross on which he was about to be crucified. The peddler ran to his aid, leaving the basket by the roadside. When he returned, he found the eggs transformed into exquisite designs of bright colors. The man was Christ; the peddler Simon. And the eggs were to become the symbol of rebirth for all mankind."

During the time of preparation for this delightful, springtime happening, dear reader, I hope that you will tell your children and grandchildren why they are coloring Easter eggs and what they represent, because I dare say most cannot tell you that when we celebrate Easter, we are celebrating a most sacred holiday.

A Garden Full of Memories

In early June of 2003 I awoke at 7:30 a.m., meandered into my living room at Silver Lake and there peeking in through our windows were 26 faces, all wearing flimsy, silky hats and a big friendly smile.

The sun had finally warmed the faces of the Irises in my flower garden. Arrayed in orchid blouses and deep purple velvet skirts, they nodded a "Good Morning, Pearl." This sparked the memory of a single face, with no name, that I had not thought of for 20 years.

Now, dear reader, you might say, "Pearl, what's so unusual about an Iris blooming in a garden?" And I will say, "My garden is no ordinary garden. It is a garden filled with perennial love. In it are perennial plants shared by numerous people - some friends, some strangers - who have enhanced my life with nature's flowering bounty.

My Memory Garden is also unusual in that it is what I call a "strip" garden. The entire area is only 4 feet wide and 24 feet long. Another unusual feature is that the garden is 10 feet beyond the house so that I can view the beauty of it from my living room windows - a must if you want to talk with your friends often.

Once I read a Chinese proverb that said, "If you wish to be happy forever and ever, make a garden." So, for two decades I have been painting this colorful landscape, clump by clump, with gifts of various plants and bulbs. Every summer, one-by-one they explode into bright blossoms that feed my soul.

Before I actually started this garden, I remember hearing of a beautiful field of Irises east of Silver Lake. One day I drove out just to take a look. I found the owner dressed in her digging clothes - a big shirt, straw hat and loose trousers. She stood surrounded by an unbelievable mixture of yellow, blue, white and purple Irises as far as the eye could see.

After we walked the field and discussed each variety, she began digging into the rich soil. With a smile as big as a half moon, she handed me three of the beautiful, purple, blooming bulbs. How, dear reader, can I ever forget her, and that smile? Those three Irises have multiplied into the 26 flowering beauties mentioned above, some with as many as 4 blossoms per stalk. Many times I have gone to the front window, paused and thanked this dear lady for the joy her gift has brought to me and to others whom I have occasionally given a bulb or two.

Another gift in my Memory Garden is a small Columbine plant. One morning, wrapped in my pink fuzzy robe, half asleep, I trod into my living room, and there nestled among the Irises were three fragile, uplifted, yellow faces greeting me. Tiny shoots of that leafy little plant had been given to me in a paper cup by a gentleman at a yard sale. Now, each summer as the blossoms appear, with gratitude I think of this unknown gardener who shared this plant of lasting beauty.

Then, also, there was another benefactor whose garden I stopped to admire out in the country at least 20 years ago. For years I did not even know her name. Finally, one summer day I traveled back to her doorstep to thank her for her gift that was the beginning of my perennial, Memory Garden. But she had moved.

After several phone calls, I did track her down. She is still a prolific gardener. Every year when that tall pink Phlox blooms, I want to stand up and shout out my appreciation. Many bouquets from that plant, as well as several sprouts, have been shared with friends. Elta, your gift has brightened my world, as well as the world of many others, and finally I am able to say "thank you" for sharing. My Phlox now has not only a face, but also a name.

And then, there's the orange Poppy plant given to me by dear Roy. In addition to sharing blooming goodness, Roy also, for many years, showered us with fresh corn and rhubarb from his vegetable garden. Although he is gone now, I can still talk to Roy when the orange Poppies burst forth with gusto every spring.

The orange Poppies, pink Phlox, yellow Columbine and purple Irises are only a few of the twenty perennials that continue to fill the view from my window. Most have names, each has a face. In every blossom there is a beautiful memory that lives on in my heart.

A flower garden filled with gifts from others, dear reader, is a peaceful place where you can visit a friend and be close to the heart of God at the same time.

God Almighty first planted a garden.
And, indeed, it is the purest of human
pleasures.
. . . Francis Bacon

A Dying Will

Most everyone knows about "Living Wills," but because of the unnecessary agony suffered when my mother died, I now have a "Dying Will." Simply stated, once I am deceased, no heroic efforts will be made to bring me back to life.

For three agonizing weeks in the hospital Momma wrestled with life, begging to die in peace. Finally at 6:15 one morning I heard an awful sound. There was no struggle, just a rasping, sucking in of the last cool breath of life. In a semi-conscious state, I jumped from my bedside cot. Now, free of pain, Momma's face glowed, even seemed wrinkle-free at eighty-eight years of age.

I thought I was ready to let her go, but ironically and instantaneously I pushed the nurse's call button and screamed, "Come, quickly!" Within seconds her dark-haired nurse rushed in. She glanced at the stillness. Then, without hesitation, she pressed another button and yelled, "Code Blue!"

Moments later white-coated men whisked Momma's body to the 7th floor. For twelve hours in a back-to-life factory, hospital personnel tried to pump life back into her. Although I fiercely objected to both the nurses and her doctor, their curt answer was always the same, "Hospital Rules!"

Just once I peered into that awful room. My beautiful Momma lay propped up midst a hodgepodge of machines and tubes. Strands of chestnut hair fell across her now ashen face. One eye was shut and the other stared straight ahead like some one-eyed monster. A metal, gag-like apparatus pried her mouth open to allow air to be pumped into her lungs through a black, vacuum-cleaner-size hose. Her chest heaved and fell, heaved and fell, while another machine forcing blood through collapsed veins clacked and thumped, throbbing like the struggling pump of a dry oil well.

Horrified, I ran from that door where death reigned into the hospital waiting room, now filled with Momma's grieving children, grandchildren and great grandchildren. Too many hours passed and too many tears fell. Pacing the corridors for hours, I prayed the medical personnel in charge would accept her death. Finally, at 6:00 p.m. a change-of-shift nurse called me into her office. "I'm sorry. We just couldn't get her heart beating again. Where would you like the body sent?"

212

At last, the inhumane torture to my beloved Momma, as well as the agony suffered immeasurably by loved ones as they watched, had ended.

How thankful I am to know, dear reader, that there is an alternative to Code Blue. With a "Dying Will" my children and theirs will be spared such heart-wringing, doctor-versus-God action.

And He shall wipe away all tears
from their eyes; and there
shall be no more death,
neither sorrow nor crying,
neither shall there be any more
pain.

. . . Revelation 21:4

Tears of Joy

Dear, dear readers, on December 8, 2005 I had surgery for colon cancer, followed by six months of chemo. The recovery period was long and difficult,

However, it was the many get-well wishes and prayers from devoted readers of my *Pearls* columns that cheered me on. I read and reread, often with tears of joy, kind notes that lovingly expressed concern for my full recovery.

One reader wrote: "Pearl, you do not know me, but we get together every time you write a column." Another wrote, "Through your Pearls, 'you have put gladness in my heart'...Psalm 4:7." A minister e-mailed me: "I read about your surgery in the Journal and I have prayed for you. You don't know me. I am just a "dear reader."

A very creative lady from Naperville, Ill. wrote: "If prayers were butterflies, I imagine 'bout now you'd be covered in monarchs." She was right! People from California to Massachusetts and from Japan to the Netherlands were praying for me. Then, she added, "I hope you mend quickly so you can keep those wonderful stories coming."

Indeed, these are words that touch one's heart, especially a writer who hopes that with every publication of a *Pearl* someone will glean a thought worth remembering.

There were long, caring, up-lifting letters from other unknown readers, one a 65 year old grandmother whose cancer was in remission. Another from Missouri assured me that "according to Oncologists, cancer colon is one of the easiest to cure."

And so, it was you, dear readers of *Pearls*, that brought me tears of joy, and it is for you that I continue to write gems stored up in my heart – gems that express my love for you and for the One who created and cares for us all.

When irritations enter our lives,
dear reader, we, like the oyster,
can make pearls.

A Miracle Gift from the Sea

Every Christmas Tree Needs a Star

A Miracle Gift from the Sea

Christmas in Florida? Bah-humbug! Missing is the sweetness of a snowflake melting upon my tongue and the sound of cherry wood crackling in our fireplace. Missing are candles glowing in tall windows and our grandchildren hugging Grandpa. And where are the church bells chiming out *Silent Night, Holy Night?*

These were my thoughts as Bill and I, in swimsuits, trudged barefoot along our Treasure Coast beach in December, 1983. My heart felt as empty as the bucket I carried for collecting shells.

"Bill, know what I want this year for Christmas?" I blurted out, "A lovely crèche for our yard with Mary and Joseph and shepherds."

Looking rather shocked, he said, "You crazy, Pearl? What would I use for tools to build it, and where would we store it? It's out of the question. Besides, on our trailer lot there's just no room."

The "no room" stung, dear reader. He was right, of course. Still, I longed for visible signs of the miracle of Christmas - love, hope, peace and joy. I had not found these midst the swishing bonneted palms of retirement. "Perhaps I could buy a tiny crèche," I mumbled.

Suddenly, thirty feet down the beach the ocean's frothy arms tossed up several thick, large, flat pieces of glistening coral. I pulled my hand from Bill's and raced to inspect Neptune's latest fling. There in front of my very eyes was the most magnificent Wiseman robed in sand and crowned with shells. And in his hands he unmistakably carried the precious frankincense.

"Bill," I yelled above the ocean's roar. "Look what I've found! And here's another one, and another!" I ran from piece to piece of etched coral, standing them upright on the beach.

Bill ambled over, chuckled something about a "great imagination" and then walked on. My heart throbbed in my chest. In my excitement I ignored the sharpness of broken shells cutting into my feet. Here, within a twenty-five foot circle, lay a perfect gift for someone in search of Christmas.

As I fashioned a crèche in the sand, I marveled at a beautiful, 10" serene Mary, a compatible, hovering Joseph and a creviced manger - all crudely carved by an ancient hand. And there were more! Two kneeling shepherds, two curly sheep, a four-humped camel and a cow with horns lay reverently in the sand. All were waiting to become a part of Christmas in our trailer park on Nettles Island. The sight was a magic, holy one.

"But something is missing," I spoke to the wind. "The Baby! Where is the Baby?" I began clawing through the sand and shells.

"What are you doing?" Bill suddenly returned from his lone jaunt down the beach.

"Oh, Bill, look at the Nativity! It's perfect! It's small! I love it! It's a miracle!"

He glanced kindly at the creation and without a word headed toward the park entrance. My hopes fell for a moment. Then he turned and called out, "Guess I'll have to bring the car to pick up your treasures."

I quickly hid Mary, Joseph, the Wiseman, the shepherds and the manger in the dune grass. I loaded the animals into my plastic bucket and trekked homeward, eyes glued to the beach. Just as a wave washed up a new batch of coral, I knelt to examine it. Again, I began to claw through the sand, still hoping to find a Baby Jesus.

"Pardon, Missus?" A strange, soft voice asked. I peered up at a stooped, elderly gentleman clad in swim trunks. His body, like tanned leather, had the appearance of a beach bum. But he spoke with a broken eloquence, which I later learned was that of a German doctor vacationing in Florida. "You search for something special?" His questioning continued.

"Well, yes, Sir. I'm looking for Christmas." I straightened up and smiled. He smiled back, his smile a little crooked and puzzled.

"In the sand, Missus? You look for Christmas?"

I motioned to the hidden treasure and gushed out the story of the coral nativity and the missing Christ Child. Just as I lowered my eyes to attest the bucket full of animals, he lowered his to view the proof that I had indeed found Christmas on the beach. There, to our amazement, lying between our bare feet was a perfectly smooth, round, sea-washed stone with tinges of brown outlining a baby's fine hairline.

My new friend picked it up, smiled a smile of belief, and then placed it in my hand. In his foreign accent, he said, "Truly a miracle, Missus. A miracle gift from the sea."

"Yes, yes it is!" I clasped his hand and wished him a very blessed Christmas. Then I hurried on, eager to show Bill my latest find. I pedaled my bike across A1A, bucket swinging. Swishing palms lining the island boulevard seemed to join the song in my heart, dear reader, - a song of hope that this special gift would make Christmas more meaningful for the residents, as well as the many visitors from the North who come each December in search of sun and sea - and miracles.

Every Christmas Tree
Needs a Star

Yes, every Christmas tree needs a star. After all, wise men followed a bright star to Bethlehem to worship a newborn Baby wrapped in swaddling clothes lying in a manger. A shiny star atop a Christmas tree reminds us all of the true meaning of Christmas.

After Christmas in 2002, I threw out our dull, fake Christmas tree and trimmings, including the dusty angel, which had adorned its top for twelve years in Florida.

As I dismantled the tree, memories of long ago Christmases lit up my mind. Each year Daddy cut down a simple, sparse-limbed pine tree and dragged it down from our Kentucky mountain. There were no strings of glittery lights. But, it was beautifully decorated with red and green paper chains we children had made and many, shiny, icicles bought at the dime store for ten cents a box. However, the decoration I remember most was the large star at the top - a star Momma had made with cardboard and covered with silver tinsel.

In early December the following year, trying to decide whether to buy a real Christmas tree from the North, I thought, "Why not use a palm tree? After all, the Holy Land is a country of palm trees." There are no "traditional" Christmas trees in Bethlehem. Bethlehem, not far from the Mediterranean Sea, is located on a sandy camel path leading out into the desert where palm trees have always been a sign of joy and a symbol of life.

Pondering these thoughts, I went out into my tiny yard and, with shovel in hand, dug up a scrubby four-foot type of palm tree with clumps of spiky fronds. I shoveled dirt into a big clay pot. Bill, thinking me insane, carried it into our trailer living room. "It will be beautiful when I finish," I cheerily announced. He shook his head in disbelief. But his lack of interest did not daunt my spirits. Remembering Momma's star, I now had a plan for the plain, little palm tree.

I quickly rushed to the closet storing ancient, glistening glass balls. I had really never noticed before that some were painted with ringing red bells, some with golden angels singing above a Nativity and some with star-filled skies, all symbols of that night so long ago when Christ was born. I hung them carefully one by one on the few spiky branches. With each hanging, the little tree slowly, but surely, became a Christmas tree. But, wait! It needed one more ornament! Yes, a shiny star at the top!

Not once did I consider buying a beautiful, store-bought star, but I had no tinsel like Momma's. So, I simply brought out my scissors and cut out a big cardboard star, covered it with aluminum foil, and wired it to the top of my new creation. I was now ready for my neighborhood Christmas party. I stood back and declared the tree perfect. Different, perhaps, but the star in all its radiance certainly would speak reams to all who would view it. "Just what every Christmas tree should have," I gloried in the thought - a star at the top!

But, dear reader, when friends came, some laughed at my Christmas tree. One commented that they loved my old Christmas tree with the purple velvet ribbons, red holly berries, and the angel at the top. Another, no doubt because of its scrubby simplicity, called it "A Charlie Brown tree." And all laughed - all but one kind gentleman who said, "I like your shiny, big star, Pearl. That star says it all." Then, my heart beat with Christmas joy.

Later, during our festive, Christmas dinner, we discussed palm trees in Bethlehem while listening to carols, including There's a Song in the Air, which sings of "the star in the sky and a baby's low cry, a star which rains its fire while many sing, announcing the manger that cradled a King."

Yes, for more than two thousand years, dear reader, that Star of Wonder has guided us to a more perfect Light. Shouldn't every Christmas tree have a star at the top?

Joy to the world!
The Lord is come!
Let earth receive
Her King!
. . . Isaac Watts
1674-1748

Yes, Bananas!

Dear reader, as I write this *Pearl*, I am so excited. It's not about winning the lottery or anything like that. It's about a miracle happening right out my back door. A huge stalk of bananas is ripening in my little tropical plantation of banana trees!

Please don't laugh at this Appalachian gal. But where I cum frum the only fruit trees on our mountain when I wuz growin' up wuz apple, mulberry and pawpaws. But them's not what I'm tellin you about. I'm a talkin' about bananas! I never in my life seen one of them big-leafed trees till I cum to the sunny state of Florida.

In 1995 a neighbor gave me a single spindly plant about three feet tall and three inches in diameter. After scratching up a circle of not-too-rich Florida sand and anemic dirt, I stuck the little tree in the ground and fertilized it with potash like my neighbor suggested. Then, lo and behold, from that little "stick" sprang a whole plantation of eight trees. Three years later the original little tree became the talk of our neighborhood with a stalk bearing 35 beautiful yellow bananas!

Watching a banana develop, dear reader, is truly a miraculous experience. When a tree is nearly full-grown, a purplish-red, pregnant, foot-long "ear" pokes through huge, bright green leaves. I simply could not believe that from under each shuck of the "ear" fifteen or twenty bananas emerge. Each morning I would run out to catch the miracle unfolding. Sure enough, every few days a half-moon row of little buds, looking like creamed, shriveled balloons, had popped out from under a curled-up, purplish-colored leaf. This leaf protects tender buds until very tiny, green bananas are formed, then it falls off. A few days later, another leaf begins to curl and another row, called a "hand of fruit," appears, each hand having 5 bananas on it.

After the one stalk of bananas matures, that tree dies and is cut down. New shoots form and new trees spring up. Dear reader, it is indeed phenomenal! Renews one's faith in the Creator of miracles!

YES,
BANANAS!

MOMS MARCH

"DR." JAY
AT THE
CANCER CENTER

Give of Yourself

Albert Schweitzer, a renowned German philosopher, physician and humanitarian, who lived to be ninety, spent sixty-five years of his life as a volunteer serving others in Africa. He wrote many books in his lifetime and one of the quotes he left the world was:

"We all must give time to our fellowmen. Even if it is just a little thing, do something for others, something for which you get no pay but the privilege of doing it."

This is a simple statement made by a great man, but one which each of us could use as a guide for our own busy, self-centered existence. Volunteering provides a wonderful opportunity for personal development as well as self-fulfillment.

As I think back on my Momma's unselfish life, I realize that her service to others influenced my way of thinking about volunteerism.

In 1949 at age 23, I served as a volunteer Gray Lady at the Veterans Hospital in Grand Rapids, Michigan. Although I worked as a secretary at Hope College, once a week I drove 20 miles to the hospital. I read to disabled veterans but soon learned that what they needed most was to have someone hold their hand and listen to terrifying stories of how they were injured in WW II. They also told heart-wrenching stories of their loneliness away from families. A volunteer job such as this, dear reader, definitely makes one more compassionate toward others.

In December 2004, I was asked to present at our New Year's Eve party an annual award to the "Star Volunteer of Nettles Island." Choosing the recipient was a difficult decision as there were so many names to consider.

However, after evaluating his selfless service, the award was given to a very deserving gentleman. As a volunteer, he had spent not hours or days but twenty years helping to make our mobile home park the caring, neighborly, place it is today. When I announced his name, the 200 celebrants thunderously applauded. But Walter did not appear on the stage right away. At age 75, instead of being served, he was in the kitchen preparing a cart full of cookies and ice cream to serve to the many party goers – a good example of a devoted volunteer.

There are so many possibilities for community service. Whether a volunteer is serving in a hospital gift shop or on the floors filling water glasses for patients, his or her effort is an important gift to others.

Our schools need playground supervisors, drivers for various class outings and, most importantly, they need teacher aides in their overcrowded classrooms.

One of my most rewarding volunteer jobs in retirement was the eight years I spent as a teacher aide in Jensen Beach Elementary School in Florida. I taught reading and math to first grade slow learners. No reward could have been greater than the smiles that greeted me as the children rushed to get a hug each morning. Countless other memories are harbored in my heart.

Historical Societies can always use guides for tours of their museums where people from all walks of life can discover and learn to appreciate their heritage.

In your community library, as a volunteer, you can read to small children, helping them to develop a curiosity and love for reading, so needed in our schools today.

Church volunteers serve parishioners in many capacities. Invaluable are those who set up tables or serve food at various community functions. Others serve by mowing, planting and keeping the grounds beautiful for all to enjoy. Church choir members also add much to the joy of Sunday worship services.

Volunteering is giving of yourself to benefit others. No volunteer, dear reader, goes unnoticed and each truly makes a profound difference.

And the King shall answer and say unto them...Inasmuch as you have done it unto one of the least of these, you have done it unto me.
... Matthew 25:40

Moonstruck

The place - our Florida Nettles Island boardwalk on the Atlantic Ocean. The date - March 21, 2002. The time - 9:30 p.m. and Spring's equinox when the sun crosses the equator, making night and day of equal length in all parts of the earth. More than 100 people clustered there to witness a lunar phenomenon - a full moon rising where the sky meets the sea.

Several grandmas and grandpas, and a few young parents, stood looking to the Atlantic horizon hoping to catch dusk's first rays of light. Bill and I joined many other couples on boardwalk benches - like new lovers eager to share the beauty of an enormous silvery moon.

I would like to say that the melodic lament of *"Moonlight and Roses"* could be heard, but 'twas not so, dear reader. At the far end of the boardwalk, rock-and-roll blared from a boom box on a picnic table. Twenty or so robust, energetic, carefree teenagers talked and laughed. None were aware of the miracle that was about to take place.

I tried to relax and mind my own business, but my brain kept saying, *"those kids are going to miss this extravaganza!"* Just when the full moon's first rays appeared upon the ocean's dancing waters, I ran toward the young strangers and in desperation screamed out, "Hey, you guys, you are missing it!"

"Missing what?" an interested, muscular young man with baggy, oversized pants blurted out. Then, practically in unison the group turned to me and loudly questioned, "What's hapnin?"

"The moon, the moon!" I shouted.

"What moon?" said a soft-spoken young lady clad in cut-off jeans and a Mickey Mouse shirt.

"The moon, a *full* moon is coming up!"

"Where?" Several of the gang chimed in.

"There!" And with a sweep of my arm I directed attention to the brightness splintering the horizon. Then in disbelief I heard this:

"Why is it coming up there?" a puzzled, little blonde asked.

"Honey," I said, somewhat bewildered, "the moon always comes up in the East - there!"

Some snickered. Then, a tall, lanky, dark-haired young man wearing glasses slapped my hand and roared, "Give me five, Grandma!"

They all turned to the light, as if moonstruck, and wondered at the moon's brilliant curve emerging from the Atlantic Ocean, bathing the darkness surrounding them with Heaven's light. Then, one crew-cut teen marveled aloud, "I never saw that before! Now that's awesome, man!"

I slipped away back to our bench where Bill and I drank in the beauty of the spectacle.

However, dear reader, that scene troubled me well into the night. Flashbacks appeared of Momma reading about the creation of light from her great black Bible. How excited I was to run out and glimpse the moon coming over our mountain - always and forever from the East.

Of course, none of us knew then that a full moon appears every 29 ½ days. Nor that the moon's diameter is 2,160 miles. Nor that it is more than 238 thousand miles from the earth. But we children were always thrilled when a full moon in all its glory dusted each stone and each tree branch with a soft, silvered light that illuminated our entire, secluded Kentucky holler.

At a young age, children everywhere need to hear the reading of Genesis 1:16, as well as be taken by the hand and led into the dark so they might experience the magic of God's miraculous gift, the moon.

And God made two great lights; the greater light to rule the day and the lesser light to rule the night.
. . . Genesis 1:16

Lessons Learned
From Bird Watching

Dear reader, I am so ecstatic! For the first time in my life, I have experienced the miracle birth of baby robins. When we first returned to Michigan in May of 2004, I noticed that just outside my sliding glass door a mama robin had made a nest in our small spruce tree.

Her snug little home had been perfectly designed of string, sticks and straw. During two weeks of wet, cold days, she sat patiently waiting for the big event. After two or three days of almost constant watching, I clocked Papa Robin's actions. Each day he would fly in, drop off Mama Robin's breakfast of a big fat worm at approximately 8:00, lunch at 12:00 and dinner around 5:30. This continued every day until the eggs hatched. I never once had a chance to count the eggs, as I could never catch mama robin off her nest.

Then, finally, one morning she began pecking on the eggs. Her head bobbed up and down in quick little jerks. I was glued to my perch, the Lazy Boy by the window, knowing that soon the long-awaited birth would come. Sure enough, the following day, which was warm and sunny, mama flew out of the nest and I quickly slid the door open and leaned out for a quick glimpse of four pink, little bare-skinned, sleeping bodies. However, Mama Robin, who was sitting on a piece of driftwood about 30 feet away watching my every move, squawked as if mad at me and immediately flapped her way back to cover her newborns.

Every day I faithfully watched, mesmerized by the dedicated attentiveness of not only a mama protecting her children, but also of the actions of the papa robin. Like clock work, he loyally continued to bring home the worms, first for mama and then for his four, tiny, now fuzzy, helpless offspring. Their survival was totally dependent on her body to keep them warm and his three daily flights in to supply food for his family of five.

After three weeks of watching, I couldn't help but compare the birth and life of robins to that of humans. How simple their life style. They have no clothes except the feathers they are wearing. Whereas, our closets are filled with clothes we don't wear. Robins don't store up food for the winter, but must forage each day for every simple morsel. Some humans, on the other hand, have shelves filled with staples. They can grocery shop once a week in a warm store for a variety of gourmet foods and bottled water that they consider essential to civilized life.

Robins enjoy a personal liberty of which we can never boast, but they don't use their personal liberty to party on weekends, abuse their spouses, or shirk caring for their children. They would not be considered civilized because they live just like their bird ancestors did a thousand years ago. We, dear reader, would call that old-fashioned and laugh at anyone who tried to live as his dad did – even 50 years ago.

But, robins don't have to keep up with the Joneses. They don't burden themselves with a multitude of "things" so they can be considered civilized. Their lives are spent working and singing. Neither do they labor an entire lifetime laying up goods for the little robin offspring to quarrel over after they are gone to bird heaven. Finally, robins, like all feathered creatures, get their eats by the sweat of their brows, so to speak, and they don't sit back and say, "The world owes me a living."

I continued to observe and listen. All of the little nestlings now chirped weakly, their mouths opening wide between chirps for Mama Robin's special treat. It seemed the "weenagers" could never be filled up as the devoted mama was flying out every five minutes to search for more worms.

Finally, the robin's nest was bursting at the seams with four, wing-feathered youngsters. Then, one bright day Mama Robin pushed them out one at a time, forcing them to fly and scratch for themselves. They were free to work and sing and bring other beautiful little robins into the world for us to enjoy.

Observing this day-to-day miracle, dear reader, reminded me that we all should strive for simplicity in our lives. So let us tune up our music boxes at daybreak each morning, like the robins, and try singing a new, cheerful song.

A Tree for Tanya

I think that I shall never see,
Anything as beautiful as Tanya's tree.

Red-haired Tanya, a new kid in school, worked feverishly coloring her Christmas tree at the first-grade classroom table. When finished, with a heart-melting smile she held her paper high for me to praise. "It's beautiful, simply beautiful," I bragged.

Then, with a frown, she leaned forward and whispered, "My Mom says we can't have no tree this Christmas because my Daddy's out of work."

Her words, *"no tree,"* troubled me all day long. I was only a volunteer teacher-aide in Tanya's first grade class, but felt the need to brighten this little girl's Christmas. The family had no phone. When I related the story to the school principal, he gave me permission to contact them at home. The following day Tanya's mother, looking weary, appeared at the door of their two-room shabby duplex. After a short visit, she said, "Yes, Maam, a tree would be nice for the children." And so the search began.

Local thrift shops were scoured and finally a lovely, new, four-foot, artificial tree was found. Before I had a chance to shop for decorations, a neighbor asked, "Pearl, could you use a bag of Christmas odds and ends?" The bag, dear reader, was filled with pink, green and red glass balls and lots of shiny tinsel - perfect for Tanya's tree. At a flea market on Saturday, I trudged up and down the aisles. Several children's character ornaments and a beautiful angel for the top were found. Unbelievably, most vendors refused money, saying, "Nah, it's Christmas. They're free."

On and on the giving continued. Through our Theatre Guild's drive for toys, a doll named Rita with *red* hair, and a bright blue truck and football for Tanya's brothers were donated. When the presents were wrapped and I was contemplating whether to buy one or two strings of lights, the phone rang.

A friend called to donate a $50.00 gift certificate for Tanya's family's Christmas dinner. What had started out as a simple little tree for a

228

precious little girl had snowballed into a wonderful, Christmas-giving experience for many and a promising, bright holiday for an entire, poverty-stricken family.

On the day of delivery Tanya met Bill and me at the door. Then, surprisingly, her parents invited us to join them in the trimming. We stood the little tree in a dark corner of their scantily furnished, small living quarters. Bill strung two sets of lights while I placed a mountain of ornaments onto their kitchen table.

The children squealed with delight as they chose a special branch on which to hang each shiny ball, a Christmas Snoopy, a holly-capped Santa, and a tiny red-scarfed teddy bear. Then, they shook each present before placing it beneath the tree. Tanya, overwhelmed, ran from her mom to her dad to me, hugging us all.

When the three hundred mini-lights were flicked on, squeals resounded and the children's world was transformed into a fairyland. How I wished at that moment that all those who had had a part in making this happen could share the joy in that room.

In the blaze of lights, freckles on Tanya's face seemed to dance. A more beautiful child nor a more beautiful tree I shall never see.

Every Christmas, dear reader, you will have an opportunity to *give* to someone you don't know. Think of a Tanya out there whose life you could light up with a Christmas dinner, a special toy, or a *tree* with an angel at the top. Your Christmas, I promise, will be a very merry one.

Give, and it shall be given unto you; good measure, pressed down, shaken together and running over.
. . . Luke 6: 38

Compliments Keep On Giving

All human beings love to receive compliments – words, verbal or written - that praise their appearance, actions, or achievements. But not everyone realizes how important it is to freely praise someone whenever the opportunity arises.

I remember receiving a compliment when I was eleven from my mountain grandmother. At my request, she had handed me a small, brown paper sack and a stubby pencil. I quickly jotted down my thoughts as I looked out across a ravine at a sea of daffodils dancing in the sun's early morning breeze. I had written only a few lines when she reached for the paper sack and squinted at the scribbles. Because she could neither read nor write, she asked if I would read what I had written.

Upon hearing the phrase, "daffodils planted by God," Grandma looked down at me and said, "Why, child, them's good words. I can see them yellow flowers right there on that sack. Some day, if you keep on scribblin', you might just be one of them poem writers." Truly, just remembering those simple, long-long-ago words of encouragement make me happy to this day. Grandma had given me a gift that keeps on giving!

In the summer of 2006, my usual activities curtailed while receiving chemotherapy, I began to be more aware of outstanding characteristics of individuals with whom I met along my journey to and from the Cancer Center. Suddenly, I decided that there are many folks who need to hear positive thoughts about themselves. Thus, I began to toss a few compliments to deserving children, teenagers and young people in the work place, as well as mothers, nurses, interns, and doctors. I would like to share a few of my joyful encounters with you, dear reader, hoping you too will realize the happiness derived from compliments you may give to others.

Once, returning from the Center, I stopped for coffee in the small resort town of Pentwater, Michigan. Before entering the restaurant, I noticed a mother frantically trying to entertain her year-old daughter by wheeling her back and forth in a stroller on the sidewalk. The child was fretting and the mother distraught. Although I was feeling a little weak and off balance, I bent to tease the fussy, curly-haired baby who immediately began to smile. Her blue-eyes sparkled with sustained tears, but she began to kick her chubby little legs and reach for her admirer. Her mother, pleased with my compliments on such a beautiful child, also began to smile and thanked me for noticing and changing both of their attitudes. We chatted for five minutes. The mother's burden was lifted as she wheeled the now content baby on down the street. Indeed, my own spirits soared.

A few days later, I was checking out at a clothing store. A very pleasant young man wearing a sleeveless tee shirt rang up my purchase. He was very patient as I exchanged a pair of men's trousers for another. "You've been very helpful," I commented, careful not to mention or criticize the tattoos running up his arms or the jewels in his ears. He smiled and then mentioned that he is a tattoo artist. The sketches on his arms were a work of art. "You can draw like that?" I touched his arm. "Yes, since I was a little boy I have always liked sketching." "Young man, you could be a great artist, maybe even be famous some day," I honestly commented. His grin was as big as a quarter moon and he thanked me for noticing his talent.

Then, there was Kay, the nurse who hugged me every time I went for a treatment. One day, as she injected medications into my port, we shared a Mother's Day poem she had written for her elderly mother. Upon reading this, dear reader. I was deeply touched by her beautifully written tribute – a daughter recognizing and giving thanks to her Mom for her years of devotion and guidance. "Kay, you are indeed a budding poet," I commented. She, in her quiet way, smiled, hugged me again, and thanked me for a seemingly insignificant little compliment.

Finally, I just must mention a tall, handsome young pre-med intern who cheered me in so many ways. He was patient, kind and genuinely concerned about the welfare of the many cancer survivors with whom he was in contact every day. We joked about my beautiful granddaughter and her interest in becoming a doctor, no doubt a perfect match for him. The last day of my treatment I showered "Dr." Jay with compliments, I held his hand and with great gratitude said, "Jay, you will be an outstanding Oncologist one day because of your love for people. You give them hope as you look into their eyes and listen with your heart." Needless to say, Jay blushed, flashed his charming smile, and squeezed my hand, expressing his thanks for a well-deserved compliment.

Dear reader, sincere compliments can be given to those you meet with so little effort. And, believe me, the rainbow a compliment leaves can last for a lifetime – a gift that keeps on giving.

Prayer Changes Things

Dear reader, God, you know the One who made the heavens and the earth, came through again for me. In September, 2004, I switched on our TV in Michigan and heard that hurricane Frances with winds of 145 MPH was predicted to slam the shores of southern Florida. Our flimsily-built trailer home at Nettles Island was in danger of being totally destroyed in the blink of an eye.

Naturally, we were deeply concerned since we had never carried expensive wind and flood insurance. But I realized there was nothing we could do but wait. Or was there?

The more I thought about the possibility of great loss, the more I searched for peace of mind. One night, unable to sleep, a bright light suddenly flashed before my eyes. And then, I saw it - a little Bible-Belt glittery plaque that had hung on my Momma's bedroom wall for as many years as I could remember. The words, PRAYER CHANGES THINGS, sparkled a message straight to my heart.

And so, on Friday night before the hurricane eye hit on Sunday, I began praying. Not praying for what one might think though. I did not pray that our trailer and screen room would be spared total devastation. I did not pray that our roof would not be blown off. I did not pray that our windows would not be shattered. Neither did I pray that my age-old, treasured Valentine from Bill, stored for many years in a shoebox, would not be ripped to shreds.

No, dear reader, I didn't ask for any favors for myself. I just simply prayed, "God, there is nothing we can do. You are in control. We still have a roof over our heads, but God, could you just slow that hurricane down so the old, old trailer homes of widows and low-income couples will be spared total destruction."

Well, dear reader, late that Saturday night as the hurricane roared across the Bahamas, suddenly Frances was downgraded from a category 4 to a 2. Needless to say, after repeating that short prayer, I slept very well.

Of course, we were unable to make contact on Sunday to determine our loss or the loss of others. But as we sat glued to the TV, we learned

232

that the sea surge was only eight feet at Nettles Island, not 20. The highest winds were 105 MPH, not 145 as originally predicted by meteorologists at the storm center. Certainly good news!

However, we waited for four days before receiving e-mails of devastating destruction on Nettles Island. There was much damage along the beach, including a 200' boardwalk that was swept away by the high wind gusts. The ocean pool was filled with sand, deck tiles, uprooted palm trees, and miscellaneous debris. And, yes, many of the newer mobile homes, including our own, had roof shingles ripped off, and in many cases only scars remained where once there were pretty pastel strips of vinyl siding.

The driving rains, as feared, had blown through broken windows, soaking carpets, ruining furniture and life-long family treasures. Several of the more recently built stucco homes along the seawalls were condemned because of severe cracked walls and f.undations.

However, after five days of no power, no telephones, no sewers, and no drinking water, a call came through that of the 1,570 homes in the park only 70 had been severely damaged. But, miraculously, most of the older mobile units still stood, unscathed.

Yes, dear reader, like the little plaque glittering in the dark reminded me during that anxious time in our lives, prayer certainly does change things.

And whatsoever we ask,
we receive of Him, because
we keep His commandments,
and do those things that are
pleasing in His sight.
. . . I John 3:22

Ring in Happiness

The beginning of a New Year is the time to ring out the old and ring in the new - a new, happy you. Do I hear you saying, "Every year I make resolutions, but by the end of March I realize they will never be resolved?"

They will be, dear reader, if you think less on improving the quality of your life and think more on improving the quality of life for others. Let's skip the old familiar goals that have turned us all into proverbial procrastinators: "I'm going on a diet," "I'm joining an exercise class," "I'm giving up smoking." I'm, I'm, I'm!

Instead, ring in the New Year with more promising, selfless resolutions. Some are easy, others a little more difficult. Some are free, others may require sacrifice, but all are attainable:

x Pen a journal, not for yourself but for your children and grandchildren. In it put special events, dreams, trips, thoughts, funny incidents, goals and memories. Believe it or not, long, dried-up wells do spring forth. A journal will be treasured for years to come by those who have known and loved you.

x Be a listener. Ask your friends, your neighbor, and yes, your children about their thoughts and dreams. Then listen with enthusiasm. Everyone needs a sounding board. Everyone needs to know someone cares about what's happening to them.

x Brighten someone's day. "That's an old cliché," you say. Yes, but there is so much darkness clouding the lives of those around us. Praise a friend's garden or tell her how pretty she looks. Compliment a gentleman on his natty orange socks - if you really do like them.

x Write a letter to a long-lost friend. Can you imagine the excitement when she reads the return address, then slits open the envelope and finds tucked inside a sentimental poem, a joke or a prayer? Everyone enjoys receiving uplifting letters and you will reap loving responses.

x Resolve to write a letter of praise to a teenager, a parent, a school principal, or to a board member. Praise him for an act of courtesy or a job well done. A letter of praise to the editor of a local paper lets the readers know that you appreciate what's happening in your community.

x Write a letter of forgiveness.

Once, while in the hot tub in our Florida park, I heard a statement which made me so sad. "My son and I had a misunderstanding. I haven't spoken to him for years." Oh, how easy to jot down four simple words, "I love you, son." And, oh, how beautifully warm two hearts would feel! A forgiveness letter should take priority over all others because it brings boundless joy.

x Give gifts - lots of gifts without expecting anything in return. If your child, young or old, needs a boost financially, and you can give it, resolve to help him now. Or help some struggling student by establishing a scholarship. If you read about a total stranger who is hurting financially, help to relieve his fear and suffering with an anonymous gift. Blessings will flow.

x Plant a tree. Free trees are given away by some State Agriculture Departments. Even as seedlings, you will enjoy watching them grow now and others will appreciate their beauty for decades. While strolling through the woods, pocket a handful of acorns and somewhere along your travels bury one here and there. Who knows? Fifty years from now a space man returning from Mars may rest beneath the shade of your great oak tree.

x Keep a child alive. For just $15.00, the price of two cheap dinners, or one bottle of Jack Daniels, a distant, hungry child can be fed for one month. A pledge or one-time contribution can be mailed to: World Vision International, P.O. Box 9716, Federal Way, WA 98063-9716. The glow in your heart will brighten your new year.

x Donate your eyes. Give a stranger an opportunity to see the glistening sea gull dip and dive into the ocean's sudsy surf. For the small price of a stamp, a donor's card can be obtained from the Eye Bank Association of America, 1015 Eighteenth Street NW, Suite 1010, Washington, DC 20036. This is truly a great, selfless resolution and you can check it off as soon as you drop the donor card in the mailbox.

Resolve to make a difference NOW, dear reader, whether it is the beginning of a New Year or not. By facing your NEW life with the OLD Book, much happiness will toll from the bell you yourself have rung.

> The Old Year, the Old Year
> it never more can be;
> but a New Year, a New Year
> rings of peace for you and me.
> . . . a *pearl*

Hope,
A Harp for the Soul

In early December of 2006, I received a somewhat unexpected gift – just in time for Christmas. It was not in a silver box trimmed with a big red bow, but it was a spiritual gift, a gift of renewed hope for my soul.

Two weeks earlier, a very disturbing call from my cancer doctor was left on our answering machine. "The scan of your chest shows a questionable spot on your left lung. We have scheduled a complete PET scan for next Monday." Needless to say, dear reader, I was stunned. I erased the message, lay down on my bed and wept.

This was the beginning of a siege of depression never before experienced. For days, periodic thoughts denying this report erupted: Surely they were mistaken. Perhaps the spot was scar tissue from tuberculosis when I was a child. And I did remember coughing while being scanned when I was supposed to lie perfectly still. Between these sieges, exhaustion seemed to block my ability to think positive or even pray. All hope seemed to have eluded me.

Monday morning early, still feeling discouraged, I drove ten miles to the cancer center for the new scan, expecting the worst, never appreciating the usual beautiful drive along the river.

It is strange though how one upbeat person can lift your spirit. The young technician explained the two-hour procedure and after injecting me with a dye, stood by the gurney and told me his life story. Turned out he had lived his young life in West Virginia just across the Ohio River from where I grew up. I got so wrapped up in sweet memories of his life, and mine, that suddenly I realized I was no longer dwelling on what the outcome of the scan might be. His caring attitude had brightened my horizon.

At home that night, I read poetry from a new book given to me by my daughter-in-law Marilyn. One excerpt from a Longfellow poem on illness alerted me to the fact that no matter what the outcome of the report, it was not the end of my life yet:

"What then? Shall we sit down and idly say, the night hath come, it is no longer day? The night hath not yet come, we are not quite cut off from the labouring light. Something remains for us to do and dare. Even the oldest trees some fruit may bear, for age is opportunity no less than youth itself, though in another dress."

Petitions to Heaven began to flow easier and more constant. Two days later as I drove up the same river road to hear the final verdict from the doctor, the sun shown brightly. Seagulls darted to and fro overhead. Every white fluffy cloud against the blue-blue sky seemed to be swaying. I turned on the car radio. Christmas carols rang out with the promise of eternal peace and hope.

One half hour later, dear reader, still somewhat fearing what I might learn, I sat waiting on the doctor's high examining table. He greeted me with a smile and then pulled from my folder the scan report. He held up the single white sheet of paper for me to read. In very black, bold letters, the last line of the report blared out: PET SCAN NEGATIVE. Overwhelmed with relief, I almost jumped off the table to hug the doctor, but instead, threw up my arms, looked to the ceiling and cried out, "Thank the Good Lord!" I then tucked a *Pearl,* Every Christmas Tree Needs a Star, into his white coat pocket. He smiled again and said, "See you in six months for a check-up."

On the return trip home I thought about how hope is indeed a harp for the soul, but also how the music of any harp is sweeter when plucked by its own harpist. May Christmas each year, dear reader, renew hope in the realm of your life, as the gift of restored health has in mine.

Let my soul take refuge
beneath the shadow of
Your wings. Let my heart,
this sea of restless waves,
find peace in You, O God.
. . . Augustine

Psalm of Life

Life is real! Life is earnest!
And the grave is not its goal;
Dust thou art, to dust returnest,
Was not spoken of the soul.

In the world's broad field of battle,
In the bivouac of life,
Be not dumb, driven cattle!
Be a hero in the strife!

Trust no Future, howe'er pleasant!
Let the dead Past bury its dead!
Act, - act in the living Present!
Heart within, and God o'erhead!

Lives of great men all around us
We can make our lives sublime,
And, departing, leave behind us
Footprints on the sands of time;

Footprints that perhaps another,
Sailing o'er life's solemn main,
A forlorn and shipwrecked brother,
Seeing, shall take heart again.

. . . Excerpts from Longfellow's
Psalm of Life

A Friend

You are my friend, as stately and beautiful
As rustling pines viewed from my cabin window.

When birches weep and the winds of heaven
Make them sing, I think of God – and you.

Diamonds shimmer upon silvered waters, and
I think of precious jewels – and you.

Sails unfurl carrying sun-drenched sailors
To mounds of gold. I think of riches - and a
Friend far greater.

And, as the blood-red sun drops surely into
A deeper sea beyond, giving me a wondrous
Feeling of love, forgiveness, and sacredness -
I think of you.

My heart delights in your friendship,
And I shall love you, my friend – ever.

Indian Farewell

Until we meet again, may the
Great Spirit make sunrise in your heart
And, may your moccasins make tracks in
Many snows yet to come.

Thank you, dear reader, for peeking through the eaves with me to view dancing daffodils on a far-away hillside.

. . . Pearl Hauine Henson Flaherty

Biography

PEARL FLAHERTY, born in the mountains of Kentucky, is a creative, blithe spirit with a zest for living. Her *Pearls* column has been published in the Oceana Herald-Journal in Michigan for eight years and the Nettles Islander in Florida for twenty-five years. Select articles have appeared in numerous other publications including Twins Magazine, The Stuart News in Florida, The Holland Evening Sentinel in Michigan and the Ferris Girls' School Textbook in Japan.

Pearl, 82, is a committed Christian and has been married to Bill for 63 years. They have five children, ten grandchildren and one great-grandchild. She and Bill spend summers at Silver Lake in Mears, Michigan and winters at Nettles Island in Jensen Beach, Florida.

13725977R00144

Made in the USA
Charleston, SC
28 July 2012